DIVE
THE VIRGIN
ISLANDS

LAWSON WOOD

Series Consultant: Nick Hanna

Interlink Books

An imprint of Interlink Publishing Group, Inc.
Northampton, Massachusetts

T0035493

Lawson Wood has many years' experience as a diver and is among the world's leading underwater photographers. He is a Member of the British Society of Underwater Photographers and a Fellow of the Royal Photographic Society. His other books include *Top Dive Sites of the Caribbean*, *The Dive Sites of the Cayman Islands*, *The Dive Sites of Cozumel and the Yucatán* and *The Dive Sites of the Bahamas*.

First American edition published in 2009 by
INTERLINK TRAVEL
An imprint of Interlink Publishing Group, Inc.
46 Crosby Street, Northampton, Massachusetts 01060
www.interlinkbooks.com

ISBN 978 1 56656 743 5

Project development: Charlotte Parry-Crooke
Series editor: Pete Duncan
Copy editor: Paul Barnett
Design concept: Philip Mann, ACE Ltd
Design: Chris Aldridge, Alan Marshall
Cartography: William Smuts
Updater: Jack Jackson

Reproduction by Hirt and Carter, South Africa
Printed and bound in Singapore by Tien Wah Press (Pte) Ltd

Photographic Acknowledgements
All photographs taken by Lawson Wood except for the following: British Virgin Islands Tourist Board 9; British Virgin Islands Tourist Board/Karen Linnett 134; Life File/Jason Holtom 100; Lesley Orson 146; Photobank/Jeanetta Baker 28; Photobank/Peter Baker 12, 13, 31, 33 (bottom), 35, 92, 93; Jim Scheiner 147; The Stock Market 36, 97; US Virgin Islands Tourism Office/Don Herbert 29.

Front cover (main): © WaterFrame / Alamy
Front cover (left): © Lawson Wood
Front cover (middle): © Kit Kittle/CORBIS
Front cover (right): © Pictures Colour Library
Spine: © Pictures Colour Library
Back cover (bottom): © Pictures Colour Library
Back cover (top): © Pictures Colour Library.

ACKNOWLEDGEMENTS

This book would not have been possible without the support and encouragement of my wife Lesley, who is a constant source of inspiration to me and acted as my other eyes underwater when taking the photographs for the book.

I would like to thank the following people involved in our lengthy visits in both the British and United States Virgin Islands: Jimmy Dalmida, the administrator of St John; Michael Royle and Blue Water Divers; Jennifer Bonner and the Bitter End Yacht Club; Nat & Glen for touring Virgin Gorda and The Baths; Joy Blaine-Seal of the British Virgin Islands National Parks Trust; Lisa Mitchell and Claire Abrehart and the varied crews of Baskin in the Sun; André Niederhauser and the Prospect Reef Resort; Colleen Ryan and Brian Savage and the *Theta Volantis*; Annie and Duncan Muirhead and the excellent crew of the equally excellent trimaran *Cuan Law*; Christine Oliver and Charlie Hampton of the British Virgin Islands Tourist Board in London; Russel Harrigan, the BVI director on Tortola; Jenny Spurgeon and Julia Edwards from the United States Virgin Islands Tourism Office in London; Gloria Gumbs on St Thomas; Jerry Koenke on St Croix; Steve Garner and Cruzan Divers; Lorelei Monsanto on St John; Captain Ed and his wife Molly Buckley at V.I. Divers Ltd.; Hal Rosbach at the Cane Bay Dive Shop; Desmond Trim, our St Croix taxi man; Captain Ken Green at Dive In, St Thomas; Centerline Car Rentals; Claudia Huber and the Sapphire Beach Resort, St Thomas; Suzanne and Kevin Ryan, the superb hosts at Waves of Cane Bay; the St John National Parks Service; Low Key Watersports on St John; John Sawyer, an absolute mine of information; Michelle Pugh and the Island Conservation Effort; Anchor Dive Centre and the Salt River Marine Park; Dive Experience Inc.; Treasure Isle Hotel; Nanny Cay; Bert and Gayla Kilbride; Robert Ward and the superb staff at Harlequin Travel Ltd; American Express Insurance Services for our emergency help on the islands; British Airways, American Airlines and American Eagle for all air transportation.

PUBLISHER'S ACKNOWLEDGEMENTS

The publishers gratefully acknowledge the generous assistance during the compilation of this book of the following: Nick Hanna for his involvement in developing the series and consulting throughout and Dr Elizabeth M. Wood for acting as Marine Biological Consultant and contributing to The Marine Environment.

PHOTOGRAPHY

The author's photographs were taken using Nikonos V, Nikon F-801 and the Nikon F-90s. Lenses used on the amphibious Nikonos system were 15mm and 12mm. The lenses for the housed Nikons were 14mm, 60mm, 105mm, 20–40mm zoom, 28–200mm zoom and 70–300mm zoom. Housing manufacture by Subal in Austria and Sea & Sea in Japan. Electronic flash was used in virtually all of the underwater photographs; the supplier was Sea & Sea Ltd from Paignton in Devon, England, and from Japan. The flashes used were YS30 Duo, YS50, YS120 Duo and YS300. For land cameras, the Nikon SB24 and SB26 were used. Film stock was Fujichrome Velvia and Fujichrome Provia, supplied by KJP in Edinburgh through Fuji Photo. Film processing was by Eastern Visual Communications in Edinburgh. All diving equipment was supplied by the Shark Group, Amble, Northumberland.

CONTENTS

How to Use this Book

THE REGIONS
The dive sites included in this book are divided into six main regions: St Croix, St Thomas, St John, Tortola/Jost Van Dyke, the Little Sisters, and Virgin Gorda/Anegada. Regional introductions describe the key characteristics and features of these areas and provide background information on climate, the environment, points of interest, and advantages and disadvantages of diving in the locality.

THE MAPS
A map is included near the front of each main regional section or sub-section to identify the location of the dive sites described and to provide other useful information for divers and snorkellers. Although certain reefs are indicated, the maps do not set out to provide detailed nautical information, such as exact reef contours. In general the maps show: the locations of the dive sites, indicated by white numbers in red boxes corresponding to those at the start of each dive site description; the locations of key access points to the sites, such as ports and beach resorts; and wrecks. (Note: the border round the maps is not a scale bar.) Each site description gives details of how to access the dive site.

MAP LEGEND

Land	✈ Airport	1 Dive Site	Wreck
Reef	Road	· · · · International Boundary	

THE DIVE SITE DESCRIPTIONS
Within the geographical sections are the descriptions of each region's premier dive sites. Each site description starts with a number enabling the site to be located on the corresponding map, a star-rating and a selection of key symbols, as shown opposite. (Note that the anchor used for live-aboards is merely symbolic: no boat should ever drop anchor over a reef.)

Crucial practical details on location, access, conditions, typical visibility and average and maximum depths precede the description of the site, its marine life, and special points of interest. In these entries, 'average visibility' assumes good conditions.

THE STAR-RATING SYSTEM

Each site has been awarded a star-rating, with a maximum of five red stars for diving and five blue stars for snorkelling.

Diving		*Snorkelling*	
★★★★★	**first class**	☆☆☆☆☆	**first class**
★★★★	**highly recommended**	☆☆☆☆	**highly recommended**
★★★	**good**	☆☆☆	**good**
★★	**average**	☆☆	**average**
★	**poor**	☆	**poor**

THE SYMBOLS

The symbols placed at the start of each site description provide a quick reference to crucial information pertinent to individual sites.

 Can be done by diving

 Shore dive

 Can be reached by local dive boat

Can be done by snorkelling

Can be reached by live-aboard boat

Suitable for all levels of diver

THE REGIONAL DIRECTORIES

A regional directory, which will help you plan and make the most of your trip, is included at the end of each regional section. Here you will find practical information on how to get to an area, where to stay and eat, and available dive facilities. Local non-diving highlights are also described, with suggestions for excursions.

OTHER FEATURES

At the start of the book you will find practical details and tips about travelling to and in the area, as well as a general introduction to the region. Also provided is a wealth of information about the general principles and conditions of diving in the area. Throughout the book there are features and small fact panels on topics of interest to divers and snorkellers. At the end of the book are sections on the marine environment (including coverage of marine life, conservation and codes of practice in the Virgin Islands) and underwater photography and video. Also to be found here is information on health, safety and first aid, and a guide to marine creatures to look out for when diving in the Virgin Islands.

INTRODUCTION TO THE VIRGIN ISLANDS

On the edge of the Caribbean Sea, 64km (40 miles) east of Puerto Rico and 225km (140 miles) northwest of St Kitts, lie the Virgin Islands. This beautiful archipelago is considered to belong to the Lesser Antilles, though in geographical terms it is closely allied to the Greater Antilles in the west. Stretching just 80km (50 miles) from west to east and 108km (67 miles) from north to south, its islands lie mostly clustered together, with only Anegada in the north and St Croix in the south relatively isolated. Some ten of the 107 islands are inhabited.

Europeans first discovered the Virgin Islands in 1493, when Christopher Columbus was making his second exploration of the West Indies. His logbook tells of islands having 'such unspoiled beauty' that he named them 'Los Once Mil Vírgenes', after St Ursula and her legendary 11,000 virgin followers. In fact the 4th-century Princess Ursula died with just 11 maiden companions and the number grew through the pressure of tradition, yet the choice of name was apt. Columbus' patrons, Isabella and Ferdinand of Spain, badly wanted a major discovery at the time and 11,000 must have seemed a much more impressive figure than 107.

The early days of European exploration paved the way for a succession of Dutch and Spanish explorers, British privateers, marauding pirates, the Knights of Malta, Danish plantation owners, Quakers escaping from prosecution and, of course, slaves, who at one time outnumbered their overseers by ten to one. Shaped by the same forces – conquest and colonization – which affected the entire Caribbean, the islands of the archipelago share common roots, but have since become two entirely distinct nations, both politically and culturally.

To the south and west lie the **US Virgin Islands**, an unincorporated Territory of the USA, purchased from Denmark in 1917. To the east, across the stretch of water known as The Narrows, are the **British Virgin Islands**, a British Overseas Territory. Of the two countries, the US Virgin Islands are the more heavily commercialized, have a higher GDP and enjoy a largely urbanized lifestyle: the British Virgin Islands have a far slower pace of life and have stayed largely rural. Disparity has led in turn to a situation of interdependence between the

Opposite: *Little Harbour on Peter Island is a popular location for learning to dive.*
Above: *Children throughout the Virgin Islands are disarmingly friendly.*

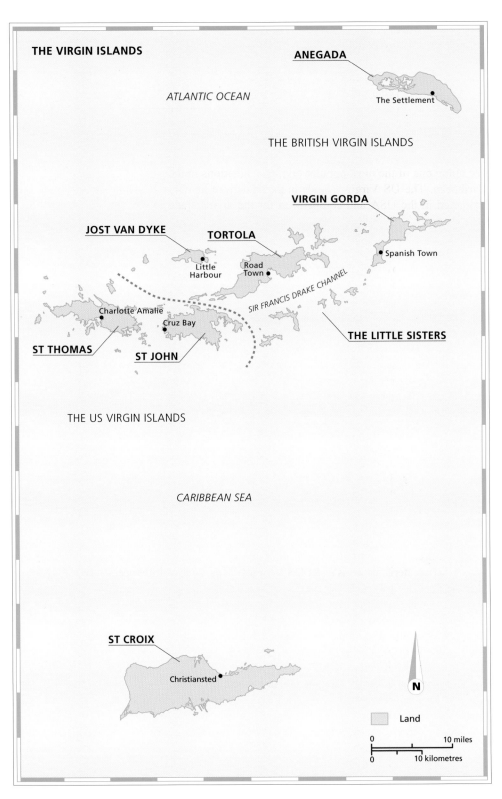

THE VIRGIN ISLANDS

ATLANTIC OCEAN

ANEGADA

The Settlement

THE BRITISH VIRGIN ISLANDS

VIRGIN GORDA

JOST VAN DYKE   **TORTOLA**

Spanish Town

Little Harbour   Road Town

SIR FRANCIS DRAKE CHANNEL

Charlotte Amalie

Cruz Bay

THE LITTLE SISTERS

ST THOMAS   **ST JOHN**

THE US VIRGIN ISLANDS

CARIBBEAN SEA

ST CROIX

Christiansted

N

Land

0   10 miles

0   10 kilometres

two countries. Despite their political differences, the working populations are extremely mobile, marrying inter-island, having children in both communities and sharing a single currency, the US dollar; change of residence is common.

Due to the vast number of safe anchorages, secluded bays and inlets, the Virgin Islands are well known for their light yacht cruising potential, and there are many companies catering specifically to the luxury end of this lucrative market. The Virgin Islands are also rapidly becoming one of the most popular diving destinations in the Caribbean. The US Virgin Islands in particular are heavily promoted in the USA and competition for the diving trade is fierce, with the result that prices are often lower than in the British Virgin Islands.

The archipelago features some world-class diving, including one of the most famous shipwrecks in the Caribbean, the Royal Mail Steamer *Rhone*, which foundered and sank during a hurricane. In addition, there are numerous coral-encrusted boulders, sculpted ravines and superb reefs such as those off Anegada. Thanks to their geographical position, placed between the Caribbean Sea and the western reaches of the Atlantic, the Virgin Islands are home to a high diversity of marine life, while the nutrient-rich Gulf Stream traverses the island chain.

PIRACY

At the turn of the 17th century, the Virgin Islands lay at the centre of a vast pirate empire which virtually controlled shipping lanes all over the eastern Caribbean and along the coast of America, extending as far as Bermuda to the northeast and Venezuela in the south. Known as the 'sweet trade', piracy flourished wherever the rewards were greater than the risks taken and attracted men and women who had nothing else to lose but their lives. Often selling their services to the highest bidder, many of the ships were privately owned and became known as 'privateers'. The privateers were so successful that over a thirty year period they almost bankrupted several major nations' treasuries. The main target was the Spanish, whose treasure-laden ships were easy pickings. However, the pirates also attacked settlements on shore. One of the most staggering and successful raids was by Captain Sir Henry Morgan, who raided Panama in 1671, carrying off gold, silver and jewels to a value of over $100 million in today's terms.

GEOGRAPHY

For the most part the islands and cays are volcanic in origin, with a mountainous landscape and large granitic boulders sculpted by time and tide, continuing into long submarine rocky reefs topped by a thin encrusting coat of coral. Good topsoil exists almost everywhere, but is rather sparse, with exposed rock showing through. The exposed and only slightly deformed rock strata suggest a possibly nearly complete record of evolution dating back 100 million years, making the islands unique in the region of the Caribbean.

St Croix is the largest of the islands, 52km (28 miles) long and 135km^2 (84 square miles) in area, and something of an exception. Although it displays many of the same physical characteristics as its sister US Virgin Islands, such as lofty peaks – the highest land is in the north and west with a maximum elevation of 350m (1165ft) at Mount Eagle – St Croix is separated from the other islands by 54km (32 miles) of deep water. It became detached from the rest of the group when a rift moved the islands apart, allying it more with Puerto Rico, and as a result the island lies completely within the Caribbean Sea. St Croix's isolation led to the formation of magnificent vertical walls of coral which drop off dramatically into depths of over 4000m (13,200ft).

The other two US Virgin Islands, St Thomas and St John, are neatly packed together with Jost Van Dyke, Tortola, the Little Sisters and Virgin Gorda – all belonging to the British Virgin Islands. Nearly all these granitic islands are surrounded

BELONGENS

Little is known about the original Belongen Treaty, other than that, if you were born a British Virgin Islander but are resident in the US Virgin Islands, you can vote in both areas. As far as working in the USVI is concerned, however, all non-USVI residents/US citizens must possess a US working permit. Reciprocal arrangements apply to the British Virgin Islands. Belongens travel across both areas with very few travel restrictions.

HURRICANES

In recent years, the Virgin Islands have been hit by several major hurricanes, including Hurricane Hugo in 1989 and Hurricane Marilyn in 1995. The latter devastated the islands, shutting down large parts of the hotel industry. Fortunately the United States views the islands as one of its top tourist destinations and millions of dollars were pumped into the island to restore services and rebuild ruined properties. There are now new marinas and shopfronts all over the islands.

by shallow boulder ridges topped with healthy coral reef and shallow sand bars. **St Thomas** is 20km (12 miles) long and covers an area of 53km² (32 square miles). Its highest point, Crown Mountain at 465m (1550ft), forms part of a broad mountain range which drops slowly towards the east, while the rugged shoreline has bays and, in the south, a huge deep natural harbour. Close by is **St John**, 14km (9 miles) long and 35km² (20 square miles) in area, with Bordeaux Mountain its highest peak at 383m (1277ft), and ending in the east in a thin neck. Two-thirds of St John is designated as a National Park.

The largest of the British Virgin Islands, **Tortola**, is also the most rugged of the Virgin Islands and virtually impossible to traverse without ascending its impressive mountain range, which peaks at 520m (1750ft) at Mount Sage. Tortola is 19km (12 miles) long and covers 32km² (21 square miles). **Jost Van Dyke** is like a mini version of Tortola, only 5km² (3 square miles) in area. To the south of Tortola, stretching from St John in the west to Virgin Gorda in the east, lie the **Little Sisters**, a rough series of small rocky islands and pinnacles. Their many channels and bays abound with archetypal tropical islands. **Virgin Gorda** reaches a height of 411m (1370ft) at Virgin Peak in its northern half, but drops to a narrow peninsula towards the southwest. Its low-lying end is best known for a collection of giant granitic boulders strewn by the water's edge, known as The Baths.

At the northernmost edge of the same plateau from which the majority of the Virgin Islands arise is **Anegada**. Unusually, it has no real peaks and is formed mostly of sand and coral, similar in nature to the low-lying islands of the Bahamas or Turks and Caicos. The

Only a short distance away by ferry, the British Virgin Islands are clearly visible from St Thomas.

Trunk Bay on St John is popular for watersports of all types, as well as just lazing in the sun.

island is 16km (10 miles) long and covers an area of 25km² (15 square miles), with numerous lagoons, marshes and salt ponds. The southern end of the island is very flat and featureless, while the northern end rises to a maximum height of 9m (30ft) above sea level, having been raised by a volcanic shift. Anegada is surrounded by a virtually unbroken series of coral reefs, for the most part in pristine condition, and is reputed to have the largest concentration of shipwrecks in the Caribbean, some 250 of which have been recorded.

CLIMATE

Categorized as having a semitropical maritime wet-and-dry climate, the Virgin Islands experience no extremes of temperature. There is only about 130cm (52in) of rainfall each year, the rainiest times being July to November and February to March. What they do have is a hurricane season, which lasts from September through to January. The Virgin Islands have been hit several times in the last few years, and large tracts of lush forest on their steep-sided mountains have been destroyed. However, the islands are still very beautiful and some original subtropical forestation remains on the higher mountain slopes. The lower slopes are largely cultivated and fringed with coconut palms.

The height of the mountain tops gives rise to regular cloud cover over the peaks, where moisture is drawn towards the islands. For most of the year, the skies appear blue with huge columbiform clouds forming over the tops of the islands, particularly in September; these clouds can give rise to fast, stormy showers that start in the morning and generally clear up by afternoon. The mean temperature is 25°C (77°F) in winter and 28°C (82°F) in summer, although

SUNTANNING

Each year, two and a half million tourists visit the Virgin Islands with the idea of going home with a suntan. However, many get burnt on their first day due to the cooling effects of almost constant light trade winds. It is important to limit your sunbathing at first and only gradually increase the length of exposure to the sun's rays. Keep yourself and any children well protected with a high factor of sun screen, paying particular attention to the top of the head (wear a hat), the nose, the backs of the knees and the tops of the feet. When snorkelling, always wear at the very least some sort of protective T-shirt.

it can sometimes soar well up to 32°C (90°F) in the height of summer. Temperatures in the water drop to about 17°C (63°F) during the winter months, but rise to a balmy 28°C (82°F) in summer.

The general direction of the winds between September and March is from the northeast. In the drier season, from April to August, the winds change to southeasterly. Wind speeds rarely rise above 25kph (15 knots), though during the infrequent hurricanes they can rise to 200kph (125 knots). In general, the islands enjoy an equable climate tempered by sea breezes.

SAILING AND WATERSPORTS

The Virgin Islands are regarded as the yachting centre of the Caribbean. With about 1800 yachts available for charter, it is no wonder they are so popular. Two types of boat are for hire: crewed charter boats with a captain and cook, and 'bareboat' charters with no crew other than the guests. Only experienced sailors are allowed to charter the latter, as the waters around the islands hide a number of treacherous shoals. First-timers can charter a crewed boat so as to be shown the ropes and taught basic sailing safety skills.

The relatively calm and shallow Sir Francis Drake Channel is the main passageway for yachts. Most prefer to base themselves on the British Virgin Islands, with its slower and easier pace of life; Jost Van Dyke, the Bitter End Yacht Club and Peter Island are particular favourites, though the southern bays of St Thomas and Cruz Bay on St John are also very popular. Throughout the archipelago there are hundreds of sheltered lagoons and natural harbours where you can find safe moorings on secure buoys and adequate onshore facilities. In the British Virgin Islands, you must register with the British Virgin Islands National Parks Trust and pay a mooring-buoy usage fee; thereafter you can moor anywhere within the island group.

Offshore deep-sea fishing is superb, and this has become another very popular activity. There are licences available for different seasons, depending on the particular fish species you want to catch. Most tour operators are able to advise on combined diving and fishing packages; also, the local tourist offices can offer advice on where and when to go for the best fishing. Resorts on St Croix, St Thomas, Tortola and Virgin Gorda all offer charter boats for deep-sea fishing, allowing you to travel to the edge of the continental shelf to try your luck for marlin, wahoo and tuna.

All the major resort hotels, as well as most tourist beaches, have windsurfing boards for hire and many offer instruction, often at little or no additional cost. With the Virgin Islands having so many secluded bays, there is usually a protected lee shore somewhere providing conditions perfect for learning to windsurf.

CLOTHING

Throughout the Virgin Islands, swimwear should be confined to the beach or swimming pool terraces. Topless sunbathing is not generally acceptable in most resort areas, although there are some secluded beaches which do allow this. It is unacceptable for women to wear bikini tops when shopping downtown, and shirts must be worn in all public buildings and banks.

Otherwise the dress code in the Virgin Islands requires only casual lightweight clothing. Some fancier restaurants and casinos may require men to wear a jacket (no tie), but in such places you'll probably want to be wearing a sweatshirt or light jumper anyway to compete with the air-conditioning.

SHOPPING

The Virgin Islands, like many of their Caribbean counterparts, have plenty of opportunities for duty-free shopping: Christiansted on St Croix, Charlotte Amalie on St Thomas and Road Town on Tortola are notable examples. These areas are also full of local artisans and craftsmen, although some of the art that you see for sale is imported from Haiti or the Bahamas. Most of the registered tourist stops have wonderful carved figures and straw goods on offer. Electrical goods are a great buy for US tourists, though European visitors should be cautious and take a close look at the voltage: the device may not be compatible at home. Most electrical goods in the British Virgin Islands are in fact purchased on St Thomas and shipped over on the daily ferries by local residents, who can move freely through the international zones between the two sets of islands.

MONEY AND TIPPING

The US dollar is the main currency in use on the islands, including the British Virgin Islands.

It is common practice to tip baggage handlers up to $US1.00 per bag depending on the weight and size of the item. All restaurants expect a standard tip of 15% and some will even expect as much as 20%; most add this automatically onto your bill, though some may still expect an additional tip! Taxis also expect a tip, especially if you expect the driver to help with your luggage. Tipping is appreciated on the day dive boats, normally at the end of your vacation.

Sunsets are always spectacular at the Bitter End Yacht Club on Virgin Gorda.

DIVING AND SNORKELLING IN THE VIRGIN ISLANDS

There is a relaxed, unhurried nature about diving here that is very appealing, and the Virgin Islands are equally popular among North American and European divers. Although there are other diving destinations in the Caribbean which are more heavily visited, the Virgin Islands are able to offer an enormous diversity within a relatively small area. This includes some of the best wreck diving in the Caribbean. Among the best known are the Butler Bay wrecks off Frederiksted (St Croix, sites 8–11), the RMS *Rhone* (Little Sisters, Site 17) off Salt Island – one of the most famous wreck dives in the world – the *Chikuzen* (Tortola, Site 5) near Anegada, and the *WIT* Shoal (St Thomas, Site 1). In addition to these photogenic wrecks, the islands boast virgin offshore reefs and pristine vertical walls which can drop 4000m (13,200ft). The northern reefs of Anegada are reputed to form the second largest continuous barrier reef in the Caribbean. There is also the bonus of exciting and challenging drift diving to the submarine peaks south of the continental shelf which borders both sets of Virgin Islands.

The main group of islands – St Thomas, St John, Tortola and Virgin Gorda – is influenced by the Gulf Stream, which passes through the archipelago from the Caribbean up into the Atlantic and carries with it a rich parcel of nutrients that makes for highly diverse fish and coral life. Although it cannot be said that marine life is profuse, the fish life to be found around the Virgin Islands is exceptionally varied. There is a curious mix of both Caribbean species and western Atlantic species, as well as a high proportion of invertebrate life in every location, with large numbers of octopus, lobster, shrimp, flamingo tongue shells and sea fans.

The Virgin Islands are also in the hurricane zone and recent years have seen major hurricanes which have caused considerable damage underwater, with forests of elkhorn coral being destroyed and huge barrel sponges ripped apart by the force of the waves. In some parts large concentrations of algae are evident where an area has been on the receiving end of storm damage in the past.

However, the local population is increasingly aware of the value of the underwater environment and most recognize the importance of dive tourism to the economy. Special

Opposite: *The aeroplane wreck off Great Dog Island (Virgin Gorda, Site 17) was used as a film prop.*
Above: *Dive BVI on Virgin Gorda has extensive experience of diving throughout the archipelago.*

PROJECT REEF

One of the most important environmental projects in the Virgin Islands is the REEF Project. Based on a programme which has been used by ornithologists with the Audubon Society, REEF involves divers completing survey sheets to give a snapshot of the area they have dived. The combined data – continually updated by hundreds of divers – should provide an invaluable knowledge bank to better understand and manage coral reefs. It is hoped that the project will eventually spread worldwide. The Baskin in the Sun dive operation, based on Tortola, is a REEF Field Station; the staff are able to help in all REEF matters. For further information, see page 155.

UNDERWATER FORMATIONS

Breaker: a rock close to the surface which is only shown when waves break over it

Pinnacle: a large coral head, tower-shaped and generally separated from the rest of the reef

Spurs: narrow ridges of coral separated by a sand channel and running perpendicular to the shore

Groove: the sand channel between coral spurs

Canyon: a vertical slice in the coral reef or rocky cliff which opens out to sea, sometimes known as a swim-through, ravine or crevice

Tunnel: a hole running through the reef

Chimney: usually a narrow tunnel running vertically up through the edge of the reef

Shelf: the outer edge of the coral reef before it drops into deep water

Wall or Drop-off: the vertical or steeply sloping coral cliff below the shelf

Sand chute: a sandy gully which runs down the reef to the depths below

Sand plain: a flat sandy area, usually between fringing and barrier reefs

Fringing reef: a coral reef which is very close to the shore

Barrier reef: a coral reef which lies offshore, running parallel to the shore and acting as a 'barrier' against the worst of the wave action

projects in conjunction with the Reef Environmental Education Foundation (REEF) have been able to harness and direct the skills of scuba divers into important scientific research. Conservation policies are such that there is a total ban on anchor drops anywhere near a coral reef and mooring buoys have been placed all around the popular dive areas. Spearfishing is completely banned, while the area surrounding the RMS *Rhone* has been declared a Marine National Park, as have several offshore cays and smaller islands.

There are hundreds of recorded dive sites around the Virgin Islands, and the majority are marked by permanent mooring buoys. Yachts touring the inner islands are encouraged to drop anchor only in confined sandy areas, away from where any corals could possibly be damaged. Local dive resorts cater specially for visiting yachts by offering the option of 'rendez-vous diving'. This allows people on a yacht to be met by a local dive boat wherever they happen to be, then taken for a dive and returned later to the yacht.

Generally the operators' on-board dive masters will plan your dive and dive time, though the importance of doing your own pre-dive planning – and sticking to that plan – should not be overlooked. There is very little shore diving done in the northern Virgin Islands and all the diving operations here have boats leaving at regular times from their dock, catering for divers with a wide variety of skills and experience. St Croix is slightly different, featuring a number of superb shore diving sites such as Cane Bay along its northwest coast and under Frederiksted Pier, truly one of the best dives on the island, in only 6m (20ft) of water.

Night diving is possible and there are a number of popular locations fairly close to the dive centres, certainly within 30 minutes' travel time by dive boat to a safe mooring point over a low boulder reef or wreck. The *Rhone* has both deep and shallow moorings for this very purpose, while the Coral Garden off northern Dead Chest (Little Sisters, Site 15) is also excellent. Night diving availability can be rather limited, however, as a number of operators only do a couple of night dives each week. It is sensible to check in advance whether a night dive is taking place and reserve your space on the dive boat, as night dives are always popular.

DIVING CONDITIONS

Virtually all diving in the Virgin Islands is done by boat and the first dives of the day are always treated as deep dives. However, with the average depth being only 21m

The dive boat of Kilbride's Sunchaser Scuba operates around the northern Virgin Islands.

(70ft) around the main group of islands, the excess nitrogen risk to divers is reduced. It is only along the north wall of St Croix, and on the deeper parts of the *Rhone* and the *Inganess Bay* (Little Sisters, Site 20) in the British Virgin Islands that divers are likely to run into decompression problems.

During November to March, oceanic swell rolling in from the North Atlantic can create some difficult surge conditions, particularly along the Dog Islands off the northern British Virgin Islands, and sometimes reaching as far south as St Croix. These conditions can make diving tiring and rather difficult when you're close to coral-encrusted boulders and caves and find yourself pushed against the corals. If you are caught in a strong tidal surge, the sensible thing is to swim with the surge – when the pull is against you, do not fin against it, but wait until the pull reverses. Care should also be taken when doing a shore dive as an ill-timed wave can make entries or exits quite hazardous.

There are also currents, with the strongest located between the narrow passes that separate the islands around St

ST THOMAS RECOMPRESSION CHAMBER

The closest hyperbaric chamber is located on St. Thomas in the USVI Schneider Regional Medical Center, Roy L. Schneider Hospital, 9048 Sugar Estate, St. Thomas USVI.
Recompression chamber: tel (340) 776 2686, (340) 776 8311 ext. 2226
VHF Hospital Frequency 1 or 2
Nurse on call (beeper): tel (340) 772 8392
US Coastguard (San Juan): tel (787) 729 6770/7778

EL NIÑO

The weather phenomenon known as El Niño is now a key factor in the prediction of hurricanes in the Caribbean. After 10 years of research by the Tropical Ocean Global Atmosphere (TOGA) it was discovered that more accurate weather prediction could be made by monitoring the effects of El Niño. El Niño depends on a relationship between the sea and the atmosphere that develops in the equatorial Pacific Ocean, causing a wave of warm water to progress eastwards (the opposite direction of its normal flow pattern). This is not a new phenomenon, as sailors in the 1800s regularly noted the anomaly and speculated that magma was oozing from the earth's crust. In the 1920s, British scientist Sir Gilbert Walker identified the influences of a mix of sea water, temperature, atmosphere and rain when trying to predict monsoons in India. He discovered that, when atmospheric pressure rises in the west, it falls in the east. Now it is widely thought that when El Niño is raging in the Pacific, hurricane force winds are unlikely to hit the eastern Caribbean.

Thomas and St John and near the *Inganess Bay*, where the Gulf Stream passes through the islands upwards into the Atlantic. The on-board dive masters will always check if there is current before you enter the water and, if it appears too strong, will move to a different location.

Visibility is variable depending on the location and time of year. As in all the world's seas, a biannual plankton bloom clouds the water in the spring and autumn; since there is little strong tidal movement through the archipelago, the resulting 'milky' conditions can last for several weeks at a time. The shallow banks are also susceptible to periodic storms, further reducing the visibility. Generally, the water is at its clearest from April to August, when there is an average visibility of about 18m (60ft). During winter this drops to about 15m (50ft) among the inner reefs, though the water visibility around the islands does vary depending on the localized tidal stream. The further you travel south into the heart of the Caribbean, the better the visibility. Off the edge of the St Croix wall visibility averages 30m (100ft) in the winter and well over 50m (165ft) in the summer.

Temperatures in the water drop to about 17°C (63°F) during the winter months, necessitating the use of full wetsuits or even drysuits for those undertaking long repetitive dives. However, during the summer water temperatures rise to about 28°C (82°F), and 'shorty' wetsuits or bathing costumes are all that is required, though it is sensible to wear at least a Lycra skin suit for protection against coral abrasions and planktonic sea stingers.

DIVE BOATS

With most diving undertaken by boat, experienced dive boat operators will choose a site to suit the average diver's ability. However, divers are always consulted as to where they would like to dive next, and with most dive sites lying less than 30 minutes' boat ride away, there is lots of scope for choice. A number of the more popular sites have several moorings, so it is not uncommon to find several dive boats at the same location. Wreck dives such as the *Rhone*, *Inganess Bay*, *Major General Rogers* and *WIT* Shoal are planned well in advance as they take more time to reach and are potentially deep dives, necessitating more caution.

Virtually all the dive boats are day boats, with only a few live-aboards available – including the *Cuan Law*, the largest trimaran in the world fitted out exclusively for dive exploration. The *Cuan Law* is capable of extended stays at sea, and can explore the less accessible outer reefs and submerged mountain ranges around Anegada. Night dives are also scheduled every evening for clients on board. Most

> ### MOORING BUOYS
>
> Increasing anchor damage caused by visiting yachts and dive boats prompted the BVI Diving Operators Association, in collaboration with the BVI National Parks Trust, to start installing in 1989 a set of mooring buoys in all the busy anchorages. Originally developed for Key Largo Marine Sanctuary in Florida, the mooring pins are now located on all the popular dive sites around the British Virgin Islands, as well as many in the US Virgin Islands. Each mooring buoy comprises a steel pin cemented into either fossilized coral substrate or hard rock bottom, with a line attached to a float on the surface. Another floating line is attached to the bu   oy to allow boats to pick up the mooring without adding undue strain to the steel securing pin. This design eliminates the kind of damage to coral reefs caused by the scouring of the seabed by more traditional buoying systems.
>
> There are still areas where boats are allowed to drop anchor, such as the sand hole anchorages on the west coast of St Croix, but then only onto a sandy seabed and not on coral or eelgrass nursery beds.

Opposite: *Colourful sponges, anemones and sea fans are common on most shallow reefs.*
Below: *Schoolmaster grunt (Lutjanus apodus) form small schools on the reef crest.*

DIVERS ALERT NETWORK (DAN)

DAN is a diver safety organization which includes a medicare insurance specifically aimed at helping and treating divers worldwide. Payment covers medical air evacuation and assistance; recompression chamber treatment; travel insurance; upkeep of recompression chambers; training and education of recompression chamber staff worldwide; research into diving safety practices; safety and educational seminars for the sport diver and full assistance in any diving related incident.

US tel (919) 684 4326, (919) 684 8111 Medical Information Line: US toll free tel (800) 446 2671; tel (919) 684 2984

charter yachts might also come into the live-aboard category, particularly with 'rendez-vous diving' on offer, allowing people the flexibility to cruise the islands and be picked up to dive as and where they like.

On the day boats, the usual programme is a twin-tank dive in the morning and a single-tank dive (or training dive) in the afternoon. The morning dives will be a deep dive to approximately 18–30m (60–100ft), followed within 40 minutes by a much shallower dive on a nearby reef or suitable shallow wreck to depths of less than 12m (40ft). Night dive trips are usually in exchange for one of the day dives, as most dive centres will rarely do more than three dives each day. However, when there is enough demand, dive resorts may offer more boat trips with the chance to dive at least four times per day. Times to the dive sites by boat are relatively quick, as the boats only venture a short radius from their home. Entry into the water from the dive boats is generally from the rear of the craft, by a giant step forward, by a backwards roll or by slipping over the side while keeping one hand on the boat.

LEARNING TO DIVE IN THE VIRGIN ISLANDS

Scuba diving is the most rapidly growing recreational pastime in the world, and many hundreds of scuba divers visit the Virgin Islands each year. Most are well versed with the area's dive sites and knowledgeable about particular locations they want to explore, such as the *Rhone* or the Salt River (St Croix, sites 19–20). Nevertheless, many people also come to the Virgin Islands to learn to dive, while others may wish to upgrade their existing diving skills.

When choosing a dive operation, make sure that it is affiliated to one of the major schools of instruction, such as PADI, NAUI or BSAC International. These are the world's leading diver training organizations and all train to the very highest standards. PADI (Professional Association of Diving Instructors) is probably the top-rated association in use throughout the islands. NAUI (National Association of Underwater Instructors) is not as widely known but has a superb record of instruction. BSAC (British Sub Aqua Club) International is now strengthening its position in the Caribbean and has a number of affiliated schools in the Virgin Islands.

You must gain certification before you are allowed to rent equipment and head off to dive independently with a buddy. The most popular way to start is to enrol in a resort course, known around the world as the Discover Scuba Programme. This 2–4 hour basic instruction course is a combination of lectures, swimming pool techniques and open water work designed to give you a taste of diving, fire your enthusiasm and teach basic water safety and conservation. A resort

FISH-FEEDING

Five reasons why we should not feed fish:

• The addition of nutrients alters the balance of the reef and can cause a decline in water quality around the reef.

• Fish-feeding alters natural feeding behaviour. Fish that would normally feed on algae, thereby controlling algae which might otherwise smother a reef if left unchecked, instead start to become handout feeders.

• Feeding night feeders, such as snappers and jacks, during the day disrupts their feeding pattern and normal predator–prey interactions that are necessary to keep the reef ecosystem in balance.

• As instanced at several popular fish-feeding locations around the world, hand-fed fish can become aggressive and a danger to non fish-feeders.

• The food which is fed to the fish does not meet their natural balance of nutritional requirements. By eating human food, they become malnourished and more susceptible to lesions and parasites.

The *Cuan Law* is the largest dedicated live-aboard trimaran in the world at 31m (105ft) long and with a 13m (44ft) beam. She was built at Wheatly, Ontario in Canada in 1987. Owners Duncan and Annie Muirhead created the boat to Duncan's exclusive designs and named her after their Scottish heritage (*cuan* is Gaelic for ocean and *law* means a hill). Despite her size, the *Cuan Law* has only a 1m (3ft) draft, allowing her to manoeuvre in shallow waters near coral reefs without causing damage to corals or the hull.

The triple hull provides for a massive deck area, as well as additional stability whenever the sea gets choppy. The *Cuan Law* is able to handle 20 guests in total. Guests are quartered in the outer hulls, while the ship's services, including air compressors, water maker, engine room, crew quarters and galley, are located in the larger central hull. At the heart of the ship is a spacious lounge where guests are able to relax between dives. Fitted with five sofas, a bar and an extensive library, the lounge has ten overhead hatches to let in the sun. The ten surrounding cabins all have their own hatches and are fully air conditioned.

The trimaran is a fully rigged sailing ship, and, when it is getting underway, guests are encouraged to help in setting the sails.

The Cuan Law is the world's largest dedicated live-aboard trimaran.

LIVE-ABOARD DIVING

Most diving from the *Cuan Law* is done directly off the stern by giant stride entry or from one of the two 6m (20ft) rigid-hull inflatable boats (RIBs). The RIBs also provide attendant surface support, particularly in conditions of strong current. Travel time to any dive site by means of the RIBs is never more than ten minutes from any anchorage or mooring site.

All diving equipment – including weights and weight belts – is stored under the aft-deck seating area, while air tanks are filled on a raised deck above the 21-seat video and television projection room. Full diving equipment can be rented on board, but any special requests (such as dive suit size or computer needs) should be sent in advance.

There is a full video editing suite on board as well as E-6 film processing, making it ideal for visiting photographers and videographers. Recharging of batteries and dive lights can be handled in the cabins, where there are 110-volt outlets as well as adapters for European specification equipment.

The Cuan Law offers unlimited diving (with the proviso that the boat is on the move daily to visit other sites). Non-divers are catered for with kayaks, a Hobie cat, windsurf boards and water skis. The Cuan Law's sister ship, the trimaran Lammer Law, operates in the Galápagos Islands.

Contact: Trimarine, c/o Charterport, PO Box 8309 PMB 613, Cruz Bay, VI 00831; tel (284) 494 2490; fax (284) 494 5774; e-mail:cuanlaw@surfbvi.com; website: www.cuanlaw.com

course is also highly recommended if you have only a few days' vacation. Those with a medical problem of which they are unsure should always consult their doctor first. A resort course is available to everyone over the age of 12 (teenagers up to age 18 must have full parental consent).

If you decide to take your training further and invest several hundred dollars and rather more time, you can take a five-day Open Water certification course. This gives you personal tuition by fully qualified dive instructors and teaches you to dive safely to a depth of 18m (60ft). A popular variant on this is the referral course, whereby much of the classroom work is done at home before travelling out to the Virgin Islands to complete the open water dives. The Open Water qualification course is taken by 25% of all first-time resort course participants.

Under the PADI system, divers qualified in the Open Water course are then able to go on to an Advanced Open Water course. Thereafter, a wide variety of speciality courses becomes available to divers, including wreck diving, cave and cavern diving, underwater photography and dive instruction.

Once you are fully qualified, your certification or 'C' card serves as your diving passport and is recognized worldwide. It is valid for life, but, if you are unable to dive from one year to the next, it is recommended that you enrol in a refresher course at any dive centre. As with most sports, your confidence and awareness will increase the more you partake of the sport. Also always ensure that any equipment you own is fully serviced after any lengthy break.

DISABLED DIVERS

A few diving operations in the Virgin Islands are specifically geared to cater for disabled divers. Certain boats are specially adapted for wheelchairs, and such dive centres are able to certify people of all disabilities, including paraplegics, quadriplegics and those with impaired hearing or sight, provided that the individual is medically able to dive. Any prospective student must consult a doctor prior to taking a certification course. As a general rule, any dive operator with its own jetty will be accessible for disabled divers, whereas smaller operators whose access to their dive boat is by beach cannot offer the service.

SNORKEL TIPS, TECHNIQUES AND EQUIPMENT

Entering the water for the first time wearing a mask, snorkel and fins can be quite daunting, but with the correct techniques you will quickly discover that snorkelling requires little physical effort. Only the ability to swim is essential.

Instruction is offered at nearly all top hotels and dive resorts and may take place in a dive centre's swimming pool.

Virgin Gorda's deeper reefs are sculpted into long canyons topped by sea fans and are easily negotiated.

SNORKEL ADVICE

Clean your mask before snorkelling by wetting it first, then spreading saliva or a light detergent with your fingers, and finally rinsing it out thoroughly; this should prevent the mask from 'fogging'. When putting the mask on, make sure that your hair does not become trapped under the seal of the mask, as water may enter as a result. If water enters the mask, breathe out through your nose while holding the top of the mask firmly to the forehead, and the water should clear without difficulty. If water enters the snorkel, blow sharply through the tube to expel the water.

With instruction you will quickly be able to enjoy the many excellent snorkelling sites around the Virgin Islands. It is wise to check with the local dive shop whether the area you are planning to snorkel in is safe enough for you and your family. If in any doubt, do not enter the water, and seek advice first.

Snorkellers should take care to stay in deep enough water when snorkelling over shallow reefs, as it is easy to cause damage to the fragile corals or inflict personal injury. Never snorkel or tread water in a vertical position as flapping fins can easily break coral or disturb sediment which may in turn smother coral polyps. For the same reasons, never adjust snorkelling equipment near any coral – always swim away into a 'safe' area.

Equipment can normally be rented from a dive centre, though snorkelling is not an expensive sport and it is possible to purchase your own. Snorkelling equipment consists of a mask with an adjustable strap and toughened glass, a snorkel and flippers. The mask must cover the nose in a way that allows you to adjust the air pressure inside through your nose. Several types of mask also

Conditions for learning to dive in the Virgin Islands are nearly perfect.

have the provision for optical lenses to be installed. For those people who wear contact lenses, a close fitting, low volume mask should normally be adequate. The snorkel should not be too long or have too wide a bore, as you need to be able to clear the water out of it in a single breath if you submerge yourself too far. Some modern snorkels make use of a self-draining device which will remove any excess water. The snorkel must fit snugly in the mouth and be free of any type of restriction which might impair breathing.

Fins, or flippers as they are sometimes called, come in two different styles. The slip-on type, incorporating an adjustable ankle strap, is often worn over a pair of waterproof pumps or diving bootees. The smaller, softer kind features a moulded fitting that fits snugly around the foot. Buoyancy vests may also be worn as an additional safety measure, but for general shallow water snorkelling these are rarely used.

> ### WATER WEAR
>
> The water temperature in the Virgin Islands varies markedly during the year. Even during the warmest months of August and September, it is recommended that you wear a Lycra skin suit or thin wetsuit for diving and snorkelling to protect against coral abrasions and stings from microscopic planktonic animals and fragments of jellyfish tentacles in the water. Night dives can be particularly uncomfortable as plankton and small benthic organisms tend to move towards the surface to feed and reproduce. During February to April, a few dive shop instructors and visitors now wear dry suits.

In addition to the basic equipment of mask, snorkel and fins, it is sensible to wear either a Lycra skin suit or a thin full wetsuit. This will not only shield you from the sun's rays but also afford protection against any stinging microscopic plankton which may be found in the water. If you have no other protection, at least wear a T-shirt to keep off the sun's rays.

DIVING EQUIPMENT

Supplementing the basic snorkelling equipment, diving equipment consists of an air tank and air; a regulator or demand valve through which you breathe; a contents gauge to indicate how much air you have left in your tank; an easy-to-read depth gauge to indicate your current depth and maximum depth reached; a watch with an adjustable bezel or timer device to let you know how long you have been at a specific depth and the duration of your dive; a weight belt and weights, which help counteract the body's natural positive buoyancy; and a buoyancy compensator or life jacket of some description that allows you to adjust buoyancy at depth in order to remain at that depth or keep off the corals.

During the winter months the water temperature can drop as low as 17°C (63°F) and it's advisable to wear a full wetsuit instead of the much thinner Lycra suit. There is no real need for equipment such as dry suits or hoods in the Virgin Islands, although some people like to wear a hood when diving at night. A small knife may be worn, in case you need to use it to cut yourself free from impediments such as fishing line loose in the water. A computer is recommended for more experienced divers who are on an unlimited dive package, to assist them with repetitive dive profiles.

When storing diving equipment at the end of a dive vacation, make sure that it is rinsed thoroughly and that all salt concretions have been removed. Have your regulator serviced and pack equipment carefully: remove any batteries from electronic equipment and torches; roll dive suits carefully rather than hanging them; treat rubber items with silicone spray and store everything away from direct sunlight. Knife blades can also be cleaned and treated with silicone rubber spray.

THE US VIRGIN ISLANDS

With a resident population of around 100,000, the US Virgin Islands are one of the most important tourist destinations in the Caribbean. Officially an unincorporated US Territory, they comprise St Croix, St Thomas and St John, plus a host of smaller islands, cays and rocky outcrops. For the most part, the islands are volcanic in origin, excepting St Croix, which is partly coralline and is set apart in the Caribbean Sea.

The largest of the three main islands, **St Croix** (pronounced *Saint Croy*), measures 45km (28 miles) long and covers 130 km² (82 square miles). This fertile island was once almost completely planted with sugar cane by early Danish settlers, but with the end of slavery the plantations ceased, and now the land is dotted by dairy and cattle-breeding farms. It contains two major towns, Christiansted and Frederiksted, as well as some fine beaches on Buck Island, which is protected as a National Monument.

St Thomas is the capital island of the US Virgin Islands and the most developed, with much of the business centred around Charlotte Amalie and its massive natural harbour. There appears to be very little free island space on the eastern hillsides surrounding Charlotte Amalie. The twisting and narrow winding roads are dotted with houses and any accessible tourist beaches have been developed, with adjacent hotels offering all manner of watersports. Thatch Cay to the north is the largest of several smaller satellite islands, while Outer and Inner Brass, Saba Island, Water Island, Birsk Island, Capella Island and Great St James Island are all popular for diving.

Due west of St Thomas, on the other side of Pillsbury Sound, is **St John**, the smallest and least developed of the three islands, which has a relaxed atmosphere much more like that of the nearby British Virgin Islands. The island is considered the least spoiled by tourist pressure and one of the most beautiful in the Caribbean with its richly forested volcanic interior and world-famous beaches. Over two-thirds of the island are given over to a National Park. Several nature and hiking trails lead through the park, and there are camping grounds for those not staying in one of the sumptuous resorts. The largest of the offshore cays are Leduck Island, Congo Cay and Grass Cay.

Opposite: *Charlotte Amalie on St Thomas is the self-crowned cruise ship capital of the Caribbean.*
Above: *Brilliantly coloured wild flowers line the hillside above Magens Bay on St Thomas.*

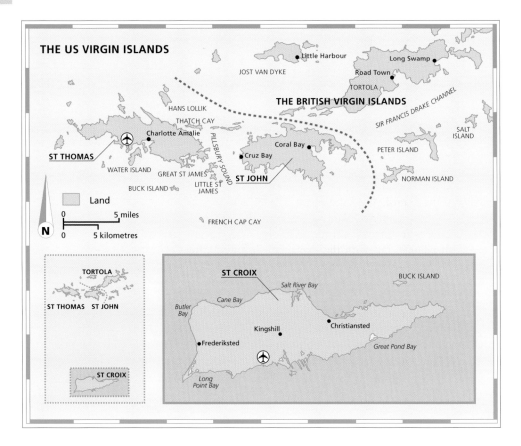

HISTORY

During Christopher Columbus's second voyage in 1493, his fleet of 17 ships was blown off course from Dominica by a southwesterly gale and ended up at an island known as Ay Ay by its Carib inhabitants. He renamed the island Isla de la Santa Cruz (St Croix), but was soon driven off by the warlike Caribs from their settlement at present-day Salt River; the headland they battled over became known as Cabo de Flechas, or Cape of Arrows.

In the 1620s the Dutch, English and French started to settle on St Croix, long after the native inhabitants had been taken off to work in the gold mines of Santo Domingo by the Spanish. The Dutch abandoned the island in 1645 and the English were driven off shortly afterwards when Spanish forces attempted to assert their claim to the island in 1650. The French, however, stood firm and persuaded the Spanish to leave for Puerto Rico. For a while St Croix remained under French occupation, prospering through plantations and slavery, and during this time the island was formally deeded to the Knights of Malta.

> ### QUELBE
>
> Quelbe is a style of music associated with St Croix, also known as 'scratch music' from the sounds corrugated gourds make when scraped by bands for percussion. Quelbe is featured in night clubs on St Croix and throughout the US Virgin Islands.

Meanwhile, following a charter by the King of Spain in 1672, the Spanish ceded their claim to the island of St Thomas to Denmark; the Danish soon asserted their authority over neighbouring St John. Following a major slave revolt in St John in 1733 Denmark also purchased St Croix from France. Although Denmark was the first European nation to formally end its participation in the slave trade, in 1802, illegal trade continued, centred on St Thomas, while the plantations flourished on St Croix. Only after an uprising in 1848 by the slaves on St Croix was slavery brought to an end. This was followed by failures of the sugar cane crop and a rise in sugar beet production in Europe, and the islands' economy crashed.

By this time St Thomas had risen to be an important staging point for cargo vessels entering the Caribbean, thanks to its capacious natural harbour at Charlotte Amalie. Allegiances gradually shifted towards the United States and in 1917, for reasons of national security, the USA purchased the Danish West Indies for $25 million in gold. The United States entered WWI a week later. The period between the wars proved rather unstable, as for many Caribbean islands, but with the expansion in travel after WWII the United States started to allocate substantial sums of money for development. The subsequent economic rise in the islands was massive.

The US Virgin Islands now boast the highest per capita income in the Caribbean. Residents of the US Virgins are governed by US laws and pay the same taxes as on the US mainland. The tourist trade is the single largest source of

PRIVATEERS IN CHARLOTTE AMALIE

The pirates who once patrolled the waterways of the Virgin Islands archipelago were superb navigators and seamen. With one of the earliest co-operative organizations, they looked after the welfare of their men. Crew members who were disabled during skirmishes were looked after and given extra bonuses to be certain their welfare would be seen to when ashore.

Charlotte Amalie, with its natural harbour, was a centre for the privateers and virtually every pirate ship would have anchored in her bay at some time or other to sell or exchange goods under a flag of truce.

However, life ashore on St Thomas was another matter – records suggest it was much safer to stay on board:

Here come the pirates to St Thomas Town,
With pockets of gold and nary a frown.
It's up and away for Charlotte's Bay,
Where the liquor is good and the lasses are gay!

The preserved sugar mill at Annaberg on St John is well worth a visit.

income in the islands and the largest employer, though there is also some heavy industry and the Hess oil refinery in St Croix is an important employer.

TRAVELLING TO THE US VIRGIN ISLANDS

The US Virgin Islands receive almost two million tourists each year, with over 85% coming from the United States. Of these, two-thirds arrive by cruise ship, mainly to St Thomas. The cruise ships usually visit as part of a weekly eastern Caribbean cruise which also takes in the Bahamas, Cayman Islands and Jamaica. Other US visitors arrive on regular daily flights via a number of different airlines, flying to St Thomas or St Croix from major hub airports such as San Juan in Puerto Rico and Miami. The flight time from Miami is about two hours; from San Juan it is just 40 minutes.

> ### VIRGIN ISLANDS NATIONAL PARK, ST JOHN
>
> Visitors to the Virgin Islands National Park should be aware of a few park rules and safety tips. Tourists (this includes hikers) should wear a T-shirt or other form of full-cover-up. Although the island is mainly looked after by the National Park, there are many private properties within its perimeter – please respect these landowners' rights and do not trespass. Stick to the proper hiking trails. Be careful of any vehicular traffic as the roads are winding and narrow, and remember to drive on the left (British-style).

Although there are no direct flights from Europe, connecting flights are available through major US airlines. American Airlines fly to St Thomas from Miami, New York and Raleigh/Durham, allowing for international connections. Continental Airlines use Newark as a connecting hub to St Thomas for flights from Boston, Chicago, Detroit and Philadelphia. Delta fly direct from Atlanta to St Thomas, continuing on to St Croix, while US Air fly direct to St Thomas from Baltimore. All other flight services from the USA connect through San Juan.

Numerous services are available from other Caribbean islands. Windward Island Airways (WinAir), Leeward Island Air Transport (LIAT), Coastal Air Transport, Bohlke International Airways, American Eagle and Air Anguilla all offer connecting services through St Thomas from most of the eastern Caribbean islands – including Beef Island and Virgin Gorda in the British Virgin Islands.

There are twice-daily connections between St Croix and St Thomas by commercial air carriers, seaplanes and hydrofoils. The only services between St John and St Thomas are by ferry. The crossing takes 20 minutes, with many services continuing to the British Virgin Islands: Island Son is one of the most popular.

The international airport on St Croix lies southwest of Christiansted and midway to the other main population centre of Frederiksted. The airport is quite spacious with both an international and a domestic terminal. St Thomas' airport is located in the far southwest of the island, where the land is much flatter, from where it is about 10 minutes' drive to the capital, Charlotte Amalie. There are no airports on St John, though Medivac helicopters are able to land at numerous locations in the event of emergency transportation to the hospital on St Thomas being required.

US VIRGIN ISLANDS TOURISM OFFICES

USA

Atlanta: United States Virgin Islands Tourist Office, Marquis One Tower, Atlanta, GA 30303; e-mail: usviatl@aol.com

Los Angeles: Suite 412, 3460 Wilshire Blvd., Los Angeles, California CA 90010; tel (213) 739 0138; email: usvila@msn.com

Miami: Suite 907, 2655 LeJune Road, Coral Gables, Miami, Florida FL 33134; tel (305) 442 7200; email: usvimia@aol.com

New York City: Suite 2108, 1270 Avenue of the Americas, New York NY 10020; tel (212) 332 2222; email: usviny@aol.com

Washington, D.C.: Suite 298, 444 North Capital Street, North West Washington DC 20001; tel (202) 624 3590; email: usvidc@sso.org

Canada

Suite 3120, Centre Tower, 3300 Bloor Street West, Toronto, Ontario M8X 2X3; tel (416) 233 1414; email: jsintzel@travelmarketgroup.com

Denmark

Park Allé 5, Aarhus Center, Denmark DK 8000; tel (86) 181933; email: usvi@danskvestindiskturist.dk

United Kingdom

Molasses House, Clove Hitch Quay, Plantation Wharf, London SW11 3TN; tel (171) 978 5262; email: usvi@destination-marketing.co.uk

Italy

Via Gherardini 2, 20145 Milan, Italy; tel (2) 331 05841; email: mail@themasrl.it

Above: *Ferries to St John from St Thomas and Tortola dock at Cruz Bay.*
Below: *'Jitneys' carry visiting tourists around the islands to notable scenic spots.*

US VIRGIN ISLANDS LOCAL TOURISM OFFICES

St Croix: PO Box 4538, Christiansted, St Croix, VI 00822; tel (340) 773 0495; fax (340) 773 5074

St Thomas: PO Box 6400, St Thomas, VI 00804; tel (340) 774 8784; fax (340) 774 4390

St John: PO Box 200, Wharfside Village, Cruz Bay, St John, VI 00831; tel (340) 776 6450; fax (340) 777 9695

All US Virgin Islands tourist offices share a common website: www.usvitourism.vi.

CUSTOMS AND IMMIGRATION

All foreign citizens must carry a full passport when entering the US Virgin Islands, and require a standard US visa (or appropriate waiver). For US citizens a normal identification card is all that is required. Tourist cards need to be filled in by all people wishing to enter the country from the British Virgin Islands, though a tourist pass is available for those making regular trips between the US and British Virgin Islands. The only exemption is for 'belongens' – residents of either set of islands – who can pass through the international barriers without too much trouble. You must retain part of your immigration slip to hand over when you finally exit whichever island you are staying on.

Most customs officers in the US Virgin Islands are well used to divers arriving with lots of baggage and will generally let you walk straight through, after a cursory examination of your documents and questions about your diving destination. If you are carrying lots of photographic equipment it is advisable to write down a list of all contents, any serial numbers and the value of each item, as a precaution against importation problems. This can then be presented to customs and stamped. The list should later be checked and cleared on your departure.

TRANSPORT

Taxis from airports to your hotel or condominium work on a fixed scale of charges, which is displayed at the airport. With taxis elsewhere it is always a good idea to ask what the fare will be before getting into the taxi. Your hotel should be able to give you an indication of the going rate. Many visitors to St Thomas and St John choose to tour these islands on regular open-sided tour buses, or 'jitneys', which offer pre-arranged stops for taking scenic photographs and tourist sales. Horse-drawn 'surreys' are another way to get about the main areas around Charlotte Amalie, offering an informative and inexpensive guided tour (about $5 per person for about 25 minutes). However, one of the best ways to see the sights is by hiring a taxibus and driver for half a day between four people. If you ask in advance, you may be able to get the driver to give you the unofficial guided tour – a great way to see the area and inexpensive.

Car hire is an obvious alternative. You must have a valid driver's licence from your country of origin and must purchase and carry proof of car insurance. Rental agencies take a signed credit card imprint as a deposit; without a credit card you will not be able to hire a car.

Hire cars are available on all of the islands and are mainly four-wheel-drive Suzukis or Honda saloon cars. Saloon cars are generally considered better for security purposes. Collect your rental car or jeep early in the day as otherwise the better models may already have been taken. Check the vehicle before you rent it, so as to avoid problems later on; especially look at the tyres – some stretches of road are rough, particularly on St Croix.

Unlike the rest of the United States and its territories, driving in the US Virgin Islands is on the left-hand side of

PERSONAL SECURITY

Use hotel safes wherever possible, either in your room or at reception, to store travel documents and valuables. Keep a note of your passport number, flight details and booking-confirmation numbers separate from all other documents, just in case of disaster. Do not carry large-denomination notes around with you (many shops will not exchange bills over $US50; use travellers' cheques as the preferred method of payment. Carry your own baggage unless you are prepared to keep an eye on it and are prepared to tip.

The beaches and bays of the US Virgin Islands are regarded as some of the most scenic in the Caribbean.

the road, with overtaking on the right. This practice dates back to the time when the first cars arrived on the islands; these were British right-hand-drive, and the custom has never changed. Nevertheless, all hire cars are left-hand drive models and the majority of hirers are American, not accustomed to driving on the 'wrong' side of the road – inevitably this creates confusion and can lead to accidents, so take care if driving. All distance markers are in miles. Some larger resorts have scooters and bicycles for hire or for guests' local use.

ACCOMMODATION
On St Thomas, St John and St Croix there is a wide variety of choice, from small guest houses to converted old plantation estate houses. Virtually all resort hotels are located on the coast or a short walk away. The larger facilities have access to golfing facilities and most have watersports available, including diving, snorkelling and parasailing. Prices vary tremendously depending on the category and location.

Hotel packages are based on the Modified American Plan (room, breakfast, dinner) or the European Plan (room only). Guest houses tend to be less expensive as most have 'efficiency suites' – small fully fitted kitchenettes with fridge, cooker and microwave. When booking into a hotel you will be asked to sign a blank imprinted credit card slip for incidental charges. A government tax of 8% is added to all hotel bills. Many diving operations have special arrangements with a nearby hotel and offer all-inclusive packages; these are regularly advertised in the US diving press. The most popular package is a four-night/three-day bed-and-breakfast deal with three two-tank dives plus a night dive. Prices rise during the US holiday seasons around Easter and Thanksgiving.

ST CROIX

Originally called Santa Cruz by Columbus, St Croix is the largest of the US Virgin Islands at 45km (28 miles) long and 130km² (82 square miles) in area. The island is located 64km (40 miles) south of St Thomas and, unlike her sister islands to the north, falls completely within the Caribbean Sea.

At one time St Croix rivalled Barbados as the major sugar cane producer in the West Indies. After slavery was brought to an end on the island in 1848, immigrant workers arrived from Vieques Island near Puerto Rico to continue working the sugar cane plantations, and sugar cane remained the major employer and source of income until the late 1960s.

Since then much of the island has reverted to being a farming community, with mixed arable and beef farms supplying the other US Virgin Islands with locally grown produce. Now over 100 abandoned sugar mills dot the island, many of which have been converted into private homes and gallery workshops; Whim Great House, one of the former sugar plantations, is now open to the public. Today the major employers are tourism and the Hess oil refinery and aluminium-processing plant, which dominates St Croix's south shore. Locals are known as Cruzans.

The northwestern section of St Croix is dominated by rainforest, while the eastern end of the island is relatively arid. Two major settlements exist on the island. Christiansted, the island capital, is located on the north coast and forms the departure point for hydrofoil ferries to St Thomas; the town is notable for its covered pavements or 'galleries', a legacy of the island's Danish heritage. Frederiksted on the west coast now has a new cruise ship pier, built after the old pier was destroyed during Hurricane Marilyn in 1994. It is about a 30-minute drive from Christiansted along the interstate – a four-lane highway that features 10 of the 16 stoplights on the island – or a 45-minute drive through the forest.

Most diving around St Croix is done along the north and west shores. The Island Conservation Effort (ICE) is a non-profit organization that maintains 22 moored dive sites along these shores, reducing the need for dive boats to anchor and thereby avoiding

---

Opposite: *Cane Bay is one of the few areas in the Virgin Islands where you can dive from the shore.*
Above: *Fireworms (Hermodice carunculata) are commonly found on sponges.*

A notable feature of diving on St Croix are large barrel sponges.

the risk of damage to the reef. Careful dive operators also take their divers to hundreds of sites in addition to the moored ones.

The island is notable for being almost completely surrounded by a superb barrier reef. Unlike St Thomas and St John, which have principally shallow diving to about 25m (80ft) on rocky reefs with a thin covering of corals and sponges, St Croix features a spectacular coral wall running the entire length of its northern shore. In most places the wall begins at about 9–12m (30–40ft) and drops off well beyond safe diving limits, sometimes vertically 3km (2 miles) into the abyss.

Off the Salt River Landing National Historic Park and Ecological Preserve, a vertical cut in the reef allows excellent diving (sites 19–20) in quite sheltered waters with large numbers of moray eels and good quality hard corals. Two of the best dives along the north coast are easily reached from the shore (although boat diving does make it easier): Cane Bay (Site 15) includes a nice beach for non-divers as well as a protected seawater swimming pool, while North Star (Site 13), further west, is a relatively easy dive despite the rocky entry. The Butler Bay wrecks off the west coast of St Croix are accessible only by boat, but on the same coast is Frederiksted Pier (Site 3), which can be dived from the shore and is particularly rewarding by night.

ICE

The Island Conservation Effort (ICE) is a non-profit agency founded in 1988 by Mandy Walsh, who worked with government and environmental agencies to install a mooring buoy system. The result was 22 moorings (now 75) which were funded by private sponsors and the Virgin Islands government. Michelle Pugh now spearheads the group, which actively drums up support and funding for the maintenance of the mooring buoys. For further infromation, contact: ICE, tel (340) 773 3307.

1 KING'S REEF
★★★

Location: Opposite King's Beach at the Westend Saltpond.
Access: By boat only.
Conditions: Sheltered except from westerly winds and swell.
Average depth: 21m (70ft)
Maximum depth: 36m (120ft)
Average visibility: 25m (80ft)
King's Reef is a steeply sloping, overgrown spur-and-groove reef principally made up of plate corals, boulder corals and brain corals, all topped with varieties of sea fans and plumes. There is a very good chance of finding turtles in this area as they are known to nest on Sandy Point to the southwest of St Croix.

Palometa (*Trachinotus goodei*) and permit (*Trachinotus falcatus*) are often seen together, as well as large groups of jacks. This is the furthest site visited by the St Croix dive operators and only rarely dived as most visitors to this side of the island want to dive the Butler Bay wrecks.

2 SWIRLING REEF OF DEATH (DAN'S REEF)
★★★★

Location: South of Frederiksted Pier (Site 3).
Access: By boat only.
Conditions: Fairly sheltered except from westerly swells.
Average depth: 9m (30ft)
Maximum depth: 9m (30ft)
Average visibility: 15m (50ft)
This is a patch reef system surrounded by clean white sand and has been described as like diving in an aquarium, with virtually every representative of Caribbean fish life to be found around these low coral heads. There are spotted morays (*Gymnothorax moringa*), chain morays (*Echidna catenata*), jackknife fish (*Equetus lanceolatus*) and queen triggerfish (*Balistes vetula*) always excavating nests and looking for crustaceans under the sand. Good quality corals can be found and colourful sponges are everywhere. Due to this site being so shallow, it is often dived after the Butler Bay wrecks (sites 8–11) and is a favourite site for fish photography.

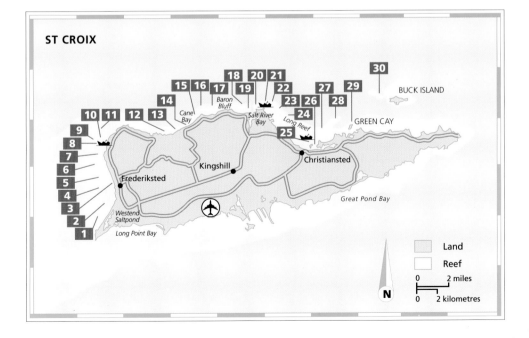

Diving under piers is one of the most rewarding easy-access options if you are looking for interesting marine life. Quite often piers are accessible only at night, for obvious reasons – they are busy places during the day. However, after a word with the harbour authorities to check whether there is any boat traffic due, you can dive at any time in safety to your heart's content.

The new Frederiksted Pier is a concrete construction and, for the most part, its pillars were left surrounded by builders' rubble upon completion – the sea is a very convenient wastebin! However, local divers have since collected all this debris and placed it in small heaps in the shaded area between the pillars.

Although seemingly inauspicious on first inspection, the new pier's pilings are now covered in a thin layer of sponges, tunicates and small corals. Around the newly arranged rubble between the pillars you can

find resident seahorses, frogfish, juvenile French angelfish and spotted drum. Furthermore, as the top of the pier is covered, casting a wide swathe of shade across the nearby water, the pier attracts a higher than average concentration of marine species that would normally be encountered only on deeper reefs or under coral overhangs.

FROM RUBBLE TO REEF

The first colonizers of any such man-made 'reef' are the encrusting sponges and algae, then slowly small hydroids, corals and sea fan larvae attach and spread out across the current. In the shallower reaches, on the outsides of the pillars, fire coral (*Millepora alcicornis*) can be found, gradually fading away as you swim around into the shade.

As time passes, slowly the physical outline of the concrete structure begins to alter as the colonizing creatures find their optimum position in relation to the sun and the prevailing current. These creatures in turn are supported by a whole host of marine fish and invertebrates, all of which appear in a situation like this to have been made specifically for the purpose.

Frequently neglected in the rush to dive the excellent reefs and wrecks to be found elsewhere, the functional structures that we see above the water are often just the ugly fences, as it were, that shield secret gardens of delight. From a photographer's point of view, they can be extremely high-yield sites: with minimum effort and all in shallow water (allowing a maximum bottom time) you can find so many good subjects that your biggest problem may simply be that of constantly running out of film.

Left: *The old pier pilings are home to large numbers of octopus, visible on night dives.*
Opposite: *Moray eels can be seen swimming free at night in search of food.*

3 FREDERIKSTED PIER

★★★★★★☆☆☆

Location: To the north of Frederiksted, opposite Cruzan Divers.
Access: From the shore.
Conditions: Calm and sheltered with little boat traffic, except infrequent cruise ships.
Average depth: 6m (20ft)
Maximum depth: 15m (50ft)
Average visibility: 15m (50ft)

The old Frederiksted pier was once known as one of the world's best macro dives. Unfortunately it was badly damaged by Hurricane Hugo in 1989, so a new pier was constructed (opened July 1994). The old pier had to be destroyed – it was barged out to a site near the Butler Bay wrecks to the north. Despite the replacement of the old pier by a new one, three 'dolphins' (small mooring-line piers) survived, and it is around these that much of the dive is conducted. At night the 'dolphins' are reminiscent of piers in Bonaire, covered in sponges and corals, orange ball

---

Sponge crabs carry around live sponges on their back for added camouflage.

anemones and thousands of guinea-chick lobsters (*Panulirus guttatus*). The pier also features the largest number of octopus you are ever likely to encounter in one location.

4 PAUL'S ANCHORS

★★★

Location: Directly out from the Frederiksted Pier.
Access: By boat only.
Conditions: Can be exposed with some current to be expected.
Average depth: 9m (30ft)
Maximum depth: 9m (30ft)
Average visibility: 15m (50ft)

This circular sandy plain and patch reef system used to be where the workboats anchored when the pier was being built. There are three anchors embedded in the sand and coral, one of of which is upright and totally encrusted in corals and sponges. Popular as a second 'rummage' dive after a deeper dive to one of the Butler Bay wrecks (sites 8–11), the site allows a maximum bottom time exploring the low corals surrounded by clean sand. Sand divers (*Synodus saurus*) and sand tilefish (*Malacanthus plumieri*) are a feature here, as are

corkscrew anemones (*Bartholomea annulata*) which always have Pederson's cleaning shrimps (*Periclimenes pedersoni*) in attendance.

5 RAINBOW
★★★★

Location: Opposite the Rainbow Beach Bar.
Access: By boat only.
Conditions: Fairly sheltered with little surge.
Average depth: 12m (40ft)
Maximum depth: 12m (40ft)
Average visibility: 15m (50ft)
This is a large section of patch reef, 3m (10ft) high and surrounded by a huge sandy plain covered in a light coating of turtle grass (*Thalassia testudinum*). Among all this can be found a few upside-down jellyfish (*Cassiopea frondosa*) and orange-spotted gobies (*Nes longus*) living in burrows excavated by a commensal snapping shrimp; this symbiotic relationship is a delight to observe.

6 HORSESHOE REEF (SPRAT HOLE)
★★★

Location: Opposite Sprat Hall Plantation.
Access: By boat only.
Conditions: Generally sheltered, except from westerly winds.
Average depth: 12m (40ft)
Maximum depth: 12m (40ft)
Average visibility: 18m (60ft)

Orange ball corallimorphs only extend their tentacles at night and are quite rare.

Horseshoe Reef is a large sandy plain surrounded by a mini-wall of coral which rises 3m (10ft) and opens out on the seaward side. Submarine tracking wires are also found in this area and serve as a useful point of reference for navigation by divers. A large 'V' cut through the reef leads to an area where huge numbers of garden eels (*Heteroconger halis*) can be found. Southern sennet (*Sphyraena picudilla*), the smaller relative of the great barracuda, are often found here, as are lots of angelfish, parrotfish and wrasse.

7 RCA
★★★

Location: South of the Butler Bay wrecks opposite the Submarine Tracking Station.
Access: By boat only.
Conditions: Sheltered from northerly storms.
Average depth: 15m (50ft)
Maximum depth: 25m (80ft)
Average visibility: 25m (80ft)
Here divers are able to follow various wires which have been placed across the reef for the Submarine Tracking Station, stretching down into deeper water. There is a definite shelf at 15m (50ft), creating a mini-wall which drops to 25m (80ft) before continuing to slope off into the depths. The corals are in good order, but many parts of these reefs have a fine algal covering, so that some sections look

Blue-striped grunt (Haemulon sciurus) are commonly found in large schools on the upper reef area.

rather untidy. Expect to find large numbers of damselfish and sergeant majors (*Abudefduf saxatilis*). Goatfish (*Mulloidichthys martinicus*) are common in the sandy areas, while filefish and pufferfish can be seen everywhere.

8 SUFFOLK MAID
★★★

Location: The most southerly wreck in Butler Bay off St Croix's west coast.
Access: By boat only.
Conditions: Fairly sheltered (except from westerly winds), with little current.
Average depth: 15m (50ft)
Maximum depth: 20m (67ft)
Average visibility: 25m (80ft)
The *Suffolk Maid*, a 42m (144ft) steel-hulled North Sea trawler, was driven ashore during a hurricane in 1984. The vessel was eventually cleaned and gutted, towed to its present site and sunk with the aid of a fire hose that filled its cargo holds with water. The vessel now sits perfectly upright in 20m (67ft) of water with her hull parallel to the shoreline. The top portions of this wreck are only 13m (44ft) deep. The huge schools of horse-eye jacks (*Caranx latus*) and blue runners (*Caranx crysos*) are always enjoyable to find on the wreck, which is now well encrusted in all manner of marine growth, particularly golden cup corals, which completely cover the undersides of the hull.

9 ROSAOMAIRA
★★★★

Location: Northern Butler Bay, 360m (400yd) northwest of the *Suffolk Maid* (Site 8).
Access: By boat only.
Conditions: Fairly calm and sheltered with some current to be expected.
Average depth: 21m (70ft)
Maximum depth: 33m (110ft)
Average visibility: 25m (80ft)

The Venezuelan container ship *Rosaomaira* had brought a cargo of cinder blocks to St Croix in 1986 when the dockers offloaded one side first, so that the ship flipped over. The hulk was towed to this site and dynamited to sink it. However, only half the dynamite went off, so that the ship was flipped back right side up as she sank. She is the largest of St Croix's wrecks and now sits upright with her bow facing shore. The wreck is fully intact, with her bow at about 21m (70ft) and the propeller touching the sand at 33m (110ft). South of this point there are almost virgin coral reefs in only about 10m (33ft) of water – they stretch along the entire west end of the island. Marine life in the area is prolific, and the ship has already acquired a good growth and is attracting a multitude of reef fish.

10 NORTHWIND
★★★

Location: East of the *Rosaomaira* (Site 9) off northeast Butler Bay.
Access: By boat only.
Conditions: Fairly calm and sheltered from the worst northerly swells, slight current to be expected.
Average depth: 9m (30ft)
Maximum depth: 14m (47ft)
Average visibility: 21m (70ft)
The *Northwind*, a 22m (75ft) steel-hulled ocean tug, was sunk by Cruzan Divers in 1986 as an artificial reef. She now sits upright in 16m (55ft) of water, completely intact. The *Northwind* was washed ashore in Frederiksted during Tropical Storm Klaus in 1985 and was subsequently used during the filming of *Dreams of Gold – The Mel Fisher Story*. The tug is ideal for photography since the top of the wheelhouse is only 4m (15ft) below the surface. The tugboat has attracted a good deal of fish life, including yellowtail snapper (*Ocyurus chrysurus*), white margate (*Haemulon album*), Bermuda chub (*Kyphosus sectatrix*), and a great many juvenile fish. Inside the hull is a school of blackbar soldierfish (*Myripristis jacobus*).

When the old pillars of Frederiksted Pier were removed to make way for the new construction, they were barged

---

PARASITES

The most commonly seen parasite in the Virgin Islands is the isopod crustacean (*Anilocra laticaudata*). These creatures attach themselves around the eyes or near gill coverings of fish and dine at leisure on the tissue. They are quite common in localized areas, often found in pairs attached to butterflyfish, angelfish, soldierfish and even small blennies. In the latter case the isopod is much larger than its host and will quickly kill the poor fish and move on to a much larger host.

---

to a site in Butler Bay near the *Northwind*. Although a lot of the attached marine life perished as a result of the trip, the remainder has the makings of a great artificial reef and will certainly improve as the years pass.

11 VIRGIN ISLANDER
★★★★

Location: About 90m (100yd) north of the *Northwind* (Site 10).
Access: By boat only.
Conditions: Fairly sheltered but with a slight current (which keeps the water clear).
Average depth: 15m (50ft)
Maximum depth: 21m (70ft)
Average visibility: 25m (80ft)
The *Virgin Islander*, a former flat barge, measures 36m (120ft) in length. Little or no penetration of the wreck is possible as it is now mostly flat metal, but it is covered in a patina of golden cup corals (*Tubastrea coccinea*) and small colourful encrusting sponges and tube worms. Sunk in 1991, the hulk is gradually becoming overgrown in larger sponges, sea fans and small hard corals. Acting as a natural oasis for fish life on this otherwise sandy plain, the wreck attracts schools of snapper and chub, as well as several large resident grouper.

12 DAVIS BAY
★★★☆☆☆

Location: North of the old plantation called Sweet Bottom, offshore from the Cane Bay Dive Shop.
Access: From the shore or by boat.
Conditions: Can be some surge and swell in the shallows.
Average depth: 6m (20ft)
Maximum depth: 25m (80ft)
Average visibility: 15m (50ft)
Davis Bay is a favourite site for diver training and one of the few areas in St Croix where there is fairly easy access down a sandy beach. This quickly gives way to an old coralline limestone shelf, pockmarked with small holes where spiny sea urchins and numerous juvenile fish and small gobies can be found. As you travel further north, the reef formation changes to a classic spur-and-groove with wide sandy platforms amid rising coral fingers, which gradually slope down into the depths. Southern stingrays (*Dasyatis americana*) are always found here as are yellowhead jawfish (*Opistognathus aurifrons*) and garden eels (*Heteroconger halis*). Wrasse, parrotfish, grouper, snapper and grunt are all common and the coral and sponge growths are quite healthy once you reach deeper waters.

13 NORTH STAR
★★★★★★☆☆

Location: 1km (1 mile) west of Cane Bay.
Access: By boat only.
Conditions: Surface chop and swell to be expected.
Average depth: 12m (40ft)
Maximum depth: Beyond 65m (210ft)
Average visibility: 30m (100ft)
The mooring for this site is set at 7m (25ft) in the middle of a nice coral garden. There are sand chutes that lead down from a flat coral shelf at 6m (20ft) to the wall, which drops to several thousand feet. Two old Danish anchors lie just to the north of the mooring in a small grotto at 20m (66ft). The wall is deeply sculpted, with some parts almost vertical and others cut by fissures and cracks. Way below the safe diving limit, two huge submarine seamounts can be seen rising up from the depths, one of them cut by an enormous shaft. The site is well known for the large schools of blue chromis and creole wrasse found at the top of the wall. North Star probably has more marine life than any other site around the island. It's not unusual to see a hawksbill turtle (*Eretmochelys imbricata*) or two, as well as stingrays and eels. You can snorkel out from the shore through a very nice coral garden, but beware of the spiny sea urchins in the shallows, especially when there is any surface swell. Descend and follow some gently sloping sand canyons between huge spurs of coral to the site.

14 WEST PALM BEACH
★★★

Location: The mooring between North Star (Site 13) and Cane Bay.
Access: By boat only.
Conditions: Surface swell and surge to be expected.
Average depth: 12m (40ft)
Maximum depth: Beyond 65m (210ft)
Average visibility: 30m (100ft)
West Palm Beach is named after what was once a rather nice palm-lined beach; alas, a passing hurricane removed the palms. The mooring is in 11m (37ft) and a rather compressed spur-and-groove reef slopes down to 18m (60ft) before becoming more vertical and dropping beyond safe diving limits. Better known for its sponges than for its coral growth, this site features rope sponges (*Aplysina cauliformis* and *Aplysina fulva*), yellow tube sponges (*Aplysina fistularis*) and brown tube sponges (*Agelas conifera*). Small featherduster worms (*Bispira* spp.) and stinging hydroids (*Gymnangium longicauda*) are interspersed everywhere, and large congregations of bluehead wrasse (*Thalassoma bifasciatum*) roam the reef crest.

15 PAVILIONS (CANE BAY WALL)
★★★★★☆

Location: Directly offshore from the Waves Hotel at Cane Bay.
Access: From shore, or by boat for the deeper sections.
Conditions: Some surge and surface swell to be expected in the shallows.
Average depth: 15m (50ft)
Maximum depth: Beyond 65m (210ft)
Average visibility: 6–25m (20–80ft)
The site lies at the east end of Cane Bay. The mooring is in 11m (35ft) right on the wall, positioned for exploring the deeper reaches of this overgrown spur-and-groove reef. It is a very beautiful wall that is alive with coral, sponges, and marine life. There are some small canyons and sand chutes leading over the wall, which drops initially to about 30m (100ft), levels off slightly, and eventually drops straight down. From the shore, there is a wide expanse of fairly flat coralline limestone rock with intermittent patches of sea fans and small knobby corals; this gradually makes way to a more defined spur-and-groove reef offering some protection and better coral growths. There are lots of golden stingrays (*Urolophus jamaicensis*) in these areas, as well as slender filefish (*Monacanthus tuckeri*) on all the sea fans and bandtail pufferfish hiding on the sand.

16 JIMMY'S SURPRISE
★★★★

Location: The western portion of the same spur-and-groove reef as Rust Op Twist (Site 17).
Access: By boat only.
Conditions: Surface surge, current and swell to be expected.
Average depth: 18m (60ft)
Maximum depth: 42m (140ft)
Average visibility: 36m (120ft)
This spectacular dive is suitable only for more advanced divers – not only is it deep, but also there is almost always a fairly strong current. The mooring is set at 17m (57ft), from where divers follow a ridge down to a huge pinnacle that starts at 18m (60ft) and drops to 36m (120ft) before becoming a vertical wall dropping several thousand feet. Near the mooring are the junction box and pipes which took seawater into a former shrimp farm in the area and now act as a useful navigation point for divers to this site. The area is well known for its large numbers of tropical fish, such as queen angelfish (*Holacanthus ciliaris*), rock beauties (*Holacanthus tricolor*), longsnout butterflyfish (*Chaetodon aculeatus*) and reef butterflyfish (*Chaetodon sedentarius*). The spurs of coral

Above: *Juvenile blue tang (Acanthurus coeruleus) hide amidst corals for protection.*
Below: *Balloonfish (Diodon holocanthus) are common on all reefs.*

are all in good order and covered in sea fans, plumes and a huge variety of sponges. Looking out to sea, you can frequently find large groups of pelagic jacks and turtle.

17 RUST OP TWIST (GENTLE WINDS)
★★★★

Location: West of Baron Bluff, offshore from the Cane Bay Reef Hotel.
Access: By boat only.
Conditions: Choppy on the surface and surge to be expected in the shallows.
Average depth: 12m (40ft)
Maximum depth: 18m (60ft)
Average visibility: 25m (80ft)
The curious name of this site comes from the name of an old plantation and is Danish for 'resting place' or 'place of leisure'. The site is midway along a 2km (1 mile) stretch of spur-and-groove reef which slopes gradually down to a sandy plain at 18m (60ft). There are well formed brain corals (*Diploria strigosa*), lettuce corals (*Leptoseris cucullata*) and spiky patches of elkhorn coral (*Acropora palmata*) which always have snapper and grunt sheltering under the extended branches. Tall stands of pillar coral (*Dendrogyra cylindrus*) are everywhere and all of them are home to large numbers of cleaning gobies. This is a fairly classic spur-and-groove reef, with all the attendant marine life to be expected.

18 ANCHOR WALL
★★★★

Location: On the western approaches to Salt River Bay.
Access: By boat only.
Conditions: Can be choppy on the surface with some current.
Average depth: 15m (50ft)
Maximum depth: Beyond 36m (120ft)
Average visibility: 30m (100ft)

This is a steeply sloping, classic spur-and-groove reef with high coral buttresses split by deep sand chutes. The dive is undertaken with the current and you traverse the coral ridges and valleys, dropping down to explore the undersides of coral ledges or swimming around the impressive sea fans and plumes. Larger pelagic fish such as tarpon (*Megalops atlanticus*) and Atlantic spadefish (*Chaetodipterus faber*) are common, as are sightings of green turtle (*Chelonia mydas*). In the sandy grooves you will find cushion sea stars (*Oreaster reticulatus*), leopard flatworms (*Pseudoceros pardalis*) and spaghetti worms (*Eupolymnia crassicornis*). It is an excellent dive, but care should be taken of your dive profile, as the coral spurs are over 6m (20ft) high and it is easy to forget the time barriers at depth, particularly when faced with so much marine life to enjoy.

19 GROUPER GROTTO
(SALT RIVER WEST WALL)
★★★★

Location: The next mooring buoy west from Anchor Wall (Site 18) before Salt River Bay.
Access: By boat only.
Conditions: Can be choppy on the surface with some current near the corner.
Average depth: 25m (50ft)
Maximum depth: Beyond 65m (210ft)
Average visibility: 30m (100ft)
This is one of the most requested boat dives along the northern coral wall, as there are countless pinnacles, canyons, ledges and recesses for divers to explore at their leisure. Several long passages under the coral ledges lead to tunnels and small caves which are quite easily negotiated. The pinnacles range in size from about 1m (3ft) in diameter to the size of a house and all topped with sea plumes (*Pseudopterogorgia* spp.). There are large green moray eels (*Gymnothorax funebris*), cero (*Scomberomorus regalis*), schools of bigeye scad (*Selar crumenophthalmus*), barracuda, snapper, grunt, wrasse and parrotfish. At night, huge basketstars (*Astrophyton*

The deeply convoluted reefs of St Croix are a delight to visiting divers.

muricatum) extend their sticky arms and slate pencil urchins (*Eucidaris tribuloides*) crawl out into the open.

20 BARRACUDA BANK
(SALT RIVER EAST WALL)
★★★★

Location: Out to the start of the coral reef which runs to the east from Salt River Bay.
Access: By boat only.
Conditions: Can be some surge and current around the corner.
Average depth: 15m (50ft)
Maximum depth: Beyond 65m (210ft)
Average visibility: 30m (100ft)
Often referred to as the 'fishiest dive on the north shore', the corner of the Salt River Canyon has huge schools of durgon (*Melichthys niger*), yellowtail snapper (*Ocyurus chrysurus*) and creole wrasse (*Clepticus parrai*). The wall rolls over at about 12m (40ft) and drops amid a number of coral gullies and sand chutes to 25m (80ft), before it drops once more into the blue. There are hundreds of coral pinnacles all along the wall where numerous species of moray eels are always found. The

corner of the wall, before it turns due south into the Salt River Canyon, is where large numbers of juvenile barracuda can be found, attracted by the mix of plankton-feeding fish. It is popular as a night dive, with the undersides of the coral ledges covered in golden cup corals (*Tubastrea coccinea*) and octopus to be seen everywhere. Also look out for tiger's tail sea cucumbers (*Holothuria thomasi*) which are quite rare in other locations of the Caribbean.

21 WHITE HORSE
★★★★

Location: At the eastern end of the reef which runs eastwards from Salt River Bay.
Access: By boat only.
Conditions: Can be strong surge and large waves in the shallows. Great care should be taken at all times.
Average depth: 4m (13ft)
Maximum depth: 8m (27ft)
Average visibility: 12m (40ft)
This is an incredibly exciting dive in shallow water, but it should not be used as a snorkelling site: the surge can be quite fierce and there is a very real danger of being

Social featherduster worms (Bispira brunnea) may be found over all of the shallow reefs.

dashed against the jagged corals which come to within a few centimetres of the surface. The reef itself is deeply scored with large open crevices, quite a large tunnel and a nice arch, under which divers can shelter from the almost continual surge from crashing waves. There are always large numbers of juvenile tropical fish, as well as schools of brown chromis (*Chromis multilineata*) and various species of damselfish which always attract barracuda and needlefish (*Ablennes hians*). When the sea is calm enough to explore the shallower reef sections, you will come across lots of evidence of ancient shipwrecks, including cannon, anchors, ballast and anchor chain. Also in the shallows you can find the rare sailfin blenny (*Emblemaria pandionis*) which is comical to watch as it darts out of its hole to snatch at passing plankton, or to attack its neighbours.

22 LITTLE COZUMEL
★★★

Location: At the northwestern end of Long Reef.
Access: By boat only.
Conditions: Current to be expected on the corner and some surge.
Average depth: 15m (50ft)
Maximum depth: 21m (70ft)
Average visibility: 25m (80ft)

The site is not named because it resembles the Mexican island of Cozumel but rather because it shares sometimes strong currents moving through from east to west. The mooring is placed in 13m (45ft) of water and is on the top of a tremendous boulder – one of two distinctive huge boulders covered in corals and sponges. These are separated by about 15m (50ft) of sand and coral rubble seabed, which is home to yellowhead jawfish (*Opistognathus aurifrons*). The sides of the boulders have plenty of coral and sponge life, while the underside of one of them has a carved out overhang that extends 6m (20ft) into the rock, which is covered in encrusting sponges and cup corals. Beyond the boulders are gently sloping walls that are filled with many gorgonians. Grouper, snapper, wrasse, barracuda and chub are common on the site.

23 CORMORANT
★★★★

Location: North of Cormorant Bay.
Access: By boat only.
Conditions: Can be some surge, slight current and surface chop.
Average depth: 15m (50ft)
Maximum depth: 25m (80ft)
Average visibility: 25m (80ft)
There are four mooring buoys on the section of Long Reef known as Cormorant. Similar to The Shack (Site 24), this section is a convoluted reef system seemingly constructed of random coral heads which jut out of a richly encrusted coral reef, covered in sponges and sea plumes. The undersides of the coral blocks are particularly fascinating, as many have created small

---

Shark-nosed gobies (Gobiosoma evelynea) are just one of the many 'cleaners' on the reefs.

swimthroughs which are home to schools of squirrelfish (*Holocentrus adscensionis*) and fairy basslets (*Gramma loreto*). Blennies and gobies appear to be located on every coral head and there are cleaning stations everywhere.

24 THE SHACK (GREEN SHACK)
★★★★

Location: Northwest of Mill Harbour to the northern section of Long Reef, opposite a shack on the headland.
Access: By boat only.
Conditions: Can be some surge and surface swell.
Average depth: 12m (40ft)
Maximum depth: 21m (70ft)
Average visibility: 25m (80ft)
The site is alternatively known as Purple Shack (its colour before Hurricane Hugo), Love Shack (by the romantics on the island) or The Shack (for those who just got tired of the name changes). The mooring is set at 11m (37ft) along a gently sloping wall that drops to about 21m (70ft), with numerous large coral heads which have created ledges and small tunnels overgrown with golden cup corals and brilliantly coloured encrusting sponges. This site is known for sightings of juvenile spotted drum (*Equetus punctatus*), occasionally a flying gurnard (*Dactylopterus volitans*) and snake eels (*Myrichthys* spp.). The corals are in good order and there are always large shoals of creole wrasse and parrotfish cruising the reef crest.

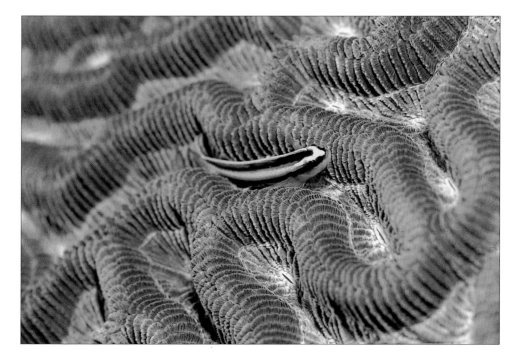

25 CHEZ BARGE
★★★

Location: Just northwest of Christiansted harbour.
Access: By boat only.
Conditions: Fairly sheltered, but lots of boat traffic.
Average depth: 22m (75ft)
Maximum depth: 28m (95ft)
Average visibility: 9m (30ft)

It is ironic that even the most obscure shipwrecks can often become exceptionally popular dive sites. The remains of this old unnamed barge with an unknown history lie just outside Christiansted harbour. It was thought to have sunk in 1975 south of Long Reef when being towed out into deeper water. Now known locally as Chez Barge, it has become a popular fish-feeding station. The old barge lies upside-down on a coral slope and is safe for divers – except for the eager attention of a huge green moray eel called Earl, which gets very close indeed. Earl is just one of a number of eels which perform for their daily fish scraps at 14.00 each day. In the interests of diver safety, no fish-feeding is done at any other time. Among the other regular residents are barracuda and numerous chub, sergeant majors and snapper. The remains of a steel crane stick out from under one side of the barge.

26 EAGLE RAY
★★★★

Location: Due north of Christiansted, just outside the harbour channel.
Access: By boat only.
Conditions: Fairly calm and sheltered, but there is danger from boat traffic.
Average depth: 12m (40ft)
Maximum depth: 20m (66ft)
Average visibility: 18m (60ft)

This site is named after a pair of eagle rays (*Aetobatus narinari*) that frequent the area, cruising along just off the mini-wall. There are various small sand chutes that lead down and away from the shallower reef crest where the mooring is set at 9m (3ft). The mini-wall slopes to 20m (66ft) amid a jumble of fairly good corals, mostly topped by algal fuzz and holding hundreds of damselfish including the brilliantly coloured juvenile cocoa damselfish (*Stegastes variabilis*) and the yellowtail damselfish (*Microspathadon chrysurus*). Being so close to shore, this is also a very popular night dive which just about always yields a dozing green turtle (*Chelonia mydas*), spiny lobster (*Panulirus argus*) and Caribbean reef octopus (*Octopus briareus*). The undersides of all the ledges are covered in golden cup corals (*Tubastrea coccinea*) which light up the reef at night.

27 EAST REEF
★★★

Location: North of Christiansted, to the eastern end of Long Reef.
Access: By boat only.
Conditions: Can be choppy on the surface with some current to be expected.
Average depth: 15m (50ft)
Maximum depth: Beyond 65m (210ft)
Average visibility: 25m (80ft)

The eastern end of Long Reef is popular with the Christiansted dive shops, due to it being only 5–10 minutes' boat ride. As one of the closest healthy reefs to the shore, it is also a very popular night diving destination. Purple vase sponges (*Callispongia plicifera*) and giant barrel sponges (*Xestospongia muta*) are common, as are angular sea whips (*Pterogorgia anceps*) and giant sea plumes (*Pseudopterogorgia* spp.). Fish life is not as profuse as on other sites, but you will find schools of blue chromis (*Chromis cyanea*) and various species of wrasse, parrotfish, grouper, snapper and grunt. The crevices are home to spiny lobster and bigeye (*Priacanthus arenatus*).

28 SCOTCH BANKS (BUCCANEER)
★★★

Location: North of the Buccaneer Hotel and northwest of Green Cay.
Access: By boat only.
Conditions: Can be choppy on the outer reef and rather exposed.
Average depth: 25m (80ft)
Maximum depth: Beyond 65m (210ft)
Average visibility: 30m (100ft)

This northeastern site is located at the northern edge of the coral wall before it turns south towards shore and shallower water. The wall has three tiers: there are steps at 12m, 39m and 50m (40, 130 and 165ft), with vertical drops at each step. Originally named after a cargo ship which lost its cargo of Scotch whisky overboard in a storm, Scotch Banks is home to thousands of Bermuda chub (*Kyphosus sectatrix*) and dogtooth snapper (*Lutjanus jocu*), which swarm around you as you enter the water, and large numbers of wrasse, snapper and grunt can be found all over the reef. Large green moray eels (*Gymnothorax funebris*) are often seen swimming about in the open, while the

The north wall of St Croix offers the only true wall diving in the Virgin Islands.

small sand patches on the deeper slopes have garden eels (*Heteroconger halis*) and heart urchins (*Meoma ventricosa*). The reef is of good quality and has survived the last few hurricanes – the site is quite popular despite the depth.

29 GREEN CAY SLOPE
★★

Location: North of Green Cay to the edge of the drop-off.
Access: By boat only.
Conditions: Can be choppy on the surface with some surge.
Average depth: 15m (50ft)
Maximum depth: Beyond 65m (210ft)
Average visibility: 18m (60ft)

The coral wall in this area is more gently sloping than the vertical drops found elsewhere along northern St Croix. Although the site is seldom dived due to the rather low-lying coral formations, there are good concentrations of fish, particularly Nassau grouper (*Epinephelus striatus*) and tiger grouper (*Mycteroperca tigris*). Hermit crabs are very common and found almost everywhere, particularly red reef hermits (*Paguristes cadenati*) and white-speckled hermit crabs (*Paguristes punticeps*). A few of the sea fans have flamingo tongue snails (*Cyphoma gibbosum*) and the algae-covered corals often feature nudibranchs and brittlestars.

30 BUCK ISLAND REEF
★★☆☆☆☆

Location: Offshore coral island to the northeast of St Croix.
Access: By boat only.
Conditions: Can be choppy, but generally sheltered off the southeast corner.
Average depth: 4m (13ft)
Maximum depth: 6m (20ft)
Average visibility: 12m (40ft)

Buck Island Reef is classed as a US National Monument and is protected by the United States National Park Service. The only dive centre with a licence to dive Buck Island is Dive St Croix, and in actual fact little diving takes place, as the island is principally used for snorkelling trips. Some of the shallower stretches of reef were damaged by Hurricane Marilyn and consequently display algal growth. However, generally the reef is recovering nicely and you can see new coral growths everywhere. There are large numbers of damselfish, sergeant majors and yellowtail snapper which are well used to being hand-fed by the snorkel tourists.

Along the eastern end of the island a barrier reef has created a safe and sheltered lagoon with a sandy floor dotted with coral heads. Here you can find an underwater trail with signs that explain the reef ecology, providing an important introduction to the marine environment for many snorkelling visitors.

Blackbar soldierfish (Myripristis jacobus) are shade-loving fish, generally found under coral overhangs.

How to Get There

Getting to St Croix is easy, with services by major airlines and many smaller airlines from their Miami, Baltimore, Atlanta and San Juan hub airports respectively before connecting to St Croix. The Henry E. Rohlsen Airport is located in the southwest of the island near the Hess oil refinery. The airport is connected by the Melvin H. Evans Highway 66 to the Queen Mary Highway 70 and takes about 30 minutes travel time by airport taxi to most of the resorts and main towns.

Direct air services are also available on Delta from Atlanta, USAir from Baltimore and a myriad of commuter flights that connect the island with San Juan and other nearby islands, such as Air Anguilla, LIAT, Coastal Air Transport, Executive Air and Vieques Air Link. Contact the Henry E. Rohlsen Airport, tel (340) 778 7105, for information. An alternative in flying inter-island is by seaplane, which links Christiansted on St Croix with St Thomas, Tortola and San Juan several times daily – this is also a great sightseeing tour. Contact Seaborne Seaplanes, tel (340) 777 4491.

There are infrequent stops in St Croix by cruise ships – less than in St Thomas, with perhaps only one ship per week and even depending on the weather, as the pier at Frederiksted is in an exposed location with any westerly swells making mooring impossible. Cruise ship guests are taken by taxi bus to Christiansted.

The Virgin Hydrofoil operates a return service between Charlotte Amalie on St Thomas and Christiansted and costs $37 one way; tel (340) 776 7417.

Getting Around

St Croix is by far the largest of the Virgin Islands and touring the island is best done in your own vehicle or by sharing a taxi van between four or six people for a more informal island tour. Due to the distances involved, touring the island will take up most of the day including a lunch stop either in Christiansted or Frederiksted. The Queen Mary Highway 70 is the fastest route along the centre of the island and Highway 69 links the airport to Cane Bay.

Car rental agencies are often at road junctions and the larger ones have an office at the airport. A number of resort hotels also have their own hire vehicles, or can arrange for a hire car to be delivered to your hotel. Rental vehicles are mainly four-wheel-drive jeeps. Although the island is mostly fairly flat, on the mountain trail to the northwest it is advisable to use the four-wheel drive facility as little of the trail is paved and it can be steep and winding in places.

Avis Rent-A-Car
Henry E. Rohlsen Airport, St Croix; tel (340) 778 9355; website: www.avis.com

Budget Rent-A-Car
Henry E. Rohlsen Airport, St Croix, P.O. Box 278, Christiansted, St. Croix USVI 00821; tel (340) 778 9636; email: budgetstx@vipowernet.net; website: www.budgetstcroix.com

Centerline Car Rentals
PO Box 1529, Kingshill, St. Croix, VI 00851, tel/fax (340) 778 0450, toll-free (888) 288 8755; email: reservations@centerline carrentals.com; website: www.ccrvi.com

Hertz Rent-A-Car
Henry E. Rohlsen Airport, St Croix; tel (340) 778 1402, toll free (888) 248 4261; e-mail: info@rentacarstcroix.com; website: www.rentacarstcroix.com

Judi of Croix Car Rentals
4017 Hermon Hill, Christiansted, St. Croix, US Virgin Islands 00820; tel (340) 773 2123; toll free (877) 903 2123

Olympic Rent-A-Car
1103 Richmond, Christiansted; tel (340) 773 8000; email: rent@olympicstcroix.com; website: www.olympicstcroix.com

St Croix Bike and Tours
PO Box 26094, Christiansted, USVI; tel (340) 773 4466; website: www.stcroixbike.com

Caribbean Taxi Service
108 La Grande Princesse, St Croix; tel (340) 773 9799

Sweeney's Safari Tours
Departs King St, Christiansted; tel (340) 773 6700

Where to Stay

There is a very wide choice of accommodation on St Croix. Most hotels also offer diving, whether provided by the company or leased out through a concession agreement with one of the major watersports operators. All the major hotels offer restaurants, bars and swimming pools and there is a more than adequate range of accommodation to suit all tastes and price structures. The main towns of Frederiksted and Christiansted are surprisingly lacking in good hotels, with most of the resorts strung out along the North Shore Road along Cane Bay and Davis Bay.

Cottages and guest houses tend to be more intimate and are usually furnished to the highest standard. As on St Thomas and St John, there are cottage colonies. These are very popular with repeat visitors to the

islands. One of the best small resort hotels is Waves at Cane Bay, which features large efficiency rooms built on the water's edge. The address of most resort accommodations is based on the former estate whose land they now occupy. As elsewhere in the USVI, an 8% local tax is added to your hotel bill unless otherwise stated.

For additional information on any of the accommodation offered, get in touch with **The United States Virgin Islands Department of Tourism,** PO Box 6400, St Thomas, VI 00804; US toll free tel (800) 372 8784; tel (340) 774 8784; fax (340) 774 4390; e-mail: info@usvi.net

Expensive
The Sun Terra Carambola Beach Resort, Estate Davis Bay, PO Box 3031, Kingshill, St Croix, VI 00851; US toll free tel (800) 228 3000; tel (340) 778 3800; fax (340) 778 1682
Located on Davis Bay, 150 spacious suites, large golf course and all watersports. 30min ride from main towns, but very secluded if you are looking for privacy.

The Buccaneer Hotel, PO Box 25200, Gallows Bay, Christiansted, St Croix, VI 00824; US toll free tel (800) 255 3881; tel (340) 773 2100; fax (340) 778 4009
Luxury self-contained beachside resort, golf course, three beaches, four restaurants and all watersports available. Admirably outfitted rooms with marble bathrooms.

Cormorant Beach Club and Villas, 4126 La Grande Princess, Christiansted, St Croix, VI 00824; US toll free tel (800) 548 4460; tel (340) 778 8920; fax (340) 778 9218; email: cormorant@viaccess.net
Rooms, suites and villas decorated to a very high standard. Secluded beachfront. Excellent restaurant and all sporting facilities.

Colony Cove Resorts, 3221 Golden Rock, Christiansted, St Croix, VI 00824; US toll free (800) 828 0746; tel (340) 773 1965; fax (340) 773 5397; email: colcove@ islands.vi; website: www.usvi.net/ hotel/colony. Tropical-style apartments surrounded by herb gardens. Comfortable condominiums, with all amenities. Large pool and full watersports centre.

Antilles Club St Croix, 321A Estate Golden Rock, St Croix, VI 00820; US toll free tel (800) 524 2025; tel (340) 773 9150; fax (340) 773 4805; email: reservations@antillesresorts.com
Luxury beachfront condominium resort. All rooms fully equipped and with ocean view. Nice restaurant. Very Caribbean and colourful in character.

Villa Madeleine Resort, 19A Teague Bay, St Croix, VI 00820; US toll free tel (800) 237 1959; tel (340) 773 4850; fax (340) 773 7518; email: jcapusvi@islands.vi
One of the best on St Croix's East End, built around a plantation Great House. 20 cottages scattered around an antiques-filled building. Very chic, very exclusive, and miles from anywhere.

Hotel on the Cay, PO Box 223329 Christiansted, St. Croix, VI 00822; US toll free tel (800) 524 2035; tel (340) 773 2035; fax (340) 773 7046; email: info@hotelonthecay.com; website: www.hotelonthecay.com
Good location in Christiansted harbour, reached by private ferry. Great Tuesday night BBQ.

Mid-range
Chenay Bay Beach Resort, PO Box 24600, Christiansted, VI 00824; US toll free tel (800) 548 4457; tel/fax (340) 773 2918; e-mail: chenaybay1@worldnet.att.net
Family resort, 5km (3 miles) east of Christiansted. Runs a special 'Cruzan Kidz' programme for children during the summer months.

Cane Bay Reef Club, 114A La Vallee, PO Box 1407, Kingshill, St Croix, VI 00820; US toll free tel (800) 253 8534; tel/fax (340) 778 2966; e-mail: cbrc@viaccess.net
Nine two-room suites with fully equipped kitchens and balconies over the sea.

Hibiscus Beach Hotel, 4131 La Grande Princesse, St Croix, VI 00820-4441; US toll free tel (800) 442 0121; tel (340) 773 4042; fax (340) 773 7668; e-mail: hibiscus@worldnet.att.net
Friendly and laid-back, at the edge of the sea. 37 rooms with sea view, very good restaurant.

Tamarind Reef Hotel, 5001 Tamarind Reef, St Croix, VI 00820; US toll free tel (800) 619 0014; tel (340) 773 4455; fax (340) 773 3989; email: reservations@tamarindreefhotel.com; website: www.tamarindreefhotel.com
New hotel, all ocean-front rooms, most with kitchenettes, two beaches, freshwater pool, adjacent to Green Cay Marina.

Inexpensive
The Waves at Cane Bay, PO Box 1749, Kingshill, St Croix, VI 00851; tel (340) 778 1805; fax (340) 778 4945; toll free (800) 545 0603
Large spacious efficiency rooms overlooking the sea. Lovely restaurant, sea swimming pool and small dive centre run by Kevin and Suzanne Ryan.

Antilles Frederiksted Hotel, 442 Strand St, Frederiksted, St Croix, VI 00840; tel (800) 524 2025; tel tel (340) 772 0500; fax (340) 719 1272; email: info@frederiksted hotel.com; website: www.frederiksted hotel.dk
Modern apartments near cruise-ship dock and perfect for diving the pier.

Pink Fancy Hotel, 27 Prince St , Christiansted, St Croix, VI 00820; US toll free tel (800) 524 2045; tel (340) 773 8460; fax (340) 773 6448; email: info@pinkfancy.com
Near the centre of town in newly refurbished Danish buildings dating from 1780. Complimentary breakfast and cocktails.

King Christian Hotel, 59 King's Wharf, PO Box 24467, Christiansted, St Croix, VI 00824; tel (340) 773 6330; fax (340) 773 2285; email: info@kingchristian.com; website: www.kingchristian.com
European-style converted warehouse, all watersports, shops and bank on premises. Reasonable restaurant and nice and close to explore the rest of town.

WHERE TO EAT

Eating out in St Croix is quite a social affair with a huge range on offer. Many of the smaller, more rural restaurants are distinctly Caribbean in style and food choice, with local specialities such as callaloo soup (made from seafood and greens) and soursop (a local fruit, mixed with milk, water, sugar and spices, popular as a drink or even ice cream). The main towns of Frederiksted and Christiansted have the obligatory 'surf and turf' (a combination of fresh lobster, fish or shrimp with steak) establishments. Most visitors, however, tend to stay in their respective hotels, as the in-house restaurants are all excellent.

Very few require reservations in advance and the dress code is casual. A service charge of 15% is usually added to your restaurant bill. A free restaurant guide is available from the Department of Tourism.

Alternatively, the Stop & Save Foodmarket, Deli & Bakery is a well stocked supermarket which also sells sandwiches, salads, dips, pastries and bread baked on the premises.

The Waves, Cane Bay, Kingshill, St Croix; tel (340) 778 1805
Balcony overlooking the sea, seafood and steak specialities.

Columbus Cove, Columbus Cove Marina, Salt River, St Croix; tel (340) 778 5771
Great breakfasts, homemade pasta and weekend brunch.

The Galleon, Green Cay Marina, St Croix tel (340) 773 9949
Mixed French and Italian style, extensive menu and wine list.

The Bombay Club, 5A King St , Christiansted, St Croix; tel (340) 773 1838
Popular BBQ, steaks and seafood pasta, air conditioning and separate TV sports bar.

Tivoli Gardens, Pan Am Pavilion, Christiansted, St Croix; tel (340) 773 6782
Dining and dancing, superb seafood dishes and homemade desserts. Try the guava cream pie.

Cultured Pelican Ristorante, Coakley Bay Condos, East End, St Croix; tel (340) 773 3333; website: www.cultured pelican.com
Home-style Italian cuisine. Closed Mondays.

Duggan's Reef, Teague Bay, St Croix; tel (340) 773 9800
Rated best beachfront restaurant on St Croix. Try the Irish whiskey lobster or do the Sunday brunch.

DIVE OPERATORS

Anchor Dive Center, Salt River Marina, PO Box 5588, St Croix, VI 00823; US toll free tel (800) 532 DIVE (3483); tel/fax (340) 778 1522; email: info@anchordivestcroix.com; website: www.anchordivestcroix.com
Great location inside Salt River and perfect for diving the northern wall.

Cane Bay Dive Shop, PO Box 4510, Kingshill, St Croix, VI 00851; US toll free tel (800) 338 3843; tel (340) 773 9913; fax (340) 778 5442; email: info@canebayscuba.com; website: www.canebayscuba.com
Great shop opposite the beach for shore diving Davis Bay and Cane Bay, lots of parking. Now rebreather friendly.

Cap'n Dick's Scuba West, ScubaWest, LLC 330 Strand Street, Frederiksted, St. Croix, US Virgin Islands 00840; tel (800) 352 0107; fax (340) 713 1459; email: adventure@divescubawest.com; website: www.divescubawest.com
Well outfitted shop opposite Fredericksted Pier and convenient for Butler Bay wrecks.

Dive Experience Inc., PO Box 4254, Christiansted, St Croix, VI 00822; US toll free tel (800) 235 9047; tel (340) 773 3307; fax (340) 773 7030; email: info@divexp. com; website: www.divexp.com
Busy shop with regular fish-feeding at Chez Barge; look out for the huge moray eels.

Cane Bay Dive Shop, PO Box 4510, Kingshill, St. Croix, US Virgin Islands 00851; toll free (800) 338 3843; tel (340) 773 9913; fax (340) 778 5442; email: info@canebayscuba.com; website: www.canebayscuba.com
Small operation, perfect for Cane Bay shore diving, very personalized diving. Now rebreather friendly.

EMERGENCY SERVICES

Police Emergency, tel 91l , (340) 778 2211 or (340) 772 9111

Coastguard Emergency, Marine Safety Detachment; tel (340) 776 3497

Air Ambulance, Bohlke Airways tel (340) 778 9177

Juan Luis F. Hospital, 4007 Estate Diamond Ruby, C'sted; tel (340) 778 6311

Golden Rock Pharmacy, Golden Rock Shopping Centre, Christiansted; tel (340) 773 7666

Recompression Chamber, St Thomas; tel (340) 776 8311

Divers Alert Network, tel (919) 684 8111

LOCAL HIGHLIGHTS

Dance the Imperial Quadrille at various festivals on the island. The dance dates back to the 18th century when the islands were under French occupation. Witty and lively, the dancers call to each other in French 'mele' – the local word for gossip.

Visit **Fort Frederik**, where the first foreign salute was given to the United States in 1776. At the Fort on July 3, 1848, Governor General Peter Von Scholten emancipated the slaves in the Danish West Indies.

Walk about **Frederiksted**: the old colonial buildings, schools and churches amid a square grid of narrow streets are well worth exploring. There are old Morovian and Lutheran Churches and St Patrick's Roman Catholic Church which was built from coral stone in 1842. In **Christiansted**, you can pick up a walking tour guide map from the Division of Tourism. Visit the outdoor market for fresh fruit and vegetables, the Steeple building where you will find a small display of Arawak artefacts and the workings of a sugar plantation, the old Customs House, Government House and Fort Christiansvaern.

Take a drive through the rainforest and stop at the old Creque Dam, where the air is filled with the scent of mountain cloves and exotic flowers. Watersports include windsurfing, jet skis, kayaks, parasailing, sailing and the famous **Buck Island National Park** with its underwater snorkel trail and beautiful white sand beach. There are huge expanses of beaches, some completely secluded and others with beach bars and restaurants.

The **St Croix Aquarium and Marine Education Center** is well worth a visit. An informative tour here takes 30 minutes, explaining all about mating behaviour, species identification, reef conservation,

Lightbulb tunicates (Clavelina picta) may be found around mangrove roots.

feeding habits and diving and snorkelling tips. At the end of each season all the aquarium exhibits are returned to the wild and the collection starts anew. Find it at 4005 Hermon Hill, Christiansted VI 00820-4430; email: txaquarium@viaccess.net; website: stcroixaquarium.org.

ST THOMAS

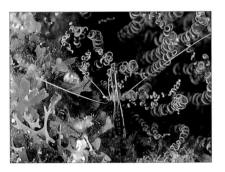

St Thomas has an area of 53km² (32 square miles) and is 20km (12 miles) long and 5km (3 miles) across at its widest point. It is easily the most heavily commercialized and developed of all the Virgin Islands – in fact, it is one of the most developed islands in the Caribbean and its main town, Charlotte Amalie, shares a similar dilemma with Georgetown on Grand Cayman in that it now has serious rush hour traffic problems.

Arriving by air or cruise ship, you cannot help but be impressed by Charlotte Amalie (which is also the capital of the US Virgin Islands), with its wonderful natural harbour enclosed by steep-sided hills. The harbour teems with cruise ships, motor boats, yachts and other vessels and congestion in the waterways has become as much of a problem as congestion on the capital's roads. The scenic appeal of the harbour is somewhat marred by the mass of buildings which spread like a rash across the surrounding hillsides. On busy cruise ship days the town itself can also be a bit of nightmare, with the streets congested with thousands of visitors.

Yet, for all this, St Thomas retains a vitality and energy which have helped it prosper over several centuries of trading ships passing through its harbour. It continues to draw in thousands of visitors thanks to its excellent hotels and top-notch nightlife (big acts fly in to perform here, earning it the nickname 'the nightclub of the Virgin Islands') as well as what many consider to be the best shopping opportunities in the Caribbean. In addition – though visitors should not expect a romantic, tropical idyll – St Thomas does have the virtue of great beaches: there are 44 on the island, of which Magens Bay on the north coast has been listed by *National Geographic Magazine* as one of the ten most beautiful beaches in the world.

Most of the accommodation on St Thomas is concentrated around Charlotte Amalie and the eastern and northeastern end of the island, where a criss-cross network of winding roads takes you around the steep-sided mountains. The western regions of St Thomas are

Opposite: *Charlotte Amalie's huge natural harbour has been used by generations of seafarers.*
Above: *Pederson's cleaning shrimp (Perilimenes pedersoni) sets up 'shop' beside a corkscrew anemone.*

largely empty, undeveloped scrub-land. However, development is still spreading around the coastline and, as the island continues to grow in popularity as a holiday destination, it seems certain that it will keep expanding commercially.

Red Hook, on the eastern tip, is the location of the main terminal for ferries from St John and Tortola in the British Virgin Islands. These ferries are always busy and the regular services are more often than not filled with 'belongens' – locals who have relatives and jobs in both the US and British Virgin Islands.

The majority of the dive sites are located around the north coast of St Thomas and its satellite islands, with a number of sites being shared with the St John operators and many dive resorts also venturing into British Virgin Islands waters to dive on the *Rhone*. Almost all diving around St Thomas is in water of less than 25m (80ft), allowing for plenty of bottom time. Identical in formation to St John, St Thomas and its smaller islands and rocky reefs are granitic in structure, covered by a thin film of coral. Nevertheless some huge, shallow coral reefs also exist around the islands, and these are popular with divers and snorkellers. Dive sites are generally within 15 minutes from a dive resorts' docks, and most dive boats will return to dock after their first dive and only stay out for a twin-tank dive when they travel to sites further afield such as Hans Lollik Island (sites 20–23), Buck and Capella islands (sites 4–5) and French Cap Cay (sites 11–12).

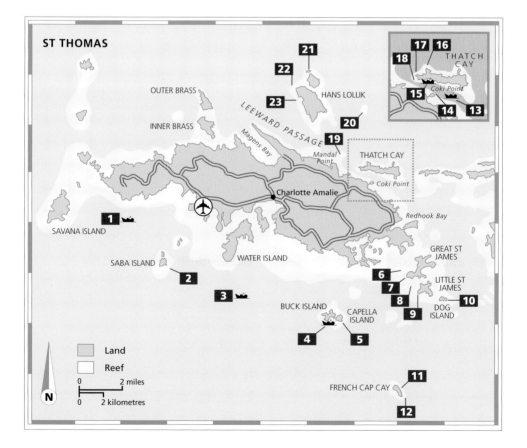

1 WRECK OF THE WEST INDIAN TRADER (WIT SHOAL)
★★★★★

Location: Southwest of the Cyril E. King Airport.
Access: By boat only.
Conditions: Current to be expected and some surge.
Average depth: 18m (60ft)
Maximum depth: 26m (85ft)
Average visibility: 30m (100ft)
Situated in an area of fairly strong tidal streams, the wreck of the *West Indian Trader* (often referred to as the *WIT*-Shoal) is located upright in 26m (85ft) of water. This West Indian Transit Company cargo ship, 150m (500ft) long, is now festooned in golden cup corals. Although the wreck is easy to penetrate, it is not recommended for inexperienced divers as there have been incidents where divers have been injured. There is also the chance of damage to the very delicate crust of marine organisms, which include sea plumes, sea fans and whips and low encrusting sponges. The ship was being towed to be sunk off the edge of the continental shelf after the end of her useful career in 1978 when she swung around and sank in much shallower water. The shallowest part of the wreck is only 11m (35ft) to the top of the wheelhouse. There is a wrecked crane over the forward hold and the propellers are still intact, now covered in marine growth.

2 SABA ISLAND
★★★

Location: Southwest of Charlotte Amalie, on the southeast reef.
Access: By boat only.
Conditions: Surge to be expected and slight current.
Average depth: 9m (30ft)
Maximum depth: 15m (50ft)
Average visibility: 25m (80ft)
This site is similar in scale and formation to the reefs found off Capella Island (Site 5) and features large boulders scattered all over the rock and sandy seabed. There is a large archway at 12m (40ft) which is easily negotiated and whose sides are pockmarked by centuries of marine growths which have burrowed into the substrate. Angelfish are common, particularly the shy rock beauty (*Holacanthus tricolor*) and hundreds of juvenile blue tangs (*Acanthurus coeruleus*) which are actually a brilliant yellow colour. The adults are often seen in large feeding aggregations moving across the reefs, eating the algae in the gardens created by damselfish. There are good stands of staghorn coral (*Acropora cervicornis*) where you will find bluehead wrasse and various damselfish.

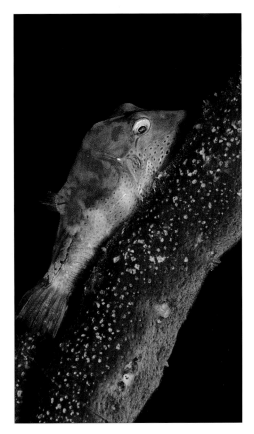

Sharp-nosed pufferfish (Canthigaster rostrata) are small reef dwellers.

3 GRAIN BARGE WRECK
★★★★★

Location: South of Charlotte Amalie.
Access: By boat only.
Conditions: Some current to be expected.
Average depth: 25m (80ft)
Maximum depth: 33m (110ft)
Average visibility: 30m (100ft)
Sitting upright, this old grain barge used to work between the Virgin Islands and Puerto Rico and was sunk at the end of her useful career. The ship is largely collapsed and smashed up due to excessive blasting by US Navy SEAL exercises. The hull is covered in golden cup corals and small lavender rope sponges (*Niphates erecta*), which are themselves always covered in large numbers of brittlestars (*Ophiothrix suensonii*). Due to the wreck being located well offshore, divers can expect to see blacktip reef sharks (*Carcharhinus limbatus*) and common Caribbean reef sharks (*Carcharhinus perezi*).

4 WRECK OF THE CARTANSER SENIOR
★★★

Location: South side of Buck Island.
Access: By boat only.
Conditions: Some surge to be expected and surface chop.
Average depth: 8m (27ft)
Maximum depth: 11m (36ft)
Average visibility: 18m (60ft)
The *Cartanser* has had an interesting life both above and below the waves. This steel-hulled cargo ship was used to transport goods in World War II and thereafter served around the Virgin Islands. She was abandoned in St Thomas in 1970 and eventually sank on her moorings. In the 1970s local diving organizations noted how the filming of the Hollywood movie *The Deep* (1977) around the RMS *Rhone* wreck in the British Virgin Islands had brought beneficial publicity, and resolved to relocate the *Cartanser* in a clear-water location as an artificial dive site.

In 1979 the wreck was moved to a cove on the southern shores of Buck Island and allowed to sink. The vessel lies in 15m (50ft) and, though largely smashed up by storms, the wreckage is still photogenic. It is completely encrusted in marine organisms and is surrounded by fish.

It is important to maintain correct buoyancy when you approach the reef, to avoid risk of damage.

5 CAPELLA ISLAND
★★★

Location: Capella Island, 4km (2 miles) southeast of Charlotte Amalie.
Access: By boat only.
Conditions: Some surge, but sheltered from current.
Average depth: 9m (30ft)
Maximum depth: 21m (70ft)
Average visibility: 25m (80ft)
The rocky ridges of Capella Island continue underwater in a series of massive boulders which are strewn all about, creating hundreds of gullies and canyons, small swimthroughs and dead-ends that are filled with schools of snapper and grunt. Pillar coral can be found, as well as small patches of brain corals. Sea fans, plumes and whips are common and, although much of the area has suffered due to hurricane damage, the reefs are improving yearly, despite the excessive algal growth.

6 COW AND CALF ROCKS
★★★★

Location: South of the Jersey Bay Marine Reserve, to the west of Great St James Island.
Access: By boat only.
Conditions: Some surge to be expected in the shallows and choppy on the surface.
Average depth: 9m (30ft)
Maximum depth: 15m (50ft)
Average visibility: 15m (50ft)
There are two separate dives around these coral reefs at the edge of the Jersey Bay Marine Park (founded 1995). Marked by mooring buoys, they are very similar, with numerous tunnels, swimthroughs, gullies and canyons which are easy to negotiate. Fire coral (*Millepora alcicornis*) covers the shallow sections and care, as always, should be taken when nearing the reef. There are large numbers of yellowtail snapper (*Ocyurus chrysurus*) and schools of jacks in the shallows. The sandy seabed at the bottom of the reef is home to hundreds of yellowhead jawfish (*Opistognathus aurifrons*) and many of the old coral heads have secretary blennies (*Acanthemblemaria maria*) and roughhead blennies (*Acanthemblemaria aspera*) living in old worm tubes.

7 THE STRAGGLERS
★★★

Location: The line of rocks which extends southwest from Great St James Island, situated between St Thomas and St John.
Access: By boat only.
Conditions: Can be some surge and surface chop.
Average depth: 9m (30ft)
Maximum depth: 14m (47ft)
Average visibility: 18m (60ft)
This low line of rocks includes numerous gullies and canyons under which nurse sharks are seen regularly.

The rocky outcrops are pretty and covered with tube sponges, encrusting corals and sea fans. The site is well known for its large numbers of tropical fish, such as queen angelfish (*Holacanthus ciliaris*), French angelfish (*Pomacanthus paru*), spotfin butterflyfish (*Chaetodon ocellatus*) and longsnout butterflyfish (*Chaetodon aculeatus*), all of which swim around in their lifelong mating pairs.

8 RAYS RISE
★★★★

Location: The channel between Great St James Island and Little St James Island.
Access: By boat only.
Conditions: Slight current flowing northeast or southwest, depending on the tide.
Average depth: 12m (40ft)
Maximum depth: 18m (60ft)
Average visibility: 18m (60ft)
This is done as an easy drift dive between the two islands – the tide is never so strong as to be overpowering. The seabed is sand at 18m (60ft), where you will always find southern stingrays (*Dasyatis americana*), garden eels and sand tilefish. A huge dome of coral can be found midway between the islands and, unlike in other locations, this is all coral and not made up of tumbled boulders. Creole wrasse, blue chromis and chub abound as well as large numbers of snapper and grunt.

9 LEDGES OF LITTLE ST JAMES
★★★★

Location: Reef off the southwest side of Little St James Island.
Access: By boat only.
Conditions: Some current and surge is to be expected.
Average depth: 7m (25ft)
Maximum depth: 15m (50ft)
Average visibility: 18m (60ft)
Little St James is well known for the interesting ledges which cut deep into the island on the southwestern flanks and its huge stands of pillar coral (*Dendrogyra cylindrus*), which grow 3m (10ft) tall. There are three moorings in this vicinity for the dive boat to tie onto, allowing for different entry and exit points for the dive. Much of the best area is in shallow water of less than 9m (30ft), allowing for lots of bottom time to explore the ledges and caverns where you can find large schools of French grunt (*Haemulon flavolineatum*) and blackbar soldierfish (*Myripristis jacobus*). Overall, the marine life around these

southern rocks is much better than around the northern islands. The island is owned by the multi-millionaire founder of Revlon Cosmetics.

10 DOG ROCKS
★★★ ★ ★ ★

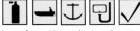

Location: Along the northeast shore of Dog Rocks, which are found southeast of Dog Island, in the same chain of islands as the St James's.
Access: By boat only.
Conditions: Some surge and surface chop to be expected, with slight current.
Average depth: 11m (36ft)
Maximum depth: 17m (45ft)
Average visibility: 18m (60ft)
A sand-hole anchorage lies along the northern portion of these rocks in 11m (36ft) of water. From here, travelling in an easterly direction, there is a superb rocky ledge which drops from 11 to 17m (36 to 45ft). This ledge is home to red-lipped blennies (*Ophioblennius atlanticus*) and roughhead blennies (*Acanthemblemaria aspera*) which live in disused tube worm holes in the reef. There are lots of lobsters all over and large numbers of juvenile rock beauties (*Holacanthus tricolor*).

11 LEDGES AT FRENCH CAP CAY
★★★★

Location: A 60min boat ride south of east St Thomas.
Access: By boat only.
Conditions: Surge to be expected and some current.
Average depth: 15m (50ft)
Maximum depth: 23m (75ft)
Average visibility: 45m (150ft)
Isolated between St Thomas and St Croix, French Cap Cay has much better visibility than around the inner islands. A site called the Deep Ledges is located off the northeastern shore, where the igneous rock has been sculpted by wave action into gullies and indented ledges roomy enough to explore and to allow divers to pass up through a chimney into open water. Caribbean octopus (*Octopus briareus*) are seen, as are barracuda, jacks, Bermuda chub (*Kyphosus sectatrix*) and even Atlantic spadefish (*Chaetodipterus faber*), regarded as quite rare elsewhere. The smaller ledges have bigeye (*Priacanthus arenatus*) with attendant banded coral shrimps (*Stenopus hispidus*) to clean them.

Golden cup corals (Tubastrea coccinea) light up many coral overhangs at night.

12 PINNACLE AT FRENCH CAP CAY
★★★★

Location: Off the southern tip of French Cap Cay.
Access: By boat only.
Conditions: Surface chop to be expected as well as surge and some current.
Average depth: 18m (60ft)
Maximum depth: 29m (97ft)
Average visibility: 45m (150ft)
This site is often done as a deeper, first dive before moving on to the Ledges (Site 11), but only when weather and sea conditions are near perfect as it takes about an hour to reach the site: even then it can be difficult and is recommended for experienced divers only. The pinnacle is actually two massive sheets of rock, turned on end and rising to within 13m (43ft) of the surface – where large barracuda can always be found. Eagle rays may be found, though only the first divers into the water are likely to enjoy the spectacle. Hawksbill turtles (*Eretmochelys imbricata*) are quite common as are nurse sharks (*Ginglymostoma cirratum*). You have to travel a long way to get to this site, but it is generally worth the effort: the visibility is excellent and you have the chance to see large pelagic animals and fish.

White-spotted filefish (Cantherhines macrocerus) are the largest of the Caribbean filefish.

13 WRECK OF THE MAJOR GENERAL ROGERS
★★★★

Location: South of Thatch Cay, mid-channel eastern mooring buoy.
Access: By boat only.
Conditions: Can be some current, boat traffic to be expected.
Average depth: 15m (50ft)
Maximum depth: 19m (62ft)
Average visibility: 18m (60ft)
The *Major General Rogers* was a steel-hulled auxiliary coastguard buoy tender, 36m (120ft) long. Sunk deliberately in 1972 as an artificial reef, the wreck, just three minutes from Chris Sawyer's dive shop dock, sits upright and completely intact. The mooring buoy is attached to the top of the deck in 12m (40ft). Penetration of the wreck is unobstructed and there are always schools of snapper, grunt and big barracuda to be found. The hull is completely festooned in marine growth, particularly golden cup corals (*Tubastrea coccinea*) which transform the ship

Venus sea fans (Gorgonia flabellum) occur on all of the reef crests.

at night. Unfortunately this area is often subjected to strong currents, sometimes making diving on the wreck impossible.

Some 60m (200ft) due north of the bow of the *Major General Rogers* is the wreckage of a small barge called the *Mary King*, which was sunk in 1976. Lying upside-down in 19m (62ft), the wreck cannot be penetrated. Large jewfish (*Epinephelus itajara*) have been seen in the vicinity.

14 LEEWARD PASSAGE DRIFT
★★★★

Location: North of Coki Point on the St Thomas side of the Leeward Passage, between St Thomas and Thatch Cay.
Access: By boat only.
Conditions: Very strong current to be expected.
Average depth: 15m (50ft)
Maximum depth: 21m (70ft)
Average visibility: 18m (60ft)
This is a fast-moving drift dive along the northern edge of a classic spur-and-groove reef which extends north of Coki Point. The spurs are over 6m (20ft) apart and are principally coral, with very little rock substrate visible. The site is rarely dived due to the strong current, and divers will come across huge barrel sponges (*Xestospongia muta*) hundreds of years old, many of them bent into rather convoluted shapes due to the current. You can also find deepwater sea fans (*Iciligorgia*

schrammi) which extend perpendicular to the current to catch the passing planktonic particles. Look out for old bottles on the seafloor, as thousands of ships have passed through this water passage since the islands were first settled. Creole wrasse (*Clepticus parrai*) are common, as are large schools of boga (*Inermia vittata*).

15 VETI BAY DRIFT
★★★

Location: The north side of the Leeward Passage, south of Stoney Bay on Thatch Cay.
Access: By boat only.
Conditions: Current to be expected and some surface traffic.
Average depth: 12m (40ft)
Maximum depth: 18m (60ft)
Average visibility: 18m (60ft)
This site is only done as a drift dive when the tide is running through from Pillsbury Sound, travelling west. The best part of the dive is along the rocky substrate where much of the bedrock is covered in sea plumes and sea fans. There are lots of overhangs and, although you are never able to stay long enough in any one area, you will catch sight of lots of spiny lobsters (*Panulirus argus*) and large channel clinging crabs (*Mithrax spinosissimus*). Large stands of pillar coral (*Dendrogyra cylindrus*) can be found near the wreckage of a small cruiser which was sunk by Hurricane Marilyn in 1995.

An important need for many underwater creatures is to be able to exist alongside each other with the minimum of conflict. Over millennia the underwater world has refined numerous sets of fascinating commensal and symbiotic relationships to enable creatures to live in harmony.

Numerous marine animals are host to commensals. Sponges, sea cucumbers, corals, anemones, sea urchins, clams, featherstars and basketstars all have various specialized hitch-hikers. These can be in the form of small worms, shrimps, crabs, molluscs, fish, tunicates, other anemones or sponges. Many commensals are simply very small creatures living on or around a much larger host for protection, but others more obviously derive mutual co-operation and beneficial arrangements. Many hosts can be found without commensals, but few commensals are ever found without their host. If they are on their own, they are likely to be in search of a new host.

UNDERWATER PARTNERSHIPS

The classic example of living in harmony in the Caribbean is undoubtedly the symbiotic relationship between several species of shrimp and a variety of anemones. The red snapping shrimp (*Alpheus armatus*) lives within the protective embrace of the corkscrew anemone (*Bartholomea annulata*),

while among the shallow turtle-grass beds of the Virgin Islands the spotted cleaner shrimp (*Periclimenes yucatanicus*) can be found in the up-turned tentacles of the upside-down jellyfish (*Cassiopea frondosa*).

Cleaning stations on the reef are a well documented part of harmonious reef living – where, for instance, several varieties of goby act as cleaners to larger predatory fish. Fulfilling a vital role in the reef ecology, cleaning gobies remove parasites and dead or decaying skin and scales from fish.

One of the most interesting associations on the reef is the symbiotic relationship between several species of sand goby and various shrimps. The almost blind snapping shrimp's primary role is of burrow maintenance. Constantly excavating its hole, it is warned when it is safe to emerge with the excavated material by a flick of the goby's tail. When danger threatens, the fish dives into the hole and so protects the shrimp.

However, perhaps the least noticed of all harmonious relationships is that of the algae which colour coral polyps. Often appreciated only by their absence – during dramatic rises in sea temperature when the algae are expelled, leading to 'coral bleaching' – the algae provide the corals with food which they themselves have manufactured.

A particularly colourful shrimp species is the spotted cleaner shrimp (Periclimenes yucatanicus).

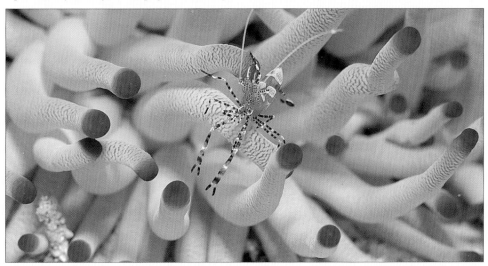

16 ARCHES AND TUNNELS OF THATCH
★★★★★

Location: North of Mother East Point to the northwest of Thatch Cay.
Access: By boat only.
Conditions: Can be surge in the gullies and current to be expected.
Average depth: 17m (57ft)
Maximum depth: 18m (60ft)
Average visibility: 21m (70ft)
It is just ten minutes from the dive centre dock at the Compass Point Marina to the mooring buoy on the site, but this dive should really be done only when there is no northerly swell. There are two particularly long tunnels, over 25m (60ft) long, six arches and a labyrinth of gullies and canyons for divers to negotiate. During the summer months clouds of silverside minnows can be seen everywhere. At the entrances to the tunnels and on top of the arches huge sea plumes (*Pseudopterogorgia* spp.) can be found as well as many other different species of sea fan. Look closely at these, as you will always find flamingo tongue shells (*Cyphoma gibbosum*) as well as slender filefish (*Monacanthus tuckeri*). A large resident green moray eel (*Gymnothorax funebris*) often frightens divers – it is alarmingly friendly and will come right out of its lair whenever it is approached. Black corals can be found in the tunnels and there are golden cup corals everywhere.

17 CANYONS AT THATCH
★★★★

Location: Off the north of Lee Point, the most westerly point of Thatch Cay.
Access: By boat only.
Conditions: Current to be expected running to the west.
Average depth: 15m (50ft)
Maximum depth: 15m (50ft)
Average visibility: 21m (70ft)
This dive is done as a drift along a winding, coral-filled canyon, with the current running to the west; it can also

---

REPETITIVE DIVING

Remember that diving three or more times each day over a sustained period is not only exhausting, but also dangerous. It can lead to residual nitrogen problems in the bloodstream and may contribute towards the 'bends'. After a few days' diving it is recommended to take some time out to do some sightseeing and allow your bloodstream and tissues to de-gas.

---

be done when there is slack water. Chris Sawyer's is the only dive centre which comes here. The tidal stream starts off quite gently at first on the drop-off point and increases in speed as you approach the corner. Divers are accompanied by a dive master with a surface marker buoy to alert the following dive boat of your exact position. Fairy basslets (*Gramma loreto*) as well as blackcap basslets (*Gramma melacara*) can be found amid the overhangs, and there are always large numbers of parrotfish and wrasse grazing on the corals and algae.

18 WEST END OF THATCH
★★★

Location: South of Lee Point on the western end of Thatch Cay.
Access: By boat only.
Conditions: Sheltered all year round, but can be some current if you travel further out into the Leeward Passage.
Average depth: 15m (50ft)
Maximum depth: 18m (60ft)
Average visibility: 18m (60ft)
This site is dived all year round due to its sheltered aspect. There are some nice small rocky ledges topped by very long sea plumes (*Plexaurella nutans* and *Plexaura flexuosa*), some of the former over 3m (10ft) tall. Closer to shore there are some rocky formations where lobsters and eels are seen on every dive. It is classed as a 'rummage' dive, where you can spend quite a lot of time exploring the ledges and finding such interesting fish as juvenile spotted drum (*Equetus punctatus*) and its close relative the highhat (*Equetus acuminatus*). Arrow crabs (*Stenorhinchus seticornis*) are also common on this site.

19 TABLE TOP (TUNNICA PINNACLE)
★★★★

Location: West of Thatch Cay, almost due north of Mandal Point on St Thomas.
Access: By boat only.
Conditions: Strong currents to be expected as well as some surge.
Average depth: 12m (40ft)
Maximum depth: 21m (70ft)
Average visibility: 25m (80ft)
This huge rock and coral platform is over 90m (300ft) in diameter and lies in depths of 12–21m (40–70ft). Strong currents whip around the rock, undercutting huge ledges beneath which nurse sharks and lobsters can be found. There are the usual sea plumes and gorgonian sea fans associated with current-swept areas, but this site is also well known for schooling French

Above: *Bigeye (Priacanthus arenatus) are shade-loving fish found in crevices on the deeper reefs.*
Below: *The roughhead triplefin blenny (Enneanectes boehlkei) often lives deep within azure sponges.*

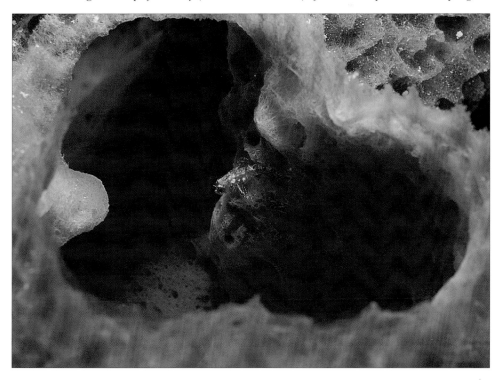

grunt (*Haemulon flavolineatum*) which mix with Caesar grunt (*Haemulon carbonarium*) and cottonwick (*Haemulon melanurum*). Blue runners (*Caranx crysos*) and bigeye scad (*Selar crumenophthalmus*) are also found in large numbers.

20 THATCH RISE (THATCH BANK)
★★★★

Location: Due north of Thatch Cay and east of Hans Lollik Island.
Access: By boat only.
Conditions: Surge to be expected.
Average depth: 15m (50ft)
Maximum depth: 33m (110ft)
Average visibility: 30m (100ft)
This is a huge rock and coral mound, over 60m (200ft) in diameter, which rises from 33m (110ft) to 13m (44ft). Much of the rock has been carved by wave and tidal action into gullies and canyons similar to true coral spur-and-groove formations. It is one of the deepest dives on the main St Thomas bank. Due to the site's isolated location, divers can expect to see spotted eagle rays (*Aetobatus narinari*), king mackerel (*Scombermorus cavalla*) and small schools of southern sennet (*Sphyraena picudilla*). The rock formations have many ledges which descend to a sand, gravel and coral rubble seabed where sand divers (*Synodus intermedius*) and peacock flounders (*Bothus lunatus*) can be found. All around this ridge are big snapper, grunt, wrasse, parrotfish and grouper as well as a large number of cleaning stations.

21 PELICAN CAY
★★★★

Location: Small islet just north of Little Hans Lollik Island.
Access: By boat only.
Conditions: Surge to be expected and slight current off the western shores.
Average depth: 18m (60ft)
Maximum depth: 26m (85ft)
Average visibility: 30m (100ft)
Pelican Cay is known for its massive boulders and steep drop-off along the leeward (west) side of the island. There are large deep canyons and two small arches which are easily negotiated by divers. This wind-protected site also features large schools of silverside minnows in the summer months, as well as glassy sweepers (*Pempheris schomburgki*) which are preyed upon by tarpon (*Megalops atlanticus*), great barracuda

(*Sphyraena barracuda*) and blue runners (*Caranx crysos*). There is little hard coral on this exposed rocky site, but there are large sea fans and plumes everywhere. The shaded areas of the gullies have small colourful encrusting sponges such as *Siphonodictyon coralliphagum* and *Phorbas amaranthus*.

22 THE PINNACLE
★★★★

Location: Northwest Hans Lollik Island.
Access: By boat only.
Conditions: Surge and current to be expected on this exposed sea mount.
Average depth: 18m (60ft)
Maximum depth: 26m (85ft)
Average visibility: 30m (100ft)
This apparent pinnacle or needle of rock juts up from the seabed to within 4m (15ft) of the surface. The Pinnacle is actually two separate flat sheets of rock which have been turned on their side by volcanic upheaval; they open out at the base where there is a natural rock tunnel covered in golden cup corals and bright encrusting sponges. At only 15m (50ft) in diameter at its widest point, The Pinnacle is a compact site, with the added opportunity of seeing nurse sharks and eagle rays.

23 THE GARDEN
★★★★★★★

Location: West of Hans Lollik Island within the more sheltered bay.
Access: By boat only.
Conditions: Sheltered site, no current.
Average depth: 9m (30ft)
Maximum depth: 15m (50ft)
Average visibility: 18m (60ft)
Generally dived as a second dive after The Pinnacle (Site 22), The Garden is a protected site within the bay on the west of Hans Lollik. There are no mooring buoys in this area and a sand anchor is dropped gently onto the sandy seabed, away from any corals. As you swim out to deeper water, there is a good spur-and-groove reef formation with large pillar corals (*Dendrogyra cylindrus*) and lots of anemones such as the giant anemone (*Condylactis gigantea*), elegant anemone (*Actinoporus elegans*) and corkscrew anemone (*Bartholomea annulata*), all of which have various cleaner shrimps in attendance, waving their antennae to attract passing fish to be cleaned of parasites.

HOW TO GET THERE

There are non-stop flights to St Thomas from Miami, Raleigh-Durham, New York Newark and Baltimore to St Thomas. All other flights are routed through San Juan first. A number of smaller airlines such as WinAir, Air Anguilla and LIAT also fly between St Thomas and the British Virgin Islands as well as neighbouring islands.

The Cyril E. King International Airport is located 2km (1 mile) west of Charlotte Amalie near Red Point at Lindbergh Bay. Built on reclaimed land, the approach to the runway almost gives the impression of landing in the sea. A wide dual carriageway connects the airport to Veteran's Drive, also known as the Waterfront Highway. Private air charters and connecting commercial flights arriving from San Juan are not required to clear customs. All other passengers arriving direct from the United States, however, must clear customs in St Thomas.

Many tourists arrive by cruise ship into Charlotte Amalie, described as the Caribbean's most popular cruise-ship port. With more than1.2 million tourists arriving by sea in over 1000 cruise ships during the year, it does get busy.

There are ferries from St John and Tortola to St Thomas, with docks at Red Hook and Charlotte Amalie. The Virgin Hydrofoil operates a return service between Charlotte Amalie and Christiansted on St Croix.

GETTING AROUND

Touring is almost obligatory for cruise ship visitors to this lush and mountainous island. Numerous 'Jitneys', or open-sided safari buses, seat up to 20 people for tours that stop at specific vantage points for photographs, particularly at Crown Mountain where a restaurant and tourist trap have sprung up to take advantage of the view. You can also rent your own vehicle or take a taxi between four of you for a more informal island tour. But be warned – due to the nature of the roads a 16km (10 mile) journey may take several hours.

Car rental agencies are found all over St Thomas and most have an office at both the airport and Charlotte-Amalie. A number of resort hotels have their own hire vehicles, or can arrange for a hire car to be delivered to your hotel. A four-wheel drive vehicle is recommended since, as on St John, the main road over the island is very steep in places.

ABC Auto and Jeep Rentals, Havensight, Charlotte Amalie; tel (340) 776 1222
Avis Rent-A-Car, Cyril E.King Airport, St Thomas; tel (340) 774 1468
Budget Rent-A-Car, Cyril E.King Airport, St Thomas; tel (340) 774 5960
Dependable Car Rental, 3901 B-Altona and Welgunst, St Thomas; tel (340) 774 2253; email: dependable@dependable car.com; website: www.dependablecar.com

Hertz Rent-A-Car, Cyril E.King Airport, St Thomas; tel (340) 774 1879
Wheatley Taxi Service & Tours, PO Box 727, St Thomas, US Virgin Islands 00804; tel (340) 473 8900; email: customerinquiry@ wheatleytaxiservice.com; website: www.wheatleytaxiservice.com

WHERE TO STAY

There is a wide range of accommodation on St Thomas, with over 2500 hotel rooms. Most hotels offer diving, whether provided by the company or leased out through a concession agreement with one of the major watersports operators. All the major hotels, many of which are all-inclusive resorts, offer restaurants, bars and swimming pools. With over 600,000 tourists arriving by air each year, there is a more than adequate range of accommodation to suit all tastes and pockets.

Possibly the most popular type of accommodation for repeat visitors is in a condominium or 'efficiency apartment' where prices are charged by the week as opposed to nightly by hotels. These self-catering apartments and villas allow you more flexibility, while culinary needs are amply catered for by the local supermarkets or by the vast number of local restaurants.

Cottages and guest houses tend to be more intimate and all are furnished to the highest standard. Cottage colonies, similar to those first started in Bermuda, are also popular with visitors to the islands. For additional information on any of the accommodations offered, contact:
United States Virgin Islands Department of Tourism, PO Box 6400, St Thomas, VI 00804; US toll free tel (800) 372 8784; tel (340) 774 8784; fax (340) 774 4390; website: www.usvitourism.vi

Expensive
Bolongo Bay Beach Resort, 7150 Bolongo, St Thomas, VI 00802; US toll free tel (800) 524 4746; tel (340) 775 1800; fax (340) 775 3208; email: reservations@ bolongobay.com; website: www.bolongo bay.com
All-inclusive resort featuring 75 select apartments all with sea views. Great restaurants, watersports and nightlife.

Colony Point Pleasant Resort, 6600 Estate Smith Bay #4, St Thomas, VI 00802-1340; US toll free tel (800) 777 1700; tel (340) 775 7200; fax (340) 775 5694; website: www.pointpleasantresort.com
134 villa-style suites on the hillside, all with great views. Own car rental, top-class restaurant, small pool, ecotrails, all watersports.

Elysian Beach Resort, 6800 Estate Nazareth, St Thomas, VI 00802; US toll free tel (800) 347 8182; tel (340) 775 1000/2700; fax (340) 779 2400; website:

www.elysianbeachresort.net
Located on Cowpet Bay, rooms stepped down hillside, spacious and luxurious with all watersports and free transport to Bolongo Club Everything.

Ritz Carlton, Great Bay, St Thomas, VI 00802-9905; US toll free tel (800) 241 3333; tel (340) 775 3333; fax (340) 775 4444; website: www.ritzcarlton.com/ en/Properties/StThomas/Default.htm
148 rooms in huge manicured estate with fine restaurants, massive freshwater pool and all watersports.

Sapphire Beach Resort and Marina, PO Box 8088, St Thomas, VI 00801; US toll free tel (800) 524 2090; tel (340) 775 6100; fax (340) 775 2403; email: sbrsales@islands.vi; website: www.sapphirebeachresort.com
Superb resort with beautiful beach, great restaurants with patio dining and full watersports.

Mid-range
Best Western Carib Beach Resort, 70-C Lindberg Bay, St Thomas, VI 00802; US toll free tel (800) 792 2742; tel (340) 774 2525; fax (340) 777 4131
Friendly and informal with only 69 rooms, all with a Caribbean flavour. Popular for weekends on the island, with a great restaurant, beach bar and pool.

Emerald Beach Resort, 8070 Lindberg Bay, St Thomas, VI 00802; US toll free tel (800) 233 4936; tel (340) 777 8800; fax (340) 776 3426
Polynesian flair in 90 rooms, secluded and romantic. Great beach, all watersports available and an all-you-can-eat BBQ on Saturday.

Marriott's Frenchman's Reef Beach Resort, PO Box 640, St Thomas, VI 00804; US toll free tel (800) 524 2400; tel (340) 776 8500; fax (340) 776 3054; email: resorts.vi@marriotthotels.com
421 rooms in a largely impersonal establishment on a secluded headland. Pools, fountains, popular beach, lively nightlife and top class restaurants.

Holiday Inn, PO Box 640, St Thomas, VI 00804; US toll free tel (800) 524 7389; tel (340) 774 5200; fax (340) 774 1231; website: www.holidayinn.st-thomas.com
Hotel overlooking Charlotte Amalie, daily complimentary transport to beaches, pools, shops and outdoor dining, next to main shopping area downtown.

Inexpensive
Galleon House Hotel, 31 Kongens Gade, PO Box 6577, St Thomas, VI 00804-6577; US toll free tel (800) 524 2052; tel/fax (340) 774 6952
14-room hotel with fantastic harbour view

of Charlotte Amalie, home cooked breakfast, freshwater pool and free use of snorkel equipment.

Island View Guest House, 11-1C Contant Charlotte Amalie, PO Box 1903, St Thomas, VI 00803; US toll free tel (800) 524 2023; tel (340) 774 4270; fax (340) 774 6167
15-room guest house high on hill overlooking Charlotte Amalie, self-catering available, small freshwater pool, lush vegetation.

Mafolie Hotel, Mafolie Hill, PO Box 1506, . Charlotte Amalie, St Thomas, VI 00804; US toll free tel (800) 225 2023; tel (340) 774 2790; fax (340) 774 4091
23 rooms high on the hill, continental breakfast and free shuttle service to town included, freshwater pool.

WHERE TO EAT

Eating out in St Thomas is generally good value, with 'surf and turf' establishments the most popular. Most visitors tend to stay in their hotels, where the food is generally buffet-style, gourmet or a mixture of local and US fare.

Very few eateries require reservations in advance and the dress code is casual. For fast-food fans, St Thomas has Hard Rock Café, Domino's Pizza, McDonalds, Dunkin' Donuts, KFC, Subway, etc. The following are establishments you will come across in the shopping areas around Charlotte Amalie, plus a few good-value restaurants near the dive resorts.

Tickles Dockside Pub, Crown Bay, St Thomas; tel (340) 775 9425
Waterside restaurant with grilled everything, very relaxed, a perfect place for après dive.

The Oasis Bar and Grill, Sapphire Beach, St Thomas; tel (340) 775 3633
Outdoor patio for steaks, seafood, pasta, salads and sandwiches, 5 minutes' walk from the beach.

Hervé Restaurant and Wine Bar, Government Hill, St Thomas; tel (340) 777 9703; email: info@herverestaurant.com; website: www.herverestaurant.com
Reservations needed, French/US cuisine with panoramic views over Charlotte Amalie.

Room with a View, Blackbeard's Castle, St Thomas; tel (340) 774 1600 ext. 340
Cool and air-conditioned, excellent food at reasonable prices, 'surf and turf', pizza and pasta.

Sandra's Terrace, Building D, American Yacht Harbor, St Thomas; tel (340) 775 2699
Local West Indian fare with plantains, conch fritters and daily steak and fish specials.

Schnitzel Haus, tel (340) 776 7198

This restaurant specializes in veal dishes and other German cuisine.

Smuggler's Steak & Seafood Grill
tel (340) 775 1510
On the grounds of the Renaissance Grand Beach Resort, this handsome tropical pavilion restaurant offers outstanding beef and fresh seafood selections.

Café Wahoo, tel (340) 775 6350
Located on St Thomas' east end adjacent to the Red Hook ferry dock, Café Wahoo boasts an eclectic menu of seafood and local favourites.

Club Rhino Tropical Café, tel (340) 777 8015
Those who need a break from Charlotte Amalie's shopping can stop for lunch at Club Rhino Tropical Café in Palm Passage. The open-air restaurant serves Caribbean-American dishes.

East End Café, tel (340) 715 1442
Formerly the Big Kahuna, the East End Café specializes in Italian and American fare with daily seafood specialties. Located in Red Hook, the restaurant's ambiance is even more enjoyable from Thursday to Saturday when live music is played.

Fungi's on the Beach, tel (340) 775 4142
Reggae Always is the motto of the newly opened Fungi's on the Beach, a bar and restaurant located on Pineapple Beach at Point Pleasant Resort. Visitors can sample local dinners and West Indian specialties, or choose from Fungi's *All Day & Night* Menu which features American fare.

Gladys' Café, tel (340) 774 6604
This café in Royal Dane Mall serves breakfast and lunch for hungry St Thomas shoppers looking for a taste of authentic native cuisine.

DIVE OPERATORS

Chris Sawyer Diving Center, 6300 Est. Frydenhoj, Suite 29, Compass Point Marina, St Thomas VI 00802-1411, toll free (877) 929 3483; tel. (340) 775 7320; fax (340) 775 9495; email: sawyerdive@islands.vi; website: www.sawyerdive.vi
A PADI 5-star facility offering excellent reef and wreck diving, referral dives and dive packages.

Admiralty Dive Center, PO Box 307065, St. Thomas, USVI 00803

Located at:
Holiday Inn Windward Passage,
Charlotte Amalie, St. Thomas
tel (888) 900 DIVE or (340) 777 9802; email: admiralty@viaccess.net; website: www.admiraltydive.com

Very experienced around the nerarshore islands, small groups catered for.

Aqua Action Dive Centre, Secret Harbor Beach Resort, St Thomas, VI 00802-1305; tel (340) 775 6285; fax (340) 775 150; email: aquaaction@aadivers.com; website: www.aadivers.com
Small operation catering for Secret Harbor guests, but also open to non-residents.

Coki Beach Dive Club, PO Box 502096, Coki Beach, St Thomas, VI 00805; US toll free tel (800) 474 COKI (2654); tel (340) 775 4220; fax (340) 779 6535; email: info@cokidive.com; website: www.cokidive.com
A PADI Gold Palm Resort, SDI Center and Universal Referral Center. Perfect for Coki Beach, very experienced, running training courses constantly.

Dean Johnson's Diving Institute, Buccaneer Mall, Suite 106-208, St Thomas, VI 00802; tel (340) 775 7610; fax (340) 777 3232
Experienced training facility to all levels of instruction.

Dive In, PO Box 5664, Sapphire Beach Resort and Marina, St Thomas, VI 00803; US toll free tel (800) 524 2090; tel (340) 775 6100 ext. 2144; fax (340) 775 2403; email: sbrsales@islands.vi
Full-service dive operation with lots of packages, good for shore and boat diving.

Drumbeat Charters, 5100 Long Bay Rd, St Thomas, VI 00802; tel (340) 774 5630; fax (340) 776 3074; email: flagshipvi@worldnet.att.net
Good operation, handling divers of all skill levels.

St Thomas Diving Club, 7147 Bolongo Bay, St Thomas, VI 00802; US toll free tel (800) LETS DIV (538 7348); tel (340) 776 2381; fax (340) 777 3232; email: info@stthomasdivingclub.com; website: www.stthomasdivingclub.com
A PADI 5-star IDC center offering boat dives twice daily along with night diving. Snorkelers are welcome on afternoon dive adventures.

Underwater Safaris, 9007 Havensight Mall, Suite C, St Thomas USVI 00802, tel (340) 774 3737, fax (340) 774 3738; email: wwo@islands.vi; website: www.scubadivevi.com
Operating since 1985, Underwater Safaris is a PADI Gold Palm Instructor Development Center Resort Facility with a record for safety unequaled by any other organization. The dive boats are US Coastguard inspected, driven by a licensed captain, and all instructors are PADI-trained with years of experience leading both certified and non-certified divers.

EMERGENCY INFORMATION

Police Emergency, tel 915; switchboard 774 2211

Coastguard Emergency, Marine Safety Detachment; tel (340) 776 3497

Recompression Chamber, St Thomas; tel (340) 776 8311

Roy Lester Schneider Hospital, 9048 Sugar Estate, St Thomas; tel (340) 776 8311

Havensight Pharmacy, 9004 Havensight Shopping Center, Suite 4, St Thomas, tel (340) 776 1235

Chelsea Drug Store, 6500 Red Hook Plaza, St Thomas, VI 00802; tel (340) 776 8300

Drug Farm Pharmacy, 2-4-9th Estate, St Thomas; tel (340) 776 7098

Drug Farm Pharmacy, St Thomas Hospital; tel (340) 776 1880

Divers Alert Network, tel (919) 684 8111

LOCAL HIGHLIGHTS

For those wishing to explore the reefs without getting their feet wet, a good option is the **Atlantis Submarine**, a fully operational submarine 20m (66ft) long and displacing 80 tons, licensed to carry 46 passengers. The submarine journeys for one hour around the coral reefs off St Thomas. Contact 9006 Havensight Shopping Center, Suite L, St Thomas, USVI 00802-2667; tel (340) 776 5650; fax (340) 776 2919; email: lbaa@atlantis submarines.com; website: www.atlantissubmarines.com

    Fort Christian is a national landmark located to the east of the Waterfront Highway in Charlotte Amalie. Painted a rather ugly colour, it was built in the 17th century and is the island's oldest building. The ancient dungeons now house a museum, open every day; free admission; tel (340) 776 4566.

    The **St Thomas Skyride**, formally Paradise Point Tramway, takes you up 210m (700ft) from the cruise-ship dock near the Havensight Mall and takes just 7 minutes for the trip to the top. Contact St Thomas Skyride to Paradise Point, 9617 Estate Thomas, St. Thomas VI, 00802, tel (340) 774 9809; fax: (340) 774 9955; website: www.paradisepointtramway.com

    Try a narrated **'flightseeing' tour** of St Thomas, St John and the western reaches of the British Virgin Islands. This 30 minute flight is a great way to get a better appreciation of the islands and their secluded bays and beaches. Contact Seaborne Adventures, 5305 Long Bay Road, Charlotte Amalie, St Thomas, tel (340) 773 5991.

Turtles are a delight to swim with, but never hold on to them.

ST JOHN

Only 14km (9 miles) long by 8km (5 miles) wide, the island of St John was named after St John the Apostle by Christopher Columbus, but is probably better known for its slave revolt in the early 1700s. Under the Danish flag, the first European settlers landed in Coral Bay in 1717; Fredericksvaern (later Fort Berg) was built overlooking the bay and within ten years over 100 sugar plantations had appeared. In 1733, however, a number of recent slave arrivals who claimed descent from African nobility refused to work on the plantations and escaped into the surrounding mountains. The rebels soon mounted an attack on Fort Berg, killing the guards and firing the cannon three times to alert other slaves to rise against their white masters. Many of the plantation owners were killed, while others fled to St Thomas, and it was six months before French soldiers specially trained in jungle warfare managed to capture some of the rebels. Those that were still at large committed suicide by throwing themselves off a cliff at Mary Point.

Today there are ruined plantation houses and mills dotted around the island, the most famous and best preserved being Annaberg. Many are worth exploring, but beware when driving around the narrow roads of St John: there are over 400 feral donkeys roaming the island; near the rural areas along the south coast and over the central highlands, pigs, goats and chickens also appear to wander freely. In addition, you may notice scavenging groups of mongooses. These were imported from India in 1872 by a Jamaican sugar planter to kill rats, and are regarded rather dubiously as the unofficial mascot of St John. Being prolific breeders, the mongooses have become something of a menace to St John's otherwise well preserved environment.

Laurence Rockefeller bought 2024ha (5000 acres) of the island in 1954 and later donated it to the US National Park Service. Since then the resulting National Park has expanded to 3846ha (9500 acres), covering about two-thirds of the entire island. Now known as the Virgin Islands National Park, with its headquarters in Cruz Bay, the park also encompasses a large stretch of mangrove beds along the southeastern coast and all of

Opposite: *The greater part of peaceful St John is designated as a National Park.*
Above: *Juvenile rock beauties (Holacanthus tricolor) are vivid yellow with a black spot near the tail.*

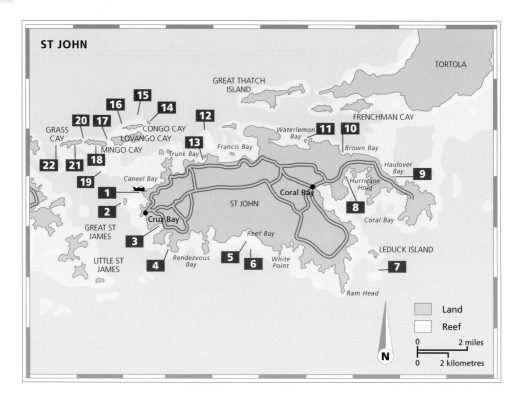

the reefs which border the north coast of the island, out to a 20m (66ft) depth contour. The highest point on the island is Bordeaux Mountain at 383m (1277ft), standing above Coral Bay.

St John is one of the few Caribbean islands to have campsites. Under the supervision of the US National Park Service, these are located at Cinnamon Bay and Maho Bay on the north coast, just ten minutes by taxi from the ferry terminal at Cruz Bay. The island also has many secluded coves and beaches which are ideal for visiting yachtsmen, and the US National Park Service has placed mooring buoys at the most favourable sites to reduce anchor damage to the surrounding reefs.

Much of the diving is to the west of St John around Congo Cay, Lovango Cay, Mingo Cay, Grass Cay and the St James's – sites also shared by the diving operators from St Thomas. The diving is all located fairly close to the shorelines of St John and its satellite islands, and for the most part takes place in water of less than 25m (80ft), allowing for maximum bottom time to explore the reefs. Although the reefs are mostly granitic in structure with a thin film of coral covering, there are also vast areas of shallow true coral reef situated between the islands. These areas are a danger to shipping, but a delight to divers and snorkellers. Due to the close proximity of some of the sites to the dive operators' bases, dive boats will tend to return to dock after only one dive and only stay out for a twin-tank dive when they travel to more distant sites.

NATIONAL PARK PROHIBITED ACTIVITIES

- Waterskiing, towing boogie-boards and use of personal watercraft such as wave runners and jet skis are prohibited in park waters.
- Spearfishing, the collection of fish and the taking of or damaging of natural resources are federal violations and not allowed in park waters.

1 LIND POINT
★★★

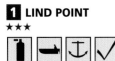

Location: Just north of the island capital, Cruz Bay.
Access: By boat only.
Conditions: Current to be expected running from east to west, otherwise fairly sheltered except for boat traffic.
Average depth: 7m (25ft)
Maximum depth: 15m (50ft)
Average visibility: 15m (50ft)

Part of the eastern reaches of the National Park, this is a rocky reef which runs parallel to the shore dropping down to 15m (50ft). The ridge is only 1m (3ft) high in profile and over 90m (300ft) long, largely undercut and host to many species of shrimp. The seabed has hundreds of yellowhead jawfish (*Opistognathus aurifrons*), small balloonfish (*Diodon holocanthus*), green moray eels (*Gymnothorax funebris*) and spotted moray eels (*Gymnothorax moringa*). Along the western part of the reef there is an old 7m (25ft) sailboat which was wrecked during Hurricane Marilyn. You can often find lobster and large crabs under the keel.

Trumpetfish (Aulostomus maculatus) often hide amidst rope sponges for camouflage.

2 STEVEN CAY
★★★★★

Location: Small island just outside the National Park boundary, due west and at the entrance of Cruz Bay.
Access: By boat only.
Conditions: Strong current to be expected through this area of Pillsbury Sound.
Average depth: 7m (25ft)
Maximum depth: 7m (25ft)
Average visibility: 18m (60ft)

A particularly strong current runs down the eastern side of this cay and, with speeds of over two knots, makes for an exhilarating drift dive. A much easier dive, however, can be had from the mooring buoy located at the northwestern point of the island. The cay is 100m (330ft) long and at the base of the rock is an undercut ledge where lobster, nurse sharks and rays can be found. There are lots of wrasse and parrotfish all along this outer stretch and the site is highly regarded for night diving when the golden cup corals (*Tubastrea coccinea*) all extend their polyps, colouring the entire reef golden yellow.

3 DEAVER'S REEF
★★★★★★

Location: Great Cruz Bay in the southwest of St John, between Contant Point and Blasbalg Point.
Access: By boat only.
Conditions: Susceptible to surge in the spring, which often stops diving within this bay.
Average depth: 7m (25ft)
Maximum depth: 12m (40ft)
Average visibility: 12m (40ft)

This is a great site for trainee divers, comprising a sandy bay with lots of boulders covered in a thin film of live corals and sponges that allow divers the chance to get close to the marine life with minimal risk of damage. A green turtle (*Chelonia mydas*) is regularly seen on this dive, as are trumpetfish (*Aulostomus maculatus*) and lots of sharp-nosed pufferfish (*Canthigaster rostrata*).

4 BOVOCOAP
★★★★★★

Location: The headland which juts out to the south of St John between Chocolate Hole and Rendezvous Bay.
Access: By boat only.
Conditions: Current running from southwest to east and some surface chop.
Average depth: 6m (20ft)
Maximum depth: 9m (30ft)
Average visibility: 15m (50ft)

This site is treated as a drift dive following Bovocoap Point around into Hart Bay at the western end of the much larger Rendezvous Bay. The dive follows over lots of coral mounds on the sea floor, which gradually give way to a hard rock substrate covered in hard corals. Sea fans are present, but there are few of the soft sea plumes. The small coral ledges are home to spiny lobsters (*Panulirus argus*) and at night the reef is teeming with red night shrimps (*Rhynchocinetes rigens*). Divers regularly see eagle rays (*Aetobatus narinari*), nurse sharks and stingrays.

5 REEF BAY
★★☆☆☆☆

Location: This is a large bay along the south coast of St John between Cocoloba Cay to the west and White Point to the east.
Access: Can be reached from the shore down the Bay Trail to Genti Bay and onto the shallow reefs, but much better accessed by boat.
Conditions: Sheltered in the shallows as the fringing reefs take away much of the surge.
Average depth: 3m (10ft)
Maximum depth: 7m (25ft)
Average visibility: 9m (30ft)
This site offers a great snorkel among shallow coral heads, which break the surface in many places. The reef is predominantly made up of old elkhorn coral (*Acropora palmata*), although this was badly damaged during a recent hurricane. However, there are also lots of small brain corals, star corals and cactus corals, all covered in a dense coat of algae. The area is teeming with damselfish of most Caribbean varieties and there are large numbers of angelfish.

6 THE LEAF
★★★★

Location: This is the deeper section of Reef Bay, directly between the two points.
Access: By boat only.
Conditions: Some surface chop to be expected, as well as slight current flowing from west to east.
Average depth: 15m (50ft)
Maximum depth: 25m (80ft)
Average visibility: 18m (60ft)
This site is usually dived during the winter months, from November to February, when the bay is at its calmest. It features coral heads in very good condition, as well as lots of lobsters to be seen everywhere. The tops of the corals have sea fans and larger gorgonians, such as black sea rods (*Plexaura homomalla*) and knobby sea rods (*Eunicea* spp.). A long coral formation – like a mini-wall,

but only 1m (3ft) high – is home to various species of grouper, snapper, grunt, wrasse and parrotfish.

7 EAGLE SHOAL
★★★★

Location: East of Ram Head to a shallow rocky reef which barely breaks the surface.
Access: By boat only.
Conditions: Surge and surface chop to be expected; only dived during the calmer winter months when the wind is predominantly from the north.
Average depth: 9m (30ft)
Maximum depth: 18m (60ft)
Average visibility: 25m (80ft)
This rocky reef shelves off steeply to the south. On approaching the rocks you will find a swim-through about halfway up, with a small tunnel encrusted with soft and hard corals as well as low encrusting sponges such as the pink lumpy sponge (*Monanchora unguifera*) and the pink-and-red encrusting sponge (*Spirastrella coccinea*). Large numbers of silversides congregate here and they are often surrounded by tarpon, jacks and barracuda. Be careful when venturing into the shallows looking for the larger cavern: the rocky surfaces are covered in fire coral.

8 HURRICANE HOLE
★★

Location: Around the mangrove shoreline which lines Hurricane Hole in the east of St John.
Access: Can be reached from the East End Road which passes next to the shoreline at Borck Creek.
Conditions: Sheltered with very little water movement, but some boat traffic.
Average depth: 1m (3ft)
Maximum depth: 6m (20ft)
Average visibility: 6m (20ft)
Hurricane Hole is just what you might expect from the name: when a hurricane is forecast, yachts hole up here for protection. In fact, hurricane or no hurricane, the site is principally a yacht mooring. The shore is lined with mangroves and, from a diving point of view, the site is really only for adventurous snorkellers, who can take a small dinghy into the reefs and mangrove beds. There are some rewards for so doing. The mangrove roots are home to thousands of juvenile fish, small shrimps, upside-down jellyfish (*Cassiopaea xamachana*) and tiny bluebell tunicates (*Clavelina picta*).

Virgin Islands reefs are home to a wide diversity of corals, sponges and fish.

9 HAULOVER BAY

★★★

Location: Northeast end of St John; can be reached by the trail which leads from East End Road to Haulover Bay.
Access: Directly from the shore.
Conditions: Can suffer from surge in the shallows November to March.
Average depth: 3m (10ft)
Maximum depth: 6m (20ft)
Average visibility: 15m (50ft)
The reef here falls within the National Park and runs parallel to the shore in a north–south direction, starting

---

The banded coral shrimp (Stenopus hispidus) is an active cleaner on deeper reefs.

directly from the access point at the water's edge. It is advisable to wear surf walkers or some type of waterproof shoe as the seashore is rather rocky. The reef is made up of elkhorn and staghorn corals (*Acropora palmata* and *Acropora cervicornis*) with lots of brain corals and cactus corals. Venus sea fans (*Gorgonia flabellum*) can be seen all over the reef crest, but a number have been damaged and are becoming overgrown with fire coral. Several species of algae are found amid the corals, making them rather untidy in appearance, but you can always find various damselfish and sergeant majors.

10 BROWN BAY

★★★★★

Location: North coast of St John; can be reached via the Brown Bay hiking trail, 45 minutes from where the trail branches off next to the Hermitage.
Access: From the shore or by boat.
Conditions: Sheltered from northerly swells by Tortola and very calm.
Average depth: 5m (17ft)
Maximum depth: 6m (20ft)
Average visibility: 15m (50ft)
Brown Bay can be reached overland, but most visitors arrive by dive boat. It is a perfect shallow bay suitable for trainees and snorkelling. Although quite rocky close

to shore, the encrusting corals are in good order and fish life is quite diverse as the bay is so little visited. Snapper, grunt, parrotfish and wrasse are the main types to be found.

11 WATERLEMON CAY
★★★☆☆☆☆☆

Location: Directly north of Waterlemon Bay and west of Leinster Point; can be reached by footpath from Annaberg parking lot (30 minutes' walk).
Access: Can be reached from the shore, but easier by boat.
Conditions: Fairly sheltered with little current, but some surface chop.
Average depth: 6m (20ft)
Maximum depth: 9m (30ft)
Average visibility: 15m (50ft)
This site is popular with trainee divers as the small island is surrounded by good coral growth that bottoms out onto a sandy seafloor where training exercises can be undertaken without risking damage to the corals. Large comet starfish (*Linckia guildingii*) are common, as are orange ridge sea stars (*Echinaster spinulosus*). Sand tilefish (*Malacanthus plumieri*) can be seen making their coral rubble nests and peacock flounders (*Bothus lunatus*) are common on the sandy plain.

Red reef hermit crabs (Paguristes cadenati) are often comical in their movements.

12 JOHNSON'S REEF
★★★★★☆

Location: North of Trunk Cay, usually marked by a large set of breakers.
Access: By boat only.
Conditions: Surge conditions to be expected and some current; only dived when it is flat calm.
Average depth: 5m (17ft)
Maximum depth: 11m (37ft)
Average visibility: 18m (60ft)
This offshore coral reef stretches approximately 150m (500ft) in a north–south direction and is susceptible to cross-current as it passes through between the islands. The reef is usually quite easy to find because of the rough water above it. On occasional calm days, however, it is always being hit by small craft, and as a result the top of the reef is rather damaged and covered in dense mats of algae. The reef consists of a huge platform of numerous species of hard corals including boulder star coral (*Montastrea annularis*) and finger coral (*Madracis formosa*). Yellowtail snapper (*Ocyurus chrysurus*) are

Among the smaller grouper to be found around the islands is the coney (Epinephelus fulvus).

common, as are striped parrotfish (*Scarus croicensis*) and bluehead wrasse (*Thalassoma bifasciatum*).

13 TRUNK BAY

★★★★★

Location: Reached by travelling east along the north shore road from the ferry terminal at Cruz Bay to the carpark at Trunk Bay (well signposted).
Access: Directly from the shore.
Conditions: Calm and sheltered, no current, but can be busy with other snorkellers.
Average depth: 3m (10ft)
Maximum depth: 5 m (17ft)
Average visibility: 9m (30ft)
Trunk Bay is protected by the US National Park Service and is St John's only designated snorkel trail. The trail is 235m (775ft) long and very popular with non-diving visitors to the island, who are able to rent snorkelling equipment from the beach. It is essentially a self-guiding trail, marked by underwater signs which identify coral reef life. There are lots of sergeant majors and snapper present as they are fed constantly by the tourists. Although the practice is not endorsed by the National Park Service, it continues to take place and consequently the fish are friendly (if rather aggressive). Corals are not very prolific,

but there are many small sea fans. There is also some fire coral (*Millepora alcicornis*) here, so care should be taken.

14 CARVAL ROCK

★★★★★★★★★

Location: Due east of Congo Cay.
Access: By boat only.
Conditions: Can be choppy on the surface with some surge during the winter months.
Average depth: 12m (40ft)
Maximum depth: 26m (85ft)
Average visibility: 25m (80ft)
Carval Rock is actually four major rocks and two smaller ones – similar to The Indians (Little Sisters, Site 7) – and is home to some of the best fish life in the area. The best diving is along the exposed north side where there is very little coral growth due to the strong currents which often sweep through. Only dived during the summer months (May to September), Carval Rock is famous for its big schools of southern sennet (*Sphyraena picudilla*) and Bermuda chub (*Kyphosus sectatrix*). At the eastern end of the rock there are some huge boulders that drop down to 26m (85ft) which are covered in gorgonian sea fans. The canyons and gullies are filled with silverside minnows in the summer.

15 EAST END OF CONGO
★★★★

Location: Just north and at the eastern end of Congo Cay.
Access: By boat only.
Conditions: Strong current passing Carval Rock and moving around Congo Cay, as well as some surge; best dived during the summer.
Average depth: 9m (30ft)
Maximum depth: 26m (85ft)
Average visibility: 25m (80ft)
When the tide is running to the north, this is treated as a drift dive, with divers being dropped off into the water on the southern end of the island, allowing the current to carry them around to the north side. Much of the dive takes place along the outer reef here, where there are weird-looking rocks (shaped like mushrooms on their sides) covered in gorgonians. In the shaded areas golden cup corals (*Tubastrea coccinea*) light up in the beam of a torch. Horse-eye jacks (*Caranx latus*) and Atlantic spadefish (*Chaetodipterus faber*) are common, as are many species of snapper and grunt. During the summer, one of the larger holes in the reef has so many silversides that the sea is black with them. Tarpon (*Megalops atlanticus*) can be seen dashing though the schools, feeding at will.

16 WEST END OF CONGO
★★★★

Location: North of Congo Point at the west end of Congo Cay.
Access: By boat only.
Conditions: Some current to be expected.
Average depth: 18m (60ft)
Maximum depth: 23m (75ft)
Average visibility: 25m (80ft)
From the mooring buoy, divers can drift around the point to the south or work their way around an extended strip reef of submerged rocks which runs for about 60m (200ft) and is between 6 and 12m (20–40ft) deep. There are numerous cracks and ledges with nice overhangs under which spiny lobsters (*Panulirus argus*) and bigeye (*Priacanthus arenatus*) can be found. To the west there is a sand chute where eagle rays (*Aetobatus narinari*) are regularly seen, as well as turtles and the occasional shark. This site is also popular for night diving and there are always sightings of a huge friendly green moray eel called General Lee.

Red clingfish (Arcos rubiginosus) are considered fairly rare in the Caribbean.

---

17 MINGO PASSAGE
★★★★

Location: Between Mingo Cay and Lovango Cay.
Access: By boat only.
Conditions: Strong current when tide is running to the north.
Average depth: 7m (24ft)
Maximum depth: 15m (50ft)
Average visibility: 18m (60ft)

Opposite: *This typical reef scene features granitic boulders topped by sparse coral growth.*
Above: *Tarpon (Megalops atlanticus) are predatory hunters, often seen near schooling silverside minnows.*

This is a strong drift dive when the tide is running to the north; yet when it flows south, the current takes another route and the area is relatively calm. The site takes the form of a low flat reef of bedrock covered in good coral growth, comprising common sea fans (*Gorgonia ventalina*), sea plumes (*Pseudopterogorgia* spp.) and long sea whips (*Ellisella barbadensis*). Caribbean reef octopus (*Octopus briareus*) are very common and the remains of their shelly meals can be seen littered all over the seabed.

18 MINGO CAY
★★★

Location: Midway along the south shore of Mingo Cay to the permanent mooring buoy.
Access: By boat only.
Conditions: Sheltered location, ideal for beginners.
Average depth: 12m (40ft)
Maximum depth: 17m (56ft)
Average visibility: 18m (60ft)
This site is similar to Grass Cay (Site 21), with large stands of good corals, although here they are fewer and smaller in size. The sandy area to the bottom of the reef is filled with garden eels (*Heteroconger halis*), which retreat into their burrows as you approach them. Also on the sand (more commonly seen at night) are red heart urchins (*Meoma ventricosa*) and tiger's tail sea cucumbers (*Holothuria thomasi*). The reef is fringed with schools of creole wrasse (*Clepticus parrai*) and blue chromis (*Chromis cyanea*).

19 TWO BROTHERS
★★★★★

Location: Middle of Windward Passage, leading southwest to Pillsbury Sound, south of Mingo Cay and due west of Caneel Bay.
Access: By boat only.
Conditions: Current to be expected and some surge.
Average depth: 7m (24ft)
Maximum depth: 9m (30ft)
Average visibility: 18m (60ft)
The Two Brothers is a pair of rocks that jut out of the water about 4m (15ft), the larger of which has a navigation light on the top. The surrounding area is made up of boulders with a living fringe of coral and some large separate heads of star coral (*Montastrea*

spp.) Due to the prevailing current passing through the passage, there are thousands of sea fans, mostly with attendant flamingo tongue shells (*Cyphoma gibbosum*) on them. This is also a good location to look out for large anemones (*Condylactis gigantea*), which have symbiotic shrimps among their tentacles. The anemone shrimp in question (*Thor amboinensis*) has vivid light spots and bands around its trunk, and quite often there may be as many as a dozen of these tiny crustaceans on each anemone.

PARROTFISH

There are 14 species of parrotfish found in Virgin Islands waters, all of which belong to the family Scaridae. They are recognized primarily by their blunt head and powerful jaws. With fused teeth that look like a true parrot's beak, they use their jaws to scrape algae and bite off chunks of living coral to extract the polyps. The fish have strong rasping or grinding plates in their mouths that grind down the limestone to remove their food source. Juvenile parrotfish are difficult to identify due to the several colour changes which they pass through to adulthood.

---

20 GRASS CAY DRIFT DIVE
★★★★

Location: Midway between Grass Cay and Mingo Cay.
Access: By boat only.
Conditions: Easy current travelling north or south through the passage between the islands.
Average depth: 6m (20ft)
Maximum depth: 17m (55ft)
Average visibility: 18m (60ft)
This is a nice easy drift dive for beginners. The tide is not too swift, so you can stop and look about you. The dive takes place along the base of the steeply sloping coral reef where it terminates on the sandy plain. It is a good-quality bank of coral covered in sea fans and plumes. Amid the coral heads are many species of small tube worm, which love this type of water movement as it allows them to trap planktonic particles that drift by on the current. They include the Christmas tree worm (*Spirobranchus giganteus*) and the larger magnificent featherduster (*Sabellastarte magnifica*).

21 GRASS CAY (THE MOUNDS)
★★★★

Location: Midway along the south shore of Grass Cay to the permanent mooring buoy.
Access: By boat only.
Conditions: Sheltered from the current; can be dived all year round.
Average depth: 7m (25ft)
Maximum depth: 12m (40ft)
Average visibility: 15m (50ft)
This is a terraced rocky reef with ledges at 6m (20ft), 13m (44ft) and 18m (60ft), with some massive heads of coral some 4m (17ft) across, consisting primarily of great star coral (*Montastrea cavernosa*). There is little coral growth on the slopes but as you work your way deeper you come across a sandy area with huge mounds of coral rising 8m (27ft) off the seabed and some 18m (60ft) in diameter. There are

over two dozen of these coral heads. Lobsters are common, as are arrow crabs (*Stenorhynchus seticornis*) and file clams (*Lima scabra*). The sandy area has large numbers of queen conch (*Strombus gigas*) and you may also be able to find the rare fingerprint cyphoma (*Cyphoma signatum*) on the sea rods. Grass Cay is a superb site for night diving as there is no current, allowing the dive boat to stay stationary on the mooring buoy.

22 JAWS REEF (MIDDLE PASSAGE)
★★★★★

Location: Off the west end of Grass Cay.
Access: By boat only.
Conditions: Can be very strong current running south.
Average depth: 9m (30ft)
Maximum depth: 18m (60ft)
Average visibility: 18m (60ft)
Named after a set of false teeth which were found on this site, Jaws Reef has some unusual tunnels at a depth of about 12m (40ft). You can swim up inside the tunnels through an upwards-twisting shaft to near the surface. All around, there are sheets of ancient rock seabed which have created mini undersea islands that drop from 4m to 18m (17–60ft). This rocky substrate is covered in lush growths of sea plumes and small rose corals (*Manicina areolata*). There are always tarpon and barracuda to be seen on the dive, as well as chain moray eels (*Echidna catenata*) and glassy sweepers (*Pempheris schomburgki*) in the tunnels.

If you follow the reef to the south, you will encounter an extended rocky ridge which has been sculpted over the centuries to form an area where fish (and divers) can rest from the current and where nurse sharks (*Ginglymostoma cirratum*) can be found regularly during the day. Much of the underside of the ledge is smothered in golden cup corals (*Tubastrea coccinea*) and there are some nice sea plumes all along the upper edge of the ridge.

Above: *The cushion sea star (Oreaster reticulatus) is fairly common on shallow reefs*
Below: *The most colourful of the small mollusc shells is the flamingo tongue (Cyphoma gibbosum).*

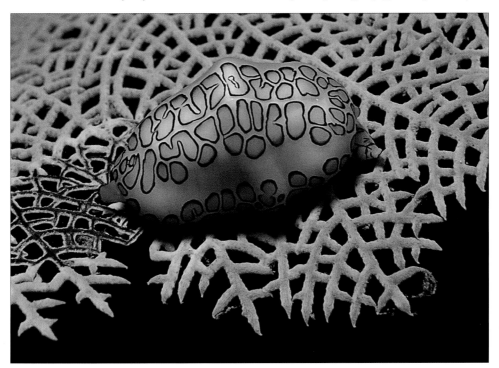

How to Get There

There are no airstrips on St John, so visitors usually arrive by private yacht charter or ferry from either nearby St Thomas or Tortola in the British Virgin Islands. There are lots of ferries that pass between St Thomas and St John, mainly from the ferry terminal at Redhook Bay on the east coast of St Thomas, near the town of Nazareth. The journey from there takes about 20 minutes. Some ferry services do run from the capital Charlotte Amalie, but they are less frequent and take 45 minutes.

From Tortola, the ferry for St John departs from West End.

Ferry services include
Native Son Inc., Veteran's Drive, St Thomas; tel (340) 775 3111; fax (340) 777 2811
Inter-Island Boat Services, PO Box 548, Cruz Bay Dock, Cruz Bay, St John; tel (340) 776 6597; fax (340) 693 7166

Getting Around

There are several ways of touring St John. You can rent your own vehicle, organize a taxi between four people or take one of the open-sided safari buses – also known as 'jitneys'; these can seat up to 20 people and are mainly for the day trippers. The buses stop at virtually every precarious vantage point to take in the superb views and the tour takes about two hours.

The main car rental agencies are found near the ferry terminal in Cruz Bay. However, a number of resort hotels have their own hire vehicles, or if not, can arrange for a hire car to be delivered to your hotel. Rental vehicles are mainly four-wheel drive, which is essential along the steeper sections of the mid-island road. Be sure to fill up with petrol at one of the two filling stations in Cruz Bay, as there is

nowhere else on the island.

Avis Rent-A-Car, 1A Cruz Bay Dock, Cruz Bay, St John; tel (340) 776 6374
St. John Car Rental, Inc, PO Box 566 Cruz Bay, St John, US Virgin Islands 00831; tel/fax (340) 776 6103
O'Connor Jeep, Cruz Bay, St John; tel (340) 776 6343
Best Rent-A-Car, 300 Contant & Enighal, St John; tel (340) 693 8177
C&C Car Rental and Taxi Service, 256 Enighed, St John; tel (340) 693 8164
Budget Rent-A-Car, 11 Contant, St John; tel (340) 776 5774
St John Taxi Services Inc., Cruz Bay, St John; tel (340) 693 7530

Where to Stay

Accommodation varies from very upmarket resorts on secluded beaches to campgrounds within the Virgin Islands National Park. Bookings for the peak season (Christmas to March) should be made well in advance. Facilities cover a wide range and all resorts include a complete watersports package. A number feature their own dive facilities. There are also a few small villas for hire through:
Caribbean Villas and Resorts Management, Islandia Building, Cruz Bay, St John; tel (340) 776 6152; fax (340) 779 4044
Tourism Division Visitor's Bureau, Wharfside Village, Cruz Bay, St John; tel (340) 776 6450

Expensive
Caneel Bay, PO Box 720, Caneel Bay, St John, VI 00831-0720; US toll free tel (800) 928 8889; tel (340) 776 6111; fax (340) 776 8280; website: www.rosewood-hotels.com
One of the island's most luxurious resorts, founded in 1955 by Laurence Rockefeller. Occupies a desirable position on a 75ha (170 acre) peninsula adjoining the Virgin Islands National Park. 171 guest cottages, all with

views over one or more of the resort's seven beaches. Famous for its gardens, which feature over 500 varieties of tropical plants. Tennis, watersports, three restaurants.

The Westin Resort, PO Box 8310, Great Cruz Bay, St John, VI 00631; tel (340) 693 8000; fax (340) 693 8888; website: www.starwoodhotels.com/westin/resorts/index.html
Recently refurbished resort with 285 guest rooms, all amenities. Set in 15ha (34 acres) of grounds, with a fine beach and a massive freshwater pool. Tennis, watersports, two restaurants.

Mid-range
Gallows Point Suite Resort, PO Box 58, Cruz Bay, St John, VI 000831; US toll free tel (800) 323 7229; tel (340) 776 6434; fax (340) 776 6520; email: gallows@islands.vi
Fully furnished, self-catering, harbour-view apartments, freshwater pool.

Serendip, PO Box 273, Cruz Bay, St John, VI 000830; tel/fax (340) 776 6646
Fully equipped, one bedroom and studio apartments.

Inexpensive
The Inn at Tamarind Court, PO Box 350, 3AE Enighed, Cruz Bay, St John, VI 000831; US toll free tel (800) 221 1637; tel (340) 776 6378; fax (340) 776 6722
Centrally located guest house, simple rooms with tropical decor, popular restaurant.

Budget
Cinnamon Bay Campground, Cinnamon Bay, St John, VI 00830; tel (340) 776 6330; fax (340) 776 6458
Bare tent sites, sites with tent-covered

Large schools of snapper and grunt can be found around most reefs.

platforms and small cottages with full self-catering equipment and linen supplied. Small shop.

Maho Bay Camps, Inc., PO Box 310, Cruz Bay, Saint John, VI 00830; US toll free tel (800) 392 9004; tel (340) 715 0501; email: mahobay@maho.org; website: www.maho.org/Scuba.cfm
Tented cabins with self-catering equipment and linen supplied. Shop and central dining area.

WHERE TO EAT

The resort hotels and guest houses on St John all offer excellent international cuisine and very few guests ever take the chance to sample the delights of the small restaurants in the main town of Cruz Bay or on the roadside as you traverse the island. These restaurants are frequented by local residents and day trippers coming over from St Thomas and Tortola in the British Virgin Islands.

The Fish Trap, A-5, Cruz Bay, St John; tel (340) 693 9994; website: www.thefishtrap.com
A tropical patio setting with nightly seafood specials, good quality and fair prices. Closed Mondays.

Mongoose Junction, Cruz Bay; tel (340) 777 3061
Full line of delicious takeouts, fresh baked goodies and picnic supplies. Air-conditioned with internet cafe. Serves breakfast and lunch.

Morgan's Mango Restaurant, 1 Enighed, Cruz Bay, St John; tel (340) 693 8141
Very popular, so best to reserve a table well in advance, creole and continental specialities, great atmosphere with lively music.

Paradiso, Mongoose Junction, Cruz Bay, St John; tel: (340) 693 8899
Excellent Italian restaurant. Food served in or out of doors.

Shipwreck Landing, Rt. 107, Coral Bay; tel (340) 693 5640
Great, lively atmosphere. Fish steaks, shrimp and lobster specialities. Excellent value in a brilliant setting.

Café Roma
Cruz Bay, tel (340) 776 6524; website: www.stjohn-caferoma.com
Extensive Italian menu with vegetarian specialities.

Panini Beach Trattoria, Wharfside Village, Cruz Bay tel (340) 693 9119; email: info@paninibeach.com; website: www.paninibeach.com

Relaxed Italian restaurant serving lunch and dinner.

DIVE OPERATORS

Cruz Bay Watersports, Inc., Cruz Bay Store, PO Box 252, St John, US Virgin Islands 00831; tel (340) 776 6234; fax (340) 693 8720; email: info@divestjohn.com; website: www.divestjohn.com

Westin Resort St. John, PO Box 8310, St John, US Virgin Islands 00831-8310; tel (340) 693 8000; website: www.westinresortstjohn.com
Large professional organization, retail stores, equipment rental, great service with fresh fruit on board and free use of wetsuits, trips all around the Virgin Islands. A PADI 5-star facility and NAUI Dream Resort.

Low Key Watersports, Wharfside Village, PO Box 716, Cruz Bay, St John, VI 00831; US toll free tel (800) 835 7718; tel (340) 693 8999; fax (340) 693 8987 website: www.divelowkey.com
A PADI 5-star IDC Training Facility. Excellent location, with a well stocked shop next door to a deli, very professional and knowledgeable, extended-range diving all over the Virgin Islands.

The Maho Bay Watersports Center, PO Box 310, Cruz Bay, St John, VI 00830; tel (800) 392 9004; tel (340) 715 0501; email: mahobay@maho.org; website: www.maho.org/Scuba.cfm
A full-service, PADI-certified dive shop just a few feet from the beautiful, secluded beach at Maho Bay Camps. Run by Maho Bay Camps, Inc.

EMERGENCY SERVICES

Ambulance/Fire/Police, tel 911
Emergency Medical Services, Cruz Bay; tel (340) 776 6222
Morris F. Decastro Clinic, Cruz Bay; tel (340) 776 6400
Chelsea Drug Store, The Marketplace, Rte. 104, Cruz Bay. tel (340) 776 4888.
Recompression Chamber, St Thomas; tel (340) 776 8311
Divers Alert Network, tel (919) 684 8111

LOCAL HIGHLIGHTS

Hiking trails can be found all over the National Park. Maps and guide books are available at the Cruz Bay Visitor Centre, a short walk from the public ferry dock. The centre also contains exhibits, a park video and brochures. Park rangers can help plan your itinerary, organize hikes and give advice on historical sites, snorkelling trails and any eco-programmes that may be held in the evenings in campgrounds

and hotels; tel (340) 776 6201; fax (340) 693 8811.

Visit the Annaberg Sugar Mill and Plantation, 20 minutes along the north shore road. The ruins of this old factory building and windmill date from 1733 and offer views of Annaberg Bay on the north coast.

The **Enighed Estate Great House** just outside Cruz Bay is an interesting restored former Danish colonial home which houses the **Elaine Ione Sprauve Library and Museum**, containing local artefacts and ancient books on the Virgin Islands. Open 1400–1700 on weekdays; tel (340) 776 6359.

Most summer weekends there is a **'Fish Fry'** around the harbour area of Cruz Bay. All the best local chefs cook locally caught fish in a hundred different ways, and there is live music and a party atmosphere (try the 'maubi' – a local drink made from ginger, herbs, sugar and bark).

The **beaches** are what visitors come to St John to enjoy. Much quieter than those on St Thomas, the six main beaches are Caneel Bay, Cinnamon Bay, Hawksnest Bay, Coral Bay, Lameshur Bay and Trunk Bay. Caneel Bay is private property and a visitor day pass must be obtained at the Caneel Bay Resort front desk. Hawksnest Bay is popular with locals and has facilities. Trunk Bay is the most popular and has a snorkel trail.

In tropical waters such as around the Virgin Islands there is a strong temptation to dive only on coral reefs, off the wall or on a wreck. As a result the surrounding sandy areas or eelgrass beds are largely ignored by divers.

The northern Virgin Islands are surrounded by vast plains of mud, sand and fine coral rubble which are in fact home to some of the most varied species of marine life found around these shores. Nevertheless, the temptation to keep on swimming over a sandy sea floor is so strong, particularly when you can see a rocky reef or wreck looming in front of you, that it is difficult to make the resolution to stop and look closely at what is under you – rather than the promise of what lies ahead. The first thing to do is to slow down, significantly enough to catch sight of fairly obvious signs of marine life such as tracks just under or across the surface of the sand. These tracks will invariably have a beginning and an end, and if you are lucky enough to follow the track in the right direction you may well be rewarded with sight of a red heart urchin (*Meoma ventricosa*) or burrowing starfish (*Astropecten articulatus*), for example.

Closest to shore, the inshore sandy area is one of the first habitats to explore. Among the soft shifting sand here queen conch (*Strombus gigas*) can often be found – a staple of the diet of many local islanders. These sandy beds are also home to snapping shrimps, which live in burrows with a species of goby (*Nes longus*). Stingrays are forever foraging in the same area for molluscs and crustaceans.

The sand diver or lizardfish (Synodus intermedius) lies under the sand in wait of its next victim.

Flounders and other types of flatfish are associated with sandy seabeds and you will invariably find various species of these fish in profusion, but other fish also like to hide under the sand and wait for their meal to pass by. Lizardfish or sand divers (*Synodus intermedius*) come into this category, lurking beneath the surface, their upturned mouths just waiting for a small blenny or shrimp to stray close enough for them to spring into action. Perhaps the most exciting find in shallow coastal waters is the Caribbean reef squid (*Sepioteuthis sepiodea*), an active night feeder seen near the surface. Attracted to divers' night lights, it will often display in front of the lights, changing colour rapidly.

DEEPER HABITATS
As you proceed deeper, the softer sand generally makes way to gravel and small stones, where wave action has not been able to move the seabed around as much. Now more stable, the rocky substrate under the sand has small ghost featherduster worms (*Anemobaea* spp.), often glimpsed only as a fuzzy appearance vanishing before you as the worms disappear into their protective tubes.

Although it is more stable, the sub-surface remains fairly soft in this area, and it is here that you are most likely to find burrowing anemones (*Arachnanthus nocturnus*), which rapidly withdraw under the sand or coral rubble whenever they are approached. On blades of sea grass, the tiny turtle-grass anemone (*Viatrix globulifera*) can be found when it extends its tentacles at night. Gravel beds are also home to a number of species of hermit crabs, eroded mud crabs (*Glyptoxanthus erosus*), box crabs (*Calappa gallus*) and of course the colourful and aggressive reef mantis shrimp (*Lysiosquilla glabriuscular*). Spaghetti worms (*Eupolymnia crassicornis*) are recognized by the long white sticky threads that fan out sometimes as much as 1m (3ft) from the mouthparts of the worm, which is always hidden away from sight. Also in these deeper regions you will find lancer dragonets (*Paradiplogrammus bairdi*) and amber penshells (*Pinna carnea*).

At night Caribbean reef squid (Sepioteuthis sepiodea) display their colour changes in front of divers' lights.

EELGRASS BEDS
Shallow eelgrass beds form the nurseries of many of the more common marine species to be found in the Virgin Islands. Apart from a range of algae, there are numerous creatures specially adapted for this environment. Amid the grass stems, you will find fire sponge (*Tedania ignis*), which can cause an irritation similar to the sting from fire coral if touched. Tiny lightbulb tunicates (*Clavelina* spp.) attach themselves to most surfaces, while mermaid's fan algae (*Udotea* spp.) always have brittlestars and small snails crawling over it at night.

Wherever there is softer sediment, you must be careful of your fin kick, as too strong a kick will disturb the sediment, perhaps smothering a delicate organism and creating havoc for any following divers. The best course of action is to emulate cave divers, using an easy sideways kick and staying off the bottom with correct buoyancy technique. Before you do settle on the bottom, check beneath first, so as to land on an area clear of sensitive marine species.

THE BRITISH VIRGIN ISLANDS

The jewel-like British Virgin Islands are located just a few kilometres from their US neighbours across The Narrows and can be reached by ferry from St Thomas or St John in as little as twenty minutes. Stretching in a southwest–northeasterly direction, this British dependency comprises some 50 islands and cays clustered around a wide, shallow channel. Largely volcanic in origin, they were once connected to what are now Puerto Rico and the US Virgin Islands. They include the remains of a huge volcanic mountain which exploded while the Caribbean was still a land-locked sea – the caldera is actually at Road Town on Tortola, with outlying islands forming the remains of the rim.

The British Virgin Islands are generally much quieter than the US Virgin Islands, with a population of only about 17,000. Tourism arrived comparatively recently: the main tourist islands are Tortola and Virgin Gorda. **Tortola** is 19km (12 miles) long by 5km (3 miles) at its widest part and resembles St Thomas and St John, with a volcanic centre and steep-sided mountain range. In its south is the capital, Road Town, while along the central ridge of the island runs a breathtaking narrow road which draws visitors when the cruise ships are in town. To the north of Tortola lie the smaller islands of **Jost Van Dyke**, Tobago Island, Guana Island and Great Camanoe. Beef Island, to the west, is where the international airport is situated

On the southern side of Tortola runs the Sir Francis Drake Channel, a wide, shallow waterway that serves as the main thoroughfare for sailors navigating these islands in search of deserted coves and interesting dive sites. Across the channel and ranging northwest towards Virgin Gorda lie the **Little Sisters**, including Norman Island, Pelican Island, Peter Island, Dead Chest, Salt Island, Cooper Island, Ginger Island, Round Rock and Fallen Jerusalem. The majority of the diving in the British Virgin Islands takes place around this string of islands, as, no matter what the weather pattern, there is always a lee shore for safe diving to take place. The RMS *Rhone*, possibly the most famous wreck in the Caribbean, is found here, to the northwest of Salt Island.

Opposite: *Tortola presents an idyllic setting, with Guana Island in the background.*
Above: *Small wooden craft-shops are commonplace on Tortola.*

Northeast of the Little Sisters but usually reached by ferry from Beef Island, **Virgin Gorda** is approximately half the size of Tortola. Its southern half is fairly flat and includes the main habitation of Spanish Town. Towards the southern tip of Virgin Gorda, giant boulder formations have created unusual grottos, caves and pools at a spot known as The Baths. Off the north coast of Virgin Gorda are The Dogs, Mosquito Island, Prickly Pear Island, Eustatia and Necker Island, popular with yachting enthusiasts due to their large number of sheltered bays and inlets. Finally, some 40km (25 miles) north of Virgin Gorda, **Anegada** is one of the largest coral islands in the eastern Caribbean, rising a mere 8.5m (28ft) above sea level.

> **BVI NATIONAL PARKS TRUST**
>
> Established in 1961, the Trust is responsible for the management of the British Virgin Islands' terrestrial and marine parks. It currently manages 14 areas, with many more parts of the islands now shortlisted. All divers and snorkellers within the Marine National Parks must have a permit. For visiting divers this costs $1.00 per person per day: it will be charged automatically by your dive resort.
>
> For further information contact: British Virgin Islands National Parks Trust, PO Box 860, Fishlock Road, Road Town, Tortola.

HISTORY

Christopher Columbus named the main island of Tortola after its abundance of turtle doves, which are still found on the island – at the same time he named Virgin Gorda ('Fat Virgin') and Anegada ('Sunken Island'). However, the first visitors to the islands came long before Columbus: a number of artefacts belonging to Ciboney, Arawak and Carib Indians can still be found on the offshore islands. These peoples were wiped out following the arrival of the Europeans.

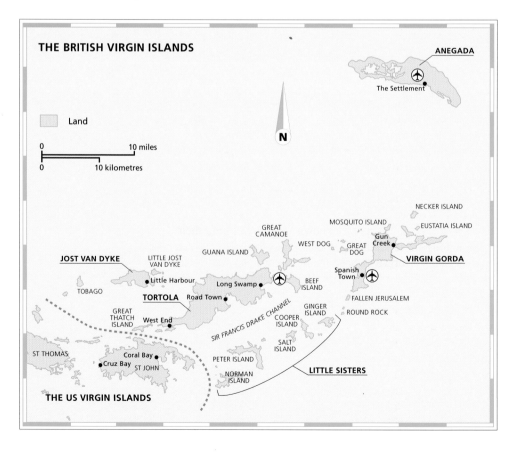

The Star Clipper is one of innumerable large yachts that visit the islands.

The islands slowly became home to a mix of predominantly Dutch settlers and rootless, marauding pirates. In 1585 Sir Francis Drake sailed through the area en route to conquering Hispaniola – hence the name of the main channel running through the islands. In the late 1600s, shortly before nearby St Thomas and St Croix were taken over by Denmark, British occupiers ousted the Dutch planters. The British Governor of the Leeward Islands annexed Tortola in 1672 and in 1680 settlers from Anguilla moved into Virgin Gorda and Anegada, establishing sugar cane plantations.

The turn of the 17th century saw the islands being used as a base for pirates, with many known to live and hide their booty among these scattered islands. They included figures such as Henry Morgan (whose main base was on Andros in the Bahamas), Edward 'Blackbeard' Teach, Anne Bonny, Sir John Hawkins, Captain 'Calico Jack' Rackam and Captain William Kidd. Most infamous of all was Blackbeard, reputed to have left 15 mutiny-minded men ashore on Dead Chest, a small but very high, scrubby island situated between Salt Island and Peter Island to the southeast of Road Town, with only a 'yo-ho-ho and a bottle of rum' between them.

Despite these shady figures, the islands prospered for a while with a high production of sugar, cotton, rum, indigo and spices. In the 1850s, the introduction of sugar beet into

ANEGADA'S FLAMINGOES

The Anegada flamingo ponds, first described in 1832 by R.H. Schomburgk, a German-born naturalist – who also described and named the glassy sweeper (*Pempheris schomburgki*) – once had hundreds of pairs of Caribbean or roseate flamingoes. However, over the decades the young birds were herded together and sold down-island for their meat, while the mature birds were hunted for their feathers. For a period of about 50 years there were no flamingoes on Anegada.

The British Virgin Islands National Parks Trust then approached the Bermuda Aquarium and Zoo which had eight birds that they were willing to part with. The first birds kept under controlled conditions did not fare well, but another 20 birds were later released onto the salt pond on Anegada and these managed to breed. It takes three years for these birds to reach sexual maturity and, although the salt ponds are capable of handling thousands of birds, it will be some time before they reach this number. Visitors to Anegada should be aware of the nesting sites and keep well away.

BVI TOURIST BOARD OFFICES WORLDWIDE

Caribbean

Tortola: BVI Tourist Board, DeCastro Street, 2nd Floor, AKARA Building, Road Town, Tortola; tel (284) 494 3134; email: info@bvitourism.com

Virgin Gorda: Virgin Gorda Yacht Harbour; tel (284) 495 5181; email: info@bvitourism.com

UK

BVI Tourist Board, 15 Upper Grosvenor St, London W1K 7PJ; tel 44-207-355 9585; email: infouk@bvi.org.uk

USA

New York: BVI Tourist Board, 1 West 34th Street, Suite 302, New York, NY 10001; tel 212-696 0400/800-835 8530; email: info@bvitourism.com

Los Angeles: BVI Tourist Board, 3450 Wilshire Blvd, Suite 1202, Los Angeles, CA 90010; tel 213-736 8931; email: info@bvitourism.com

Europe coincided with the revolt over slavery, and the plantations all but closed down, with many people leaving the islands. The emancipation of Tortola's slaves in 1834 led to new immigrant workers arriving from the island of Vieques to work the land, for minimal wages. However, conditions did not improve on the plantations and together the immigrant workers and some former slaves staged a revolt in 1853, burning the owners' estates, crops and cane mills.

There was a resurgence in trade when the Royal Mail Steam Packet Company moved their operations for refuelling and transferring passengers and goods from Charlotte Amalie to Road Harbour in Tortola and Great Harbour in Peter Island, spurred on by a serious outbreak of yellow fever and malaria in St Thomas. For a time many other transatlantic steamers avoided St Thomas and transferred operations to Tortola, but its harbour was not as sheltered as Charlotte Amalie and a number of ships came to grief on the surrounding submerged reefs.

However, any real development on the islands failed to materialize. It was only after the United States bought the Danish West Indies in 1917 and renamed them the United States Virgin Islands – much to the chagrin of the islanders, who had traded on the name 'Virgin Islands' for some time – that things picked up again. The islands began to feel the benefits of development in the US Virgin Islands, a situation that still holds today, with the largest proportion of visitors to the British Virgin Islands being incidental visitors staying on nearby St Thomas or St John.

In the 1950s Laurence Rockefeller donated three large parcels of land to the British Virgin Islands National Parks Trust, building at the same time the first luxury resort on Virgin Gorda at Little Dix Bay. Tourism began, and an upsurge in the local economy got underway. Tourism has since far outstripped all other sources of income, except offshore banking, and the British Virgin Islands has attained economic and political stability. Visitors number about 380,000 annually, of whom two-thirds are from the USA.

In 1967 the islands voted to stay under the wing of the United Kingdom, gaining a new constitution that provided for a locally elected government and a governor appointed by the Crown. With almost 100% employment and little or no serious crime, the islanders are justifiably proud of their country and like to maintain the distinction between their quiet lifestyle and that of the US Virgin Islands. Nonetheless, many local inhabitants also have family in the US Virgin Islands.

RENDEZ-VOUS DIVING

Pioneered by Underwater Safaris on Tortola over 25 years ago, this form of diving allows people on yachts to visit dive sites if they don't have scuba equipment on board. The visiting yacht radios ahead to the local dive shop giving its location in relation to the chosen dive site. Then the dive resort sends a boat carrying all the necessary diving equipment to rendez-vous with the yacht and take the passengers diving.

TRAVELLING TO THE BRITISH VIRGIN ISLANDS

For travellers from Europe, there are regular scheduled flights to the British Virgin Islands from London, serviced by British Airways, Virgin, BWIA, KLM and Iberia. However, these flights are routed through either Antigua or San Juan in Puerto Rico, as the British Virgin Islands airport runway is too short (though there are plans to extend the runway in the

The granite blocks at The Baths on Virgin Gorda are a famous tourist attraction.

future). Flights via San Juan usually connect with American Eagle for the final leg to Beef Island. Delays should be expected at San Juan and it is worth enlisting the help of a porter on arrival to avoid missing your connection. If possible make sure that your follow-on seats are protected by your travel agent. If you do have to spend extra time in San Juan, take a taxi to the Old Town, which is a delight.

From the US Virgin Islands, Tortola is serviced several times daily by ferries from St Thomas and St John. Local islanders, or 'belongens', commute daily between the islands, often doing their shopping in the US Virgin Islands where domestic goods are much cheaper. From other eastern Caribbean islands there are a number of smaller charter flight services flying into Beef Island. Cruise ships do visit the British Virgin Islands, though not in the numbers that you find on St Thomas.

> **NATIONAL PARKS MOORING BUOYS**
>
> With the help of local dive operators, the British Virgin Islands National Parks Trust has installed over 200 mooring buoys in the past decade. The colour-coding system used is:
> - yellow buoy: commercial dive and sail boats only
> - white buoy: all charter boats including diving
> - orange buoy: snorkelling and 'lunch' moorings
> - blue buoy: dinghy docks

CUSTOMS AND IMMIGRATION

All foreign citizens must carry a full passport when entering the British Virgin Islands, and a visa may be required by some nationalities. Unless you are a 'belongen' you have to present your passport and fill out a tourist card whenever you enter the country, even if it is only as part of a short day trip across The Narrows from the US Virgin Islands. However, regular commuters can get a special pass to save filling their passport with immigration stamps. You must retain part of the immigration slip to hand over when you finally exit whichever island you are staying on.

Most customs officers are well used to divers arriving with lots of baggage and will generally let you walk straight through, after a cursory examination of your documents and questions about your diving destination. If you are carrying lots of photographic equipment it is advisable to write down a list of all contents, any serial numbers and the value of each item, as a precaution against importation problems. This can then be presented to customs and stamped. The list should later be checked and cleared on your departure.

TRANSPORT

Taxis are available from the airport at Beef Island and work on a fixed scale of charges which is displayed at the airport. For onward travellers to Virgin Gorda, a small taxi ride is needed to catch the ferry at Beef Island. When travelling around the islands by taxi, particularly outside of urban areas, it is always a good idea to ascertain the fare in advance. All hotels should be able to give you an indication of the going rate.

An alternative is to hire a car. For this you must have a valid driver's licence from your country of origin and must purchase and carry proof of car insurance. Rental agencies will take a signed credit card imprint as a deposit: without a credit card, you will not be able to hire a car.

Four-wheel-drive is a must as the mountain roads are very narrow and steep and most have tight corners not originally intended for cars. Driving is on the left hand side of the road and overtaking is on the right. However, most of the hire cars are left-hand-drive US models, which can lead to confusion and the occasional accident; the rule is to take care when driving. All distance markers are in miles.

Pusser's Restaurant and Stores has outlets at several locations in the British Virgin Islands.

ACCOMMODATION

Accommodation on Tortola and Virgin Gorda is varied, with something to suit all tastes. There are small, quiet guest houses, large resort hotels, all-inclusive luxury condominiums and even converted plantation estate houses. Most larger resorts offer watersports such as diving, snorkelling, parasailing and windsurfing. Prices reach their highest during the US holiday seasons around Easter and Thanksgiving.

Hotel packages are based on the Modified American Plan (room, breakfast and dinner) or the European Plan (room only). Self-catering guest houses with 'efficiency suites' – small fully fitted kitchenettes with fridge, cooker and microwave – tend to be less expensive. When booking into a hotel you will be asked to sign a blank imprinted credit card slip for incidental charges: this is standard practice. In addition a government tax of 10% is added to all hotel bills. Although diving operators are usually situated within the grounds of a particular hotel, they often have special arrangements with other guest houses or small hotels and can arrange pick-up and transfer for a day's diving. All the dive operators offer all-inclusive packages which are regularly advertised in the US scuba diving press.

TORTOLA AND JOST VAN DYKE

The main centre of tourism in the British Virgin Islands is Tortola, with the capital Road Town situated in a sheltered harbour to the south. This rugged island is 19km (12 miles) long by 5km (3 miles) at its widest part and dominated by a lofty mountain range, with its highest peak at Mount Sage, 520m (1750ft) high. Crossing the island often involves dramatic ascents and descents along precipitous roads, such as the switch-back road leading to the beach at Brewers Bay. So mountainous is Tortola that the airstrip had to be built on neighbouring Beef Island, the northern limits of which are flat by comparison. Largely coralline in geology, Beef Island is connected to Tortola by the earliest toll bridge in the Caribbean.

Much of Tortola's original subtropical forestation was cleared for sugar cane production in the 1700s. However, the growing of sugar cane has virtually ceased and production is now only enough to supply one of the original rum distilleries in Cane Garden Bay to the north. Today cacti, mango trees, hibiscus, bougainvillaea, frangipani and wild tamarind dominate the arid hillsides, while mangroves and palm trees are found around the shoreline.

To the north of Tortola lie Green Cay, Little Tobago, Tobago, Jost Van Dyke, Little Jost Van Dyke, Guana Island, Great Camanoe and Scrub Island. Jost Van Dyke is reputedly named after an early Dutch pirate who used the island as his base, although some argue that Jost Van Dyke was rather one of the early settlers of the islands when they still came under the Danish Flag. At only 6km (4 miles) long this island is like a mini-Tortola with lush mountains dropping to rocky shores in the north and gorgeous secluded bays along the south.

In the past, these islands have been largely bypassed by divers, partly due to lack of marketing and partly due to the excellent diving to be found elsewhere in the Caribbean. The up-side, however, is that there has been much less diver pressure and the reefs are in excellent condition. The British Virgin Islands National Parks Trust has been responsible for the placing of over 200 mooring buoys since 1989. These factors, plus the ease of accessibility for divers visiting the islands with their own sailboat or powered charter yacht and the invention of 'rendez-vous diving', have made the British Virgin Islands rather special in the diving world.

Opposite: *Marina Cay off the northeastern shore of Tortola is a popular anchorage for yachtsmen.*
Above: *Vividly coloured featherduster worms (Megalomma spp.) are found on most species of coral.*

TORTOLA

It only takes a few hours by hire car to explore Tortola, but, as it is virtually impossible to traverse the island without ascending the lofty mountain range, extra time may be needed to take in the breathtaking views. Topped by the incredibly scenic Ridge Road, the dizzying heights make you stop at every turn just to gaze or snap another picture. Although there isn't much to do on the island, the original sugar cane rum distillery still operating in Cane Garden Bay is well worth a visit.

There is comparatively little diving done immediately around Tortola, and dive boats tend mostly to travel north to Jost Van Dyke, Guana Island and Great Camanoe Island – or the short distance across the Sir Francis Drake Channel to the Little Sisters in the south. Nonetheless, the north coast of Tortola has a few fabulous bays, such as Cane Garden Bay and Brewers Bay, which are protected by boulder-strewn barrier reefs. Some of the more exposed headlands are cut by huge tunnels and canyons, which become difficult to dive whenever there is a strong northerly gale.

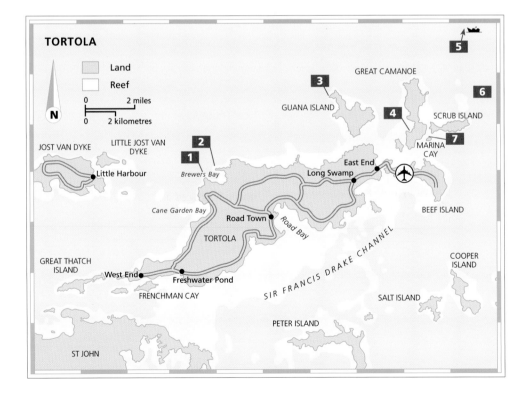

1 BREWERS BAY PINNACLES (BREWER'S DROOP)
★★★

Location: Off the western tip of the entrance to Brewers Bay, northwest Tortola.
Access: By boat only.
Conditions: Can be surge, and current usually to be expected.
Average depth: 12m (40ft)
Maximum depth: 33m (110ft)
Average visibility: 12m (40ft)
About half a dozen massive rocky pinnacles rise in varying depths, from 33m (110ft) to within 9m (30ft) at the shallowest point. The close proximity of a number of the rocky stacks has created interesting winding canyons covered in deep-water gorgonians (*Iciligorgia schrammi*), which filter nutrients from the ever-present current. The shallower reaches of the boulders are all covered in fire coral (*Millepora alcicornis*) so great care should be taken, particularly if there is any ground swell. Lobsters are common, as are angelfish and butterflyfish; cleaning gobies (*Gobiosoma genie* and *gobiosoma oceanops*) are present on the rocky surfaces and it is not uncommon to see predatory jacks lining up to be cleaned of parasites.

2 ROCKY MOUNTAIN LOW
★★★★★

Location: At the northeastern edge of Brewers Bay.
Access: Can be reached from the shore, but easier by boat.
Conditions: Surge to be expected during the winter months.
Average depth: 12m (40ft)
Maximum depth: 25m (80ft)
Average visibility: 15m (50ft)
This site is marked by two exposed rocks on the surface opposite the headland, which provide a clue to the numerous sub-surface pinnacles along this exposed northern shore. These massive boulders have schools of blackbar soldierfish (*Myripristes jacobus*) mixed with French grunt (*Haemulon flavolineatum*), creating a colourful moving wall as you explore under the deeper ledges with torchlight. Golden cup corals and red sponges are everywhere and spinyhead blennies (*Acanthemblemaria spinosa*), roughhead blennies (*A. aspera*) and secretary blennies (*A. maria*) by the dozen can be found in abandoned worm tubes, their tiny heads protruding to pick off passing planktonic particles.

3 GRAND CENTRAL
★★★★

Location: Muskmelon Bay at the north tip of Guana Island.
Access: By boat only.
Conditions: Cave-diving experience (particularly in penetrating long caves) is recommended, especially since light levels are low. Can be surge.
Average depth: 18m (60ft)
Maximum depth: 21m (70ft)
Average visibility: 15m (50ft)
Along the lowest end of the wall here, a tunnel has been carved out of the surrounding hard rock. The entrance to the northwest is in 17m (55ft) and drops down as far as 21m (70ft). This lower part is known as the Well; above this a vertical shaft called the Elevator Shaft rises up to the reef top. The Main Chamber has rounded boulders all over the bottom, shaped by the relentless pounding surge in the winter months. A small antechamber called the Telephone Booth is next on the swim-through and then you go upwards through the Corkscrew, which exits on the reef top at 3m (10ft). Playing in the shafts of light is a resident school of glassy sweepers (*Pempheris schomburgki*). The walls of the chambers are covered in spiky sponges and bryozoans. Torches are recommended on this dive, which can be undertaken only when conditions are perfect.

4 THE MOUSE TRAP (LEE BAY)
★★★★★★

Location: At the entrance to Lee Bay on the southwestern coast of Great Camanoe.
Access: By boat only.
Conditions: Potential danger from surge in the shallows.
Average depth: 9m (30ft)
Maximum depth: 18m (60ft)
Average visibility: 15m (50ft)
This is a shallow fringing reef off the southwestern shores of Lee Bay, which slopes steeply down amid a tumble of boulders and a maze of winding gullies that have been sculpted out of the bedrock. There are hundreds of sea fans and plumes everywhere and, although the corals are sparse, many of the rocky surfaces are covered in colourful sponges such as yellow boring sponges (*Siphonodictyon coralliphagum*), orange icing sponges (*Mycale laevis*) and orange encrusting sponges (*Diplastrella* spp.). Damselfish, small wrasse and parrotfish predominate, with flounders and garden eels also to be found on the sand plain. There is a sand patch at 4m (15ft) towards the shore when you exit the maze and to the east is a nice coral overhang where squirrelfish and bigeye can be found with their attendant cleaner shrimps.

5 CHIKUZEN

★★★★★

Location: 10km (6 miles) north of Great Camanoe Island to the northeast of Tortola.
Access: By boat only.
Conditions: Subject to northerly swells.
Average depth: 15m (50ft)
Maximum depth: 25m (80ft)
Average visibility: 30m (100ft)
Midway between Great Camanoe and Anegada lie the remains of the *Chikuzen*. This former Japanese refrigeration vessel was part of a derelict fleet in St Maarten. In danger of damaging the docks during a severe storm, she was towed out to sea to be scuttled by her owners. They also set fire to the ship, hoping that this would speed her sinking, but she refused to sink and drifted off in the storm, ending up in the British Virgin Islands. She was then towed out to this point and finally sunk in 1981. At 74m (246ft) long, she now rests on her port side, hatches open, her masts and rigging extended out into the water. Be warned that there are lots of hanging wires and a risk of entanglement. Much of the superstructure has fallen off due to the constant battering of the northerly swells. The ship has settled onto a featureless sand plain and is festooned with fish. Her masts, railings, propeller, winches and anchors are

---

HYDROIDS

Hydroids or hydrozoa are sedentary colonial animals which attach themselves to seaweeds, rock, stones, boat hulls and the shells of live molluscs, hermit crabs or other crustaceans.

A close relative of jellyfish, the dominant stage in the life cycle of the hydroid is attached rather than free-floating. Hydroids have erect stems or stalks on which the polyps are situated. The arrangement of the polyps along the stalk varies with the different species – they may be located singly at the end of the stalk, opposite each other or even with alternate spacing.

All hydroids feed on zooplankton, which they capture using nematocysts (stinging cells). The food can be carried via the communal gut to any part of the colony. There are several common species: some can be found on the lower shore, some attached to seaweeds, but most enjoy areas of fast-moving water where there is a rich supply of zooplankton. The most common you are likely to encounter in the Virgin Islands are the feather hydroid (*Gymnangium longicauda*) and the feather plume hydroid (*Aglaophenia latecarinata*),which should be avoided at all costs, as the nematocysts contained in its innocuous-looking 'feathers' extremely painful and can easily become embedded in the softer parts of your skin, such as unprotected wrists.

---

covered in gorgonian sea fans and encrusting sponges. This is definitely an oasis of life in the desert.

6 TOW ROCK

★★★

Location: Northwest of Scrub Island, midway to West Dog.
Access: By boat only.
Conditions: Strong current to be expected and oceanic surge from the north.
Average depth: 12m (40ft)
Maximum depth: 21m (70ft)
Average visibility: 25m (80ft)
This is an offshore rocky mound with a steep slope which drops down from 12m to 21m (40 to 70ft). Along the south there are some huge boulders which are covered on their undersides by golden cup corals (*Tubastrea coccinea*) and small colourful encrusting sponges. The rocks are topped with common sea fans (*Gorgonia ventalina*) and small knobby hard corals. Fish life is rather sparse, but there is a regular large school of horse-eye jacks (*Caranx latus*) which appears to be on constant patrol around this reef. Other pelagics such as large barracuda and the occasional turtle are also seen.

7 DIAMOND REEF

★★★★

Location: Between Marina Cay and Great Camanoe before you reach the channel between Great Camanoe and Scrub Island.
Access: By boat only.
Conditions: Sheltered but heavy with boat traffic.
Average depth: 6m (20ft)
Maximum depth: 12m (40ft)
Average visibility: 6m (20ft)
Dive boats anchor in the sand channel near the reef, and it is a simple case of swimming from here towards the shore of Great Camanoe. A fringing reef drops down from shore level to about 9m (30ft), where it reaches the sand channel. The channel then slopes gently to a series of scattered small coral heads, often covered with a film of silt or sand. An electric cable which snakes its way along the seabed can be used as a ready reference for divers. Best done as a night dive, this is one of the few sites where fingerprint cyphomas (*Cyphoma signatum*), considered very rare in other areas of the Caribbean, are commonly found, here on most of the small sea plumes. Lettuce leaf nudibranchs (*Tridachia crispata*) are also found and, although the fish life is sparse on the reef, there are interesting finds at night such as sand dollars (*Clypeaster subdepressus*) and cushion sea stars (*Oreaster reticulatus*).

Above: *Virtually all the rocky overhangs are covered in golden cup corals (Tubastrea coccinea).*
Below: *Blackbar soldierfish (Myripristes jacobus) are commonly found in caves and caverns.*

How to Get There

There are regular flights from all of the US 'hub' airports such as Miami, Houston and Chicago. Flights from the UK are first routed through Antigua or San Juan in Puerto Rico, due to the small size of the international airport on Beef Island in the British Virgin Islands. Transfers at San Juan can be slow, due to the lengthy immigration procedures, the necessity of collecting luggage and then transferring it about 300m (984ft) to the domestic terminal to catch the connecting flight to Beef Island. You cannot take any trolleys out of the arrivals terminal at San Juan, so you must enlist a porter or 'skycap'.

Beef Island International Airport is typically Caribbean, where no one is in a hurry. There is no duty-free shop, but duty-free goods can be purchased in most stores on the British Virgin Islands.

You can reach Tortola by ferry from either St Thomas (Red Hook or Charlotte Amalie) or St John (Cruz Bay). The main ferry terminal is at West End, opposite the Sopers Hole Marina. A service does run to Road Town, but this is less frequent.

Some Ferry Services
Native Son Inc., West End, Tortola; tel (284) 495 4617; Road Town tel (284) 494 5674
Inter-Island Boat Services, PO Box 548, Cruz Bay Dock, Cruz Bay, St John; tel (340) 776 6597; fax (340) 693 7166; tel Tortola (284) 495 4166
North Sound Express, Beef Island, Tortola; tel (284) 495 2138
Marina Cay Ferry, Marina Cay, Beef Island; tel (284) 494 2174 or call VHF channel 16

Getting Around

A hired four-wheel drive is the best way of getting around the island. The larger ones have a very large turning circle and require some manoeuvring on the steeper mountain passes, but these bigger vehicles have the advantage of air-conditioning. Minibus taxi-cabs are available at the airport to take you to your resort past Road Town or for the short hop to the northeast landing slip on Beef Island to catch the ferry to Leverick Bay, Little Dix Bay, Spanish Town or the Bitter End Yacht Club on Virgin Gorda.

However, many visitors to the islands travel by their own yacht or private charter craft. Bicycles are available from a few of the resorts, as most are close to town.

Alphonso Car Rental, Fish Bay (near Road Town), Tortola, tel (284) 494 8746 or (284) 494 8756
Avis Rent-A-Car, Botanic Station, Road Town, Tortola; tel (284) 494 3322
Del's Jeep & Car Rental, Cane Garden Bay,

Tortola; tel (284) 495 9356
Dollar Rent-A-Car, Prospect Reef, Tortola; tel (284) 494 6093
Hertz Car Rental, West End, Tortola; tel (284) 495 4405
International Car Rentals, Road Town, Tortola; tel (284) 494 2516

Where to Stay

Accommodation on Tortola varies from very upmarket resorts to a campground at Brewers Bay on the northwest of the island. Bookings for the peak season (Christmas to March) should be made well in advance. Facilities cover a wide range and all resorts include a complete watersports package. A number feature their own dive operations. If you'd prefer to find accommodations unfrequented by other divers, these are certainly available: there are plenty of guest houses and villas scattered around the island, which are very popular with visitors looking for privacy. Resort hotels such as Prospect Reef are large and spread out, requiring either a long walk to get anywhere, or help from the concierge taxi-bus service which also does complimentary trips into Road Town each day.

A full list of accommodation is available in the free Welcome Tourist Guide Magazine (www.bviwelcome.com), available everywhere, or you can contact the **British Virgin Islands Tourist Board**, DeCastro Street, 2nd Floor, Akara Building, Road Town, Tortola , British Virgin Islands; tel (284) 494-3134; fax (284) 494-3866 email: bvitourb@surfbvi.com; website: www.bvitouristboard.com

Expensive
Treasure Isle Hotel, Pasea Estate, PO Box 68, Road Town, Tortola; tel (284) 494 2501; fax (284) 494 2507; website: www.treasureislehotel.net
On a hillside above the town and marina. Pool, good restaurant.

Prospect Reef Resort, Slaney Point, PO Box 104, Road Town, Tortola; US toll free tel (800) 356 8937; tel (284) 494 3311; fax (284) 494 5595; website www.prospectreef.com
Large resort with a wide range of rooms, suites and villas. Five pools, health and fitness suite, two restaurants, sailing charter, shops, children's facilities and dive centre (Baskin in the Sun); underwater photography shop (Rainbow Visions Photography).

Sugar Mill Hotel, PO Box 425, Little Apple Bay, Tortola; tel (284) 495 4355; fax (284) 495 4696; email: sugmill@surfbvi.com; website: www.sugarmillhotel.com
Excellent small hotel on the hillside. Efficiency apartments, very good

restaurant located in an old sugar mill, swimming pool.

Nanny Cay, PO Box 281, Road Town, Tortola; US toll free (866) BVI-HOTEL/(866-284-4683); tel (284) 494 4895; fax (284) 494 0555; email: hotel@nannycay.com; website: www.nannycay.com; Standard and deluxe suites, pool, two restaurants, shops, yacht charter and moorings, dive centre (Blue Water Divers).

Long Bay Beach Resort, Long Bay, PO Box 433 West End, Tortola; US toll free tel (800) 729 9599; tel (284) 495 4252; fax (284) 495 4677; website: www.longbay.com
Spectacular setting on one of the best beaches in the British Virgin Islands. Two restaurants, 9-hole golf course, live music each night.

Mid-range
Sebastian's on the Beach, PO Box 441, Little Apple Bay, Tortola; US toll free tel (800) 336 4870; tel (284) 495 4212; fax (284) 495 4466; website: www.sebastiansbvi.com
Lively, popular resort. Eight beachfront rooms, plus others (at a lower price) across the road. Restaurant/bar overlooking beach.

Village Cay Hotel & Marina, Wickhams Cay, PO Box 145, Road Town, Tortola; tel (284) 494 2771; fax (284) 494 2773; email: villcay@candwbvi.net; website: www.villagecay.com
Overlooking the harbour and marinas. Close to the main shopping area and popular with yachtsmen. Small pool and fair restaurant.

Moorings Mariner Inn, Wickhams Cay II, PO Box 139, Road Town, Tortola; tel (284) 494 2331; fax (284) 494 2226
Headquarters for the Moorings charter yacht business with efficiency apartments, small pool and good-value harbourfront restaurant.

Inexpensive
Rhymer's Cane Garden Beach Hotel, Cane Garden Bay, PO Box 750, Tortola; tel (284) 495 4639; fax (284) 495 4820
Fine beach setting, efficiency apartments, beach bar and terrace restaurant.

Castle Maria Hotel, MacNamara, PO Box 206, Road Town, Tortola; tel (284) 494 2553; fax (284) 494 2111
Simple but tidy efficiency apartments close to town. Small pool and bar.

Budget
Brewers Bay Campground, PO Box 185, Brewers Bay, Tortola; tel (284) 494 3463
Tented and bare-ground pitches as well as

self-catering accommodation. Restaurant, beach bar and shop.

WHERE TO EAT

The resort hotels and guest houses on Tortola all offer excellent international cuisine (quite often buffet style). Not many visitors venture out of the resorts, but there are some delightful small restaurants in Road Town or on the roadside as you traverse the island. The restaurants are frequented by local residents and day trippers coming over from St Thomas, St John and off the irregular cruise ships. Unlike in the US Virgin Islands, there are no fast-food diners. Pusser's is the only 'chain' establishment. Note that a number of restaurants can only be reached by private yacht charter.

A free British Virgin Islands restaurant guide is available at most tourist points.

The Last Resort, Trellis Bay, Beef Island, Tortola; tel (284) 495 2520; VHF Channel 16
Entertaining one-man-show and huge buffet-style feast. Accessible only by boat.

Callaloo at the Reef, Prospect Reef Resort, Tortola; tel (284) 494 3311; email: reservations@prospectreef.com; website: www.prospectreef.com
Contemporary Caribbean cuisine with lobster and seafood specialities and table-side flambé. Very tropical and quite fancy.

Brandywine Bay Restaurant, Brandywine Estate, Tortola; tel (284) 495 2301
Try the Roast Duck with Mango and Rum. Popular and dressy. Bookings recommended.

C&F Bar & Restaurant, Purcell Estate, Tortola; tel (284) 494 4941
Award-winning Caribbean and BBQ dinners. Excellent seafood any way you want it.

Captain's Table, Inner Harbour Marina, Tortola; tel (284) 494 3885
Lobster specialities from their own pool. Great vegetarian menu.

DIVE OPERATORS

Aquaventure Scuba, PO Box 852, Inner Harbour Marina, Road Town, Tortola; US toll free tel (800) 698 6579; tel (284) 494 4320; fax (284) 494 5608; email: aquavent@surfbvi.com; website: www.aquaventurebvi.com
Popular with small groups, small shop for sales. PADI and NAUI instructors.

Works in conjunction with:
We Be Divin', tel (284) 494 4320; We Be Divin' Anegada tel (284) 541 2835/ 541 0489; email: info@webedivinbvi.com; website: www.webedivinbvi.com

Dive Tortola, Prospect Reef Resort, Road Town, Tortola; tel (800) 353 3419 or (284) 494 9200; fax: (284) 494 7264; email: divetortola@surfbvi.com; website: www.divebvi.com
Superb operation and large retail shop, very professional, friendly and knowledgeable staff.

Blue Water Divers, Nanny Cay, PO Box 846, Road Town, Tortola; tel (284) 494 2847; fax (284) 494 0198; email: bwdbvi@surfbvi.com; website: www.bluewaterdiversbvi.com
Nice location and small but well stocked shop, well informed and professional staff.

UBS Dive Center, PO Box 3283, Road Town, Tortola, British Virgin Islands; Phone: 284 494 0024; Fax: 284 494 0623; email: info@ divebvi.com; website: www.scubabvi.com
Private, personalized scuba diving specialists.

Live-Aboard Dive Boats
Trimarine, c/o Charterport, P.O. Box 8309 PMB 613, Cruz Bay, VI 00831; tel (284) 494 2490; fax (284) 494 5774; email: cuanlaw@surfbvi.com; website: www.cuanlaw.com
The *Cuan Law* is the largest dedicated live-aboard trimaran dive boat in the world, and can carry 20 guests in comfort and style. Full E-6 and video editing on board.

Promenade Sail Dive Cruises, Box 2249 Roadtown, Tortola, British Virgin Islands; tel (284) 499 2756 ; email: promcruz@surfbvi.com; website: www.yachtpromenade.com/scuba.htm
Offers a 20m (65ft) trimaran that cruises the inner islands with 12 guests. A bit cramped but good value and great food.

EMERGENCY SERVICES

Police Emergency, tel 999 or 911
Police Headquarters, tel (284) 494 2945
Virgin Islands Search & Rescue, VHF Channel 16; tel (284) 494 4357, dialling 999 or 911
Peebles Hospital, Road Town, Tortola; tel (284) 494 3497
B&F Medical Complex Pharmacy, Mill Mall Bldg., Wickhams Cay; tel (284) 494 2196

Ruth's Drug Store, Fat Hog's Bay, East End; tel (284) 495 1173
Vanterpool Pharmacy, Wickhams Cay; tel (284) 494 2702
Recompression Chamber, St Thomas; tel (340) 776 8311
Divers Alert Network, tel (919) 684 8111

LOCAL HIGHLIGHTS •

These islands have such incredible natural beauty that just driving or walking around, sampling the sights is what people most enjoy. Traversing the island you pass through the **Sage Mountain National Park**, which has gravel paths leading through the forest.

It is best to explore Road Town itself on days when the cruise ships aren't in. The narrow road known as **Main Street** retains much of its West Indian charm: it has bright, colourful buildings and a quaint colonial look. The **J. R. O'Neal Botanic Gardens** in the centre of town is well worth a visit.

There are a few ruined forts around the island. **Fort Recovery**, built by the Dutch in the 1660s, is the oldest intact structure; located at West End, it has a turreted gun emplacement and old walls 1m (3ft) thick.

The **Callwood Rum Distillery** at Cane Garden Bay is housed in its original stone plantation building. Rum is still produced in the same way as it has been for centuries, except for the fact that diesel-powered presses are now used.

Sopers Hole Marina towards the West End is worth a tour, even if only to sit under the shaded awnings watching the ferries arrive from St Thomas and St John. Some fine shops and Pusser's Store are here.

Apart from golf courses, there is also excellent game fishing out on the edge of the continental shelf.

From earliest times, man has recorded the plight of his fellow creature being stung by denizens of the deep. Aristotle first accurately described the stinging properties of stingrays and jellyfish in 350BC. Pliny described the stingray thus in *Historia Naturalis*:

'So venomous it is, that if it be strucken into the root of a tree, it killeth it: it is able to pierce a good cuirace or jacke of buffe, or such like, as if it were an arrow shot or a dart launched: but besides the force and power that it hath that way answerable to iron and steele, the wound that it maketh, it is therewith poisoned.'

The venom of underwater creatures is in most cases used purely for defensive purposes. Divers quickly learn that if an animal being approached does not swim away it probably has some form of defence. As a general rule, stinging mechanisms found around the mouth parts of an organism are for offence, while stinging parts found along the back and tail are for defence.

Different creatures have different types of toxins and potency. Most cause localized effects such as numbness, irritation or paralysis, though others can kill nerves or blood cells or attack muscles and affect internal organs. Some venoms have a cumulative effect and cause several problems at the same time – in certain circumstances such toxins can even cause death in humans. (See pages 168-9 for remedies.)

Jellyfish come in a vast army of different sizes and potency, and are primarily offensive stingers. Their stinging mechanism is in the form of a tiny hooked barb fired by a hydraulic coiled spring: these barbs are called nematocysts and are held inside a trap-door until they are released by touch or chemicals in the water. The barbs are hollow and filled with toxins which are released as soon as the stinger penetrates its victim. The primary aim is to paralyse prey as a preparation for eating it. Most jellyfish sting, but few of their stings are dangerous. The most common complaints in tropical oceans are from Portuguese men-of-war (*Physalia physalis*) and sea wasps (*Carybdea alata*).

Whenever the conditions are favourable for thimble jellyfish (*Linuche unguiculata*), there is also a chance of much smaller and almost invisible planktonic stingers in the water column. These micro-organisms are found in shallow warm water at night and are attracted to light, often swarming together. The stings they cause can be severe, leading to muscle cramps, nausea and breathing difficulties, so it is important at such times to wear protection such as a Lycra skin suit.

SEDENTARY STINGERS

Anemones, hydroids and corals have a surprisingly large number of harmful representatives. Few anemones do any harm to the relatively thick skin of your fingers, but many can inflict quite painful 'burns' on softer parts on the inside of arms or legs. Species such as the berried anemone (*Alicia mirabilis*), found in deeper shaded areas, have warty tubercles all over the stem of the anemone, each 'berry' armed with lethal nematocysts. The more common anemones use their barbs to hook and paralyse prey which swim inadvertently within their 'sticky' grasp and most can leave their poison harpoons in softer body parts.

A similar looking species is the corallimorph, which covers large areas of dead coralline limestone boulders on Virgin Islands reefs. When disturbed, they produce sticky white filaments filled with nematocysts. Hydroids such as the stinging hydroid (*Aglaophenia latecarinata*) have harmless-looking feather-like plumes which can inflict a nasty sting to the skin if you brush up against them.

Fire coral is another fairly common stinger. Attractive but potentially painful, this coralline hydroid comes in a variety of guises. The most common is branching fire coral (*Millepora alcicornis*) which tends to grow over and envelop various species of sea fan, often taking on the complete shape. A closely related variety is blade fire coral (*Millepora complanata*) which forms a hard structure very similar to that of true corals.

TOUCH-ME-NOT VASE

Even the most innocuous-looking sea creatures often have a hidden battery of stingers just waiting for something to rub against them. The touch-me-not vase sponge (*Neofibularia nolitangere*) has tiny calcium spicules which, when rubbed against, produce an effect like that of fibreglass rubbing against the softer parts of your skin. They can cause severe irritation, rashes and sores.

Fireworms (*Hermodice carunculata*), although quite cute in appearance, should never be handled, as they have clumps of white hairs along their sides which display bristles when touched. The bristles break off easily in the skin, causing a painful burning feeling and intense irritation.

A large number of molluscs also have stinging mechanisms. Some nudibranchs, for example, eat stinging hydroids and anemones and have the ability to store the stinging nematocysts of their prey in their own tentacles. When attacked by predators, the nudibranchs use the stored nematocysts in defence.

In the fish world the most lethal stings are those associated with the scorpionfish family, which have venom in the modified hollow spines that tip their dorsal fins. Also potentially dangerous, however, are the stingrays, as noted by Aristotle and Pliny. Visitors accustomed to diving at Stingray City off Grand Cayman Island should bear in mind that stingrays in the Virgin Islands are not used to human contact. Never attempt to grab hold of the tail, as this is where the stinging mechanism is located and any undue force may cause the creature to spring forward its tail in a reflex action, thus erecting the spine. As with all underwater creatures, the most important thing is to treat them with respect.

The Florida corallimorph (Ricordea florida) is common throughout the northeastern Caribbean.

JOST VAN DYKE

Now known as a 'party island' due to the large proportion of small bars and eateries along Great Harbour, Jost Van Dyke has become very popular, with great food, lively entertainment and a terrific atmosphere. There are only 140 residents on the island, all of whom are engaged in catering to the various visitors in one form or another. Power is supplied by generators and the whole island gives you the feeling of having stepped back in time. Much of the diving is in water of under 25m (80ft), with the reefs generally being in excellent condition.

Large spiny lobsters (Panulirus argus) are often found wandering about the reef during the day.

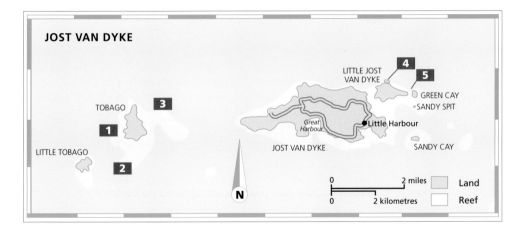

JOST VAN DYKE

LITTLE JOST VAN DYKE

4
5

GREEN CAY
SANDY SPIT

TOBAGO **3**

1

Great
Harbour

Little Harbour

LITTLE TOBAGO

JOST VAN DYKE

SANDY CAY

2

0   2 miles   Land

N

0   2 kilometres   Reef

1 WATSON ROCKS
★★★★

Location: At the northern edge of the shelf between Tobago Island and Little Tobago.
Access: By boat only.
Conditions: Surge and current to be expected, even during the best weather conditions.
Average depth: 12m (40ft)
Maximum depth: 21m (70ft)
Average visibility: 25m (80ft)
According to local dive operators, 'always expect the unexpected' on these lonely rocky pinnacles, as they act as a natural focus for many species of pelagic fish. This is also one of the few locations where blacktip sharks (*Carcharhinus limbatus*) are found. Large groups of Atlantic spadefish (*Chaetodipterus faber*) are common, as are many species of jacks and large snapper. Although the location is lacking in good corals, its sheer drama far outweighs this factor. Usually done as a second dive after Mercurius Rock (Site 3), it is always interesting. Lobsters are very common and there are numerous large crabs, including literally thousands of hermit crabs.

2 KING ROCK
★★★★

Location: At the southern edge of the shelf between Tobago Island and Little Tobago.
Access: By boat only.
Conditions: Surge and current to be expected, even during the best weather conditions.
Average depth: 12m (40ft)
Maximum depth: 21m (70ft)
Average visibility: 25m (80ft)

Similar in formation to Table Top (St Thomas, Site 19), this large, flat rocky plateau is undercut all the way round, creating interesting nooks and crannies for fish and invertebrates to hide under. Bull sharks (*Carcharhinus leucas*) have been seen here as well as Caribbean reef sharks (*Carcharhinus perezi*). This is often dived after Mercurius Rock (Site 3). The current can sweep around the southern end of the channel and thus make for an interesting drift dive, as you are taken in closer towards the fringing reef of Tobago Island. The site lacks good coral growths due to the pounding it receives from the winter swells.

3 MERCURIUS ROCK
★★★★★★★★

Location: Between Tobago Island and Jost Van Dyke to the east.
Access: By boat only.
Conditions: Surge and current are commonplace on this difficult offshore site; dived only in perfect conditions.
Average depth: 9m (30ft)
Maximum depth: 20m (66ft)
Average visibility: 25m (80ft)
Mercurius Rock can be dived only in perfect weather conditions, as the swell often reaches over 6m (20ft) deep to the tip of the rock. However, the submerged rock is difficult to find when the weather is calm without the use of GPS coordinates. The site is also more often visited by operators from St Thomas. There are actually three peaks which rise from the submarine pinnacle, which is topped in fire coral and covered on the sides by deep-water gorgonian sea fans, encrusting sponges and small cactus corals (*Mycetophyllia* spp.). Button corals (*Caryophyllia* spp.) are also found on this exposed site. At 9–15m (30–50ft) there is a tunnel that

Juvenile blue tangs are actually brilliant yellow in colour, changing to blue in their adult phase.

extends for about 30m (100ft), which is easily negotiated by divers. Slipper lobsters (*Parribacus antarcticus*) are found, as well as banded clinging crabs (*Mithrax cinctimanus*), which hide under the giant anemone's tentacles. Although the site is difficult to reach and a long boat ride, it is well worth the effort.

4 WHERE EAGLES DARE (TWIN TOWERS)
★★★★

Location: Off the northern headland of Little Jost Van Dyke.
Access: By boat only.
Conditions: Surge to be expected; usually only dived in optimum conditions.
Average depth: 15m (50ft)
Maximum depth: 27m (90ft)
Average visibility: 15m (50ft)
These exposed northern shores have an impressive array of sculpted headlands and deep tunnels cut into the barren steep-sided cliffs. Underwater, massive boulders rise up from a flat sandy plain, and in this site there are two distinctive monoliths. Although sparsely covered in coral growth, their sheer size and stature are impressive enough to warrant the dive. Known for massive shoals of silverside minnows which congregate in early summer,

the site is popular when the conditions to reach it and dive are perfect. It is also popular with some of the US Virgin Islands dive operations.

5 LITTLE JOST DRIFT (THE PLAYGROUND)
★★★★

Location: To the north and between Little Jost Van Dyke and Green Cay to the east.
Access: By boat only.
Conditions: Strong current and some surge during the winter months.
Average depth: 12m (40ft)
Maximum depth: 21m (70ft)
Average visibility: 15m (50ft)
From a central point between Little Jost Van Dyke and Green Cay, the northerly-running current can sweep you round to the east or west. Accompanied by an experienced dive master with boat cover, divers follow a leisurely drift over some excellent coral-encrusted boulders. The area between the two islands is mostly too shallow for all but the shallowest draft of boat. The site is known for its large concentrations of juvenile fish, and you can expect to find rock beauties (*Holacanthus tricolor*), foureye butterflyfish (*Chaetodon capistratus*) and hundreds of blue tang (*Acanthurus coeruleus*). Many of the boulders are overhanging, attracting species that love shade or only come out at twilight. Turtle are often seen in the shallows and some rather large barracuda always follow the divers.

How to get there

The only way to get to Jost Van Dyke is by boat, whether by private yacht charter or the occasional dive boats – which call in for lunch before exploring the surrounding islands and sea mounts. A ferry is available from Road Town to Great Harbour by arrangement; contact the Call the Jost Van Dyke ferry service, tel (284) 494 2997.

Getting around

There are only a handful of vehicles on Jost Van Dyke and no paved roads, so visitors either walk everywhere or take their boat tenders around to the various bays and islands nearby, leaving their yachts anchored safely in Great Harbour on the south of the island.

Where to stay

Soggy Dollar Bar/Sandcastle Hotel, White Bay, Jost Van Dyke, British Virgin Islands; tel (284) 495 9888; fax (284) 495 9999; website: www.sandcastle-bvi.com
Unwind on a hammock on the beach in one of four hideaway cottages, with cuisine by candlelight. The award-winning bar is home to the 'Painkiller' rum cocktail.

Sandy Ground Estates, PO Box 594, Sandy Ground, East End, Jost Van Dyke; tel (284) 495 3391; fax (284) 495 9379; website: www.sandyground.com; email: sandygroundjvd@surfbvi.com

Eight individually styled houses on the beach, can be stocked with provisions if required, have to walk to restaurants over the hill.

White Bay Campground, White Bay Beach, Jost Van Dyke; tel (284) 495 9312 Bare sites plus a few equipped with tent and electric light; small restaurant and beach bar.

Where to eat

Jost Van Dyke has something of a reputation of a party island with many yachties coming to the island, attracted by the freedom and also by the lack of the crowds associated with the larger resorts. Not a place for day trippers; the community mainly caters for visitors who want to sample fresh seafood and listen to yachting stories from around the world.

Harris' Place, Little Harbour, Jost Van Dyke; tel (284) 495 9302; VHF Channel 16 Fresh seafood and buffet pig roast nightly – not to be missed for all-you-can-eat dinners.

Foxy's, Great Harbour, Jost Van Dyke; tel (284) 495 9258; website: www.foxysbar.com
Famous BBQ buffet on Friday and Saturday. The place to be seen if you're a yachtie!

Abe's By the Sea, Little Harbour, Jost Van Dyke; tel (284) 495 9329; email: abes@candwbvi.net
Fresh lobster specialities, as well as BBQ pig, chicken and ribs.

Dive Operators

There are no diving facilities available on Jost Van Dyke.

Emergency Services

Virgin Islands Search & Rescue, VHF Channel 16; tel (284) 494 4357, dialling 999 or 911.
Peebles Hospital, Road Town, Tortola; tel (284) 494 3497
B&F Medical Complex Pharmacie, Mill Mall Bldg., Wickhams Cay; tel (284) 494 2196
Vanterpool Pharmacy, Wickhams Cay; tel (284) 494 2702
Recompression Chamber, St Thomas; tel (340) 776 8311
Divers Alert Network, tel (919) 684 8111

Local Highlights

There are few specific attractions on Jost Van Dyke. The allure of peace and quiet – other than on party nights – is what draws most visitors to the island.

The hair-like tentacles of fire coral are packed with nematocysts.

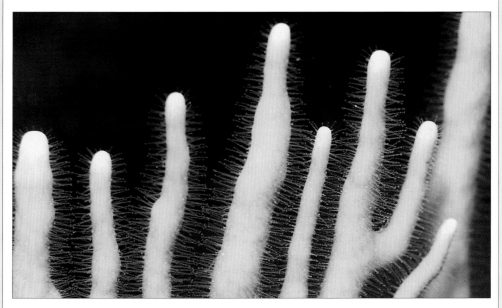

THE LITTLE SISTERS

To the south of the Sir Francis Drake Channel lie the Little Sisters, comprising Norman Island, Pelican Island, Peter Island, Dead Chest, Salt Island, Cooper Island and Ginger Island, interspersed with a number of rocky pinnacles. These are allied closely with St John in the US Virgin Islands, from which they are separated by a narrow stretch of water called the Flanagan Passage, and stretch northeast to Virgin Gorda. The islands are much smaller and lower in stature than their northern and western neighbours, resulting in a more arid profile with cactus growing at all levels, even down to the beach. Coconut plantations are found on a few of the islands, but these have long ceased to be commercially viable.

The most southerly island in the British Virgin Islands chain is **Norman Island**, reputed to be the inspiration for Robert Louis Stevenson's *Treasure Island* (although he used the shape of Unst in Scotland's Shetland Islands as the template for his fictitious island's shape). Treasure Point Caves on Norman Island has three caves at water level which yielded a treasure horde to some local islanders many years ago, and there are still tales of lost treasure buried on the island. The highest point on the island, known as Spyglass Hill, at 429m (1425ft), once gave privateers an almost uninterrupted view of all the water passages around the nearby islands, while the fabulous natural harbour known as The Bight was said to have been capable of concealing an entire armada.

Pelican Island, to the north of Norman Island, is little visited, apart from a small group of rocks known as The Indians in the west (Site 7) which attract scores of boaters, snorkellers and divers whenever the conditions are suitable. These dramatic rocks are peppered with guano and are said to resemble from a distance a Native American Indian's headdress.

The largest of the Little Sisters is **Peter Island**, with its picture-perfect bay and superb clear water at Little Harbour, always popular as an anchorage with yachtsmen. The island is home to the biggest resort in the Little Sisters, the Peter Island Yacht Club Resort at

Opposite: *Dive boats tie up to the pier at Little Harbour on Peter Island between dives.*
Above: *The banded butterflyfish (Chaetodon striatus) is a distinctive sight.*

Spratt Bay Point. The resort is serviced by Dive BVI, who have a full service shop on the island. The island's highest points are at 353m (1175ft) above Deadman Bay and 385m (1280ft) above Stoney Bay and Peter Island Bluff in the south.

Salt Island is known the world over for the remains of the RMS *Rhone* (Site 17), which foundered and sank here in 1867. The bodies that were recovered were interred in a small cemetery on the island near the ancient salt pond (the custodian of which presents a barrel of sea salt to the Queen each year in lieu of rent). Now the entire area around the wreckage of the *Rhone* is a Marine National Park, extending west to include the island of **Dead Chest**, as well as a small area north of Great Harbour where her snagged anchor was located (Site 11). A dive site to the south of the island known as Painted Walls (Site 14) is very popular, but only in flat calm conditions.

Cooper Island has two resorts, one around the superb Manchioneel Bay and the other just north of Carval Bay. The highest point is in the south of the island, at 509m (1680ft) above Black Bluff. The Cooper Island Beach Club is popular with yachting enthusiasts who enjoy the topside scenery as well as safe and easy snorkelling. Underwater Safaris also have a dive operation here and pick up at the resort each day. Between Cooper Island and Salt Island lie three wrecks, the newest being the *Inganess Bay* (Site 20), which was sunk in 1997 just out from Haulover Bay onto a flat sandy seabed where the current sweeps over the wreck, bringing nutrients and plankton to colonize the ship.

Uninhabited **Ginger Island** in the northeast is particularly rocky, with steep, dry scree slopes filled with rubble and boulders and very little beach. The highest peak is between Pond Point and Toby Bay at 350m (1165ft). South Bay is a popular anchorage for dive boats as this shallow, flat sand bay has numerous isolated coral heads, making it ideal for night diving.

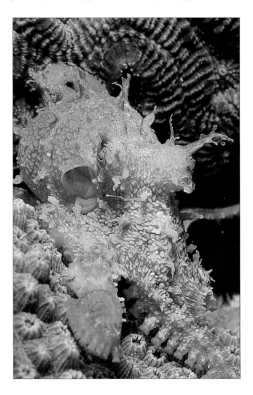

The Caribbean twospot octopus (Octopus filosus) is rarely found, and only at night.

The majority of the diving in the British Virgin Islands takes place around the Little Sisters, with their numerous sheltered bays, fringing reefs and offshore seamounts. The reefs that are most commonly visited are located between these islands and Tortola, where the water is more sheltered from the worst of any oceanic swells. Sites such as Carval Rock (Site 25) are exciting on account of their exposed locations, but take more planning and are entirely weather-dependent.

By far the most popular site is the wreck of the RMS *Rhone*, which seems almost tailor-made for diving. However, another rewarding kind of dive here is on the seagrass beds in sheltered coves such as Deadman Bay on northeast Peter Island. These huge expanses are home to an amazing array of marine life and act as important hatcheries to many marine species.

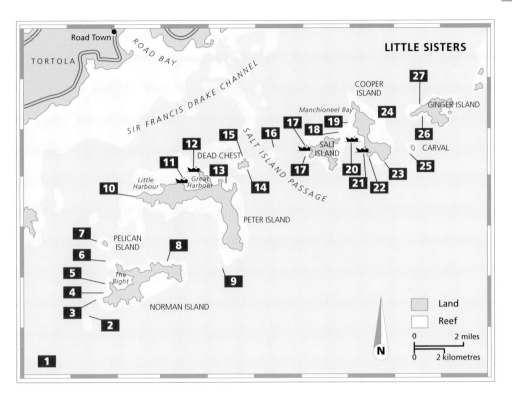

LITTLE SISTERS

Road Town

TORTOLA

ROAD BAY

SIR FRANCIS DRAKE CHANNEL

COOPER ISLAND

GINGER ISLAND

Manchioneel Bay

SALT ISLAND PASSAGE

DEAD CHEST

Little Harbour

Great Harbour

PETER ISLAND

PELICAN ISLAND

The Bight

NORMAN ISLAND

CARVAL

Land

Reef

0   2 miles

0   2 kilometres

N

1 NORMAN ISLAND DROP-OFF (BOB'S BUMP)

★★★

Location: Southwest from Norman Island to the edge of the continental shelf. This site can be found only by echo sounder.
Access: By boat only.
Conditions: Subject to oceanic swell and current.
Average depth: 45m (150ft)
Maximum depth: Beyond safe diving limits
Average visibility: 50m (165ft)
This site is considered a challenging offshore dive for experienced divers: it is by no means for novices. A weighted shot line is dropped over the side of the boat and made secure to either the boat or to a large float; you descend the line to where the continental shelf drops off into the blue. As you drift along in the current you have an above-average chance of seeing large pelagics such as shark, turtle, marlin, wahoo and barracuda. A solitary deep seamount, rising from 58 to 18m (190 to 60ft), is a special feature, providing an oasis of fish life and deep-water gorgonians.

2 SANTA MONICA ROCK

★★★★★

Location: 1.5km (1 mile) southwest of Norman Island.
Access: By boat only.
Conditions: Exposed open ocean site subject to swell, surface chop and current.
Average depth: 12m (40ft)
Maximum depth: 27m (90ft)
Average visibility: 30m (100ft)
Santa Monica Rock is named after an old wooden schooner called the *Santa Monica* which ripped out her hull and finally sank near St John. The 'rock' is in fact a cluster of huge coral-encrusted rocky pinnacles which are impossible to cover in just one dive. Dropping rapidly to 27m (90ft), the corals are home to large numbers of snapper and grunt. Turtle, barracuda and

---

FLYING GURNARDS

One of the most fascinating fish species found on the shallow banks of the Virgin Islands is the flying gurnard (*Dactylopterus volitans*), usually found in quite shallow water. Flying gurnards inhabit sand, coral rubble and sea grass areas, generally in spur-and-groove reef formations or near a fringing or strip reef. When foraging, they keep their extra-large pectoral fins folded against the side of their body and perch or walk with specially adapted ventral fin rays. Rather shy in nature, when approached or threatened they spread their pectoral fins and 'fly' away.

Variously coloured sponges and corals can be found under most coral overhangs.

other pelagic fish are always encountered here, but the site can be dived only when conditions are perfect. The top few metres are covered in fire coral and the sides are encrusted in literally thousands of sea fans. Snapper, grunt and angelfish are common, as are many different invertebrates including shells, nudibranchs and octopus. The dive is particularly scenic, with sculpted walls and gullies covered in corals, and includes thousands of fairy basslet (*Gramma loreto*).

3 ANGELFISH REEF
★★★

Location: Off the southwestern tip of Norman Island.
Access: By boat only.
Conditions: Can be some surface chop and slight current around the corner.
Average depth: 12m (40ft)
Maximum depth: 19m (64ft)
Average visibility: 18m (60ft)
Angelfish Reef is located where Norman Island shelves steeply away and features huge barrel sponges and sea fans. There are also indeed a good number of angelfish here – four species are found on every dive: the queen angelfish, grey angelfish, French angelfish and rock beauty. The dive generally starts off in deeper water where turtles are often encountered and

large southern stingrays (*Dasyatis americana*) can be found half-hidden under a fine coating of sand, after their nocturnal feeding. The reef on the corner of the island is cut by a series of narrow gullies where you might find smooth trunkfish (*Lactophrys triqueter*), trumpetfish (*Aulostomus maculatus*) and queen triggerfish (*Balistes vetula*); the latter can act quite aggressively towards divers during the breeding season (early May).

4 SANDY'S REEF (SANDY'S LEDGE)
★★★

Location: Between Angelfish Reef (Site 3) and Treasure Point on Norman Island.
Access: By boat only.
Conditions: Fairly sheltered, but can be some surge in the shallows on top of the ledge.
Average depth: 3m (10ft)
Maximum depth: 12m (40ft)
Average visibility: 15m (50ft)
Often ignored due to its shallow reef base and rocky beach, this reef is home to thousands of juvenile fish which appear to thrive in the nutrient-rich shallows. Nearly all of the sea fans have resident flamingo tongues (*Cyphoma gibbosum*) and the bases of the fans are overgrown with communal featherduster worms (*Bispira brunnea*). The turtle-grass beds feature cushion sea stars (*Oreaster reticulatus*) and red heart urchins (*Meoma ventricosa*). The top of the coral ledge is where much of the action is, with cleaning shrimps

and gobies always in attendance. There is often a great light for photography here, particularly on afternoon dives.

5 THE CAVES (TREASURE CAVES)

★★☆☆☆

Location: Off the corner of Treasure Point, west of The Bight, Norman Island.
Access: By boat only.
Conditions: Can be some surge in the caves; only to be dived or snorkelled in perfect weather.
Average depth: 6m (20ft)
Maximum depth: 12m (40ft)
Average visibility: 15m (50ft)

NUDIBRANCHS/SEA SLUGS

There are approximately 35 species of sea slug recorded in the Caribbean. Some browse on the algae that grow on dead coral and among turtle grass, others (the nudibranchs) are carnivorous, eating other nudibranchs, coral polyps, sponges, sea squirts and hydroids. Often found in shallow water and on night dives, many sea slugs have superb camouflage and can be difficult to locate without a torch to pick out their colours. The most common sea slug to be found in the Virgin Islands is the lettuce leaf sea slug (*Tridachia crispata*) which grows only to 3cm (1in) and has numerous skin ruffles along its back resembling a lettuce leaf. It feeds on algae.

Carrot Rock (Site 9) has a large cave beneath which schools of fish are always found.

The interest of this site derives partly from the fact that a local family found pirate treasure in the caves in the early 1900s. More often snorkelled than dived, the caves have large concentrations of sergeant majors (*Abudefduf saxatilis*) and yellowtail snapper (*Ocyurus chrysurus*) attracted by fish-feeding – although the practice is frowned upon by the British Virgin Islands National Parks Trust. The three caves are accessible – the northernmost cave penetrates quite far back and has walls covered in golden cup corals.

6 RING DOVE ROCK
★★★★

Location: In a line between Water Point to the northeast of The Bight on Norman Island and Pelican Island.
Access: By boat only.
Conditions: Surge, current and surface chop to be expected.
Average depth: 9m (30ft)
Maximum depth: 21m (70ft)
Average visibility: 25m (80ft)
This rocky pinnacle rises from 17m (55ft) to within 5m (17ft) of the surface and is cut by numerous gullies and fissures, creating overhangs, cracks and crevices where all manner of fish and invertebrates are found. The seabed is littered with boulders and coral heads, and on the surrounding sand plain you can see plenty of yellowhead jawfish, sand tilefish and literally thousands of gobies. The sides of the boulders feature gorgonian sea fans and a light covering of hard corals. Parrotfish, wrasse and small tropical fish dominate this popular site.

7 THE INDIANS
★★★☆☆☆☆

Location: West of Pelican Island.
Access: By boat only.
Conditions: Can be some surge and wind-generated surface chop.
Average depth: 5m (17ft)
Maximum depth: 15m (50ft)
Average visibility: 18m (60ft)
A popular location for both divers and snorkellers is The Indians, near Pelican Island. From a distance, these four rocky outcrops in a row resemble an Indian's headdress and it is only when you get closer that you can see the distinctive rugged structure of these offshore stacks. The walls are covered in a variety of sea plumes and sea fans, all of which feature arrow crabs (*Stenorhynchus*

seticornis), small molluscs and tiny attendant fish. A small tunnel can be easily negotiated and there are usually silverside minnows around in the summer months. The site can get somewhat crowded, and divers should beware of passing boats when surfacing.

8 SPYGLASS WALL (SPYGLASS)
★★★

Location: East from Benures Bay on the north shore of Norman Island.
Access: By boat only.
Conditions: Can be some surge from the north, but generally fairly sheltered due to nearby Peter Island.
Average depth: 12m (40ft)
Maximum depth: 18m (60ft)
Average visibility: 18m (60ft)
Spyglass Wall is about 450m (1500ft) long, stretching east from Benures Bay. This steeply sloping mini-wall drops from 6m (20ft) to the sandy seabed at 18m (60ft). There is a mooring buoy at the western limits and divers depart from here to the seabed, travelling along the wall at depth, and returning to the mooring in the shallower areas. The site has many sea plumes and hard corals – plus quite a lot of algae – as well as some huge purple tube sponges (*Callyspongia vaginalis*). Tarpon (*Megalops atlanticus*) and Atlantic spadefish (*Chaetodipterus faber*) are common along the wall, travelling with the current gently flowing from the east.

9 CARROT SHOAL
★★★

Location: West of Carrot Rock off the southern tip of Peter Island.
Access: By boat only.
Conditions: Subject to current, surge and surface chop; to be dived only in calm weather.
Average depth: 15m (50ft)
Maximum depth: 21m (70ft)
Average visibility: 25m (80ft)
This small rocky ridge is topped with fire coral, giving it an orange hue. The shoal is quite close to the surface and cut in several places so that it forms a series of narrow canyons, which are always filled with snapper. On the northwestern edge a large overhang has a resident green moray eel (*Gymnothorax funebris*) and hundreds of fairy basslets (*Gramma loreto*), which all

The huge propeller of the RMS Rhone (Site 17) is covered in marine growth in shallow water.

swim upside-down, aligning themselves to the cliff wall. There are also several species of hermit crab, as well as lobsters and shrimps. This can be a great dive when the conditions are perfect.

10 BLACK CORAL FOREST (BLACK TIP REEF)
★★★

Location: Off the western tip of Peter Island.
Access: By boat only.
Conditions: Current to be expected and some wind-generated surface chop.
Average depth: 15m (50ft)
Maximum depth: 20m (66ft)
Average visibility: 25m (80ft)
The mini-wall which stretches off and round to the south of the point is covered in large black coral bushes (*Antipathes* spp.) and wire corals (*Ellisella barbadensis*). The sides of the wall are pockmarked by holes and small crevices, around which congregate cleaning shrimps, fairy basslets, small blennies and gobies and shade-loving squirrelfish. The reef crest always features a mass of blue chromis (*Chromis cyanea*).

Large channel clinging crabs (Mithrax spinossisimus) roam the reefs during twilight hours.

11 THE RHONE ANCHOR
★★★

Location: North of Great Harbour, Peter Island.
Access: By boat only.
Conditions: Generally sheltered, no current.
Average depth: 16m (55ft)
Maximum depth: 25m (80ft)
Average visibility: 15m (50ft)
The RMS *Rhone*'s anchor and chain were discovered by George Marler in 1974. Now protected under the British Virgin Islands National Parks Trust, the huge anchor and chain snapped when the *Rhone* tried to escape from her mooring in front of an approaching storm. A sheltered area, this site is often chosen when other more exposed reefs are blown out due to bad weather. The 90m (300ft) of chain is draped over several coral heads and over and under mounds of sand. The huge 5m (17ft) anchor is wedged under a massive coral block, also overgrown by corals and sponges. Nearby can be seen old crockery, now embedded in coral.

12 THE FEARLESS AND WILLIE T WRECKS
★★★

Location: To the east of the northern entrance to Great Harbour on Peter Island.
Access: By boat only.
Conditions: Can be subject to northerly swells.
Average depth: 15m (50ft)
Maximum depth: 25m (80ft)
Average visibility: 18m (60ft)
The *Fearless* (said to be the sister ship of Jacques Cousteau's *Calypso*) was intentionally sunk in 1986 as an additional attraction to the mini-wall which extends westwards from northern Peter Island. The *Willie T* was a popular floating bar and restaurant which used to be moored at Norman Island; it was sunk in 1995 to the south of the *Fearless*. Both ships have a healthy covering of corals. However, they are of wooden construction and deteriorating, so penetrating them is not recommended. The nearby mini-wall is known for its black coral trees and large schools of fish.

13 DEADMAN BAY
★★★★★

Location: To the north of Deadman Bay on northeast Peter Island.
Access: By boat or from the shore.
Conditions: Generally sheltered, but does get heavy boat traffic.
Average depth: 7m (24ft)
Maximum depth: 7m (24ft)
Average visibility: 8m (27ft)
This site is often overlooked due to the fact that the shallow bay gets a lot of boat traffic and is covered in a dense mat of turtle grass (*Thalassia testudinum*). However, the field of sea grass makes a fantastic night dive, with stingrays, octopus, squid and numerous species of starfish and molluscs. Small knobby tube corals (*Cladocora arbuscula*) can be found, as well as many algal species, including the broad-leafed mermaid's fan (*Udotea* spp.).

14 PAINTED WALLS
★★★★★★

Location: The southeastern corner of Dead Chest Island.
Access: By boat only.
Conditions: Subject to surge in the wave-sculpted gullies.
Average depth: 9m (30ft)
Maximum depth: 12m (40ft)
Average visibility: 15m (50ft)

At this site the volcanic rock has been carved by centuries of wave and tidal action into long galleries, caves and tunnels, the sides of which are festooned in brightly coloured sponges – hence the name. Turtles can be seen and small Caribbean reef sharks (*Carcharhinus perezi*) often hunt in the gullies. In the third canyon, a small circular cavern faces you, covered in orange and yellow sponges, while branching to the right is a huge natural arch which is superb for photography. The best time to dive these outer rock stacks is between July and September when the sea will be flat calm and without any surge.

15 CORAL GARDEN
★★★★★★

Location: North of Dead Chest Island, onto the northerly running reef.
Access: By boat only.
Conditions: Can be some surge at times, but generally sheltered.
Average depth: 7m (24ft)
Maximum depth: 12m (40ft)
Average visibility: 12m (40ft)
Coral Garden is a series of connected coral heads rising over 3m (10ft) off the seabed in some cases, running in a northerly direction. To the east is a wide area of sand where flounders and gurnards are found. Among the coral heads large numbers of small blennies can be found living in cast-off worm tubes, their tiny heads poking out at passing plankton. The site is also favoured as a night dive and dive boats generally journey across the channel from Tortola at dusk to arrive at the site in time to moor up before complete darkness. After dark you can find turtle, nurse sharks, lobster, octopus, innumerable different invertebrates and some of the most amazing colours of corals and sponges you are likely to see anywhere in the Caribbean. Caribbean reef squid (*Sepioteuthis sepiodea*) can also sometimes be seen giving displays of colour changes.

SNAKE EELS

Snake eels are very similar in shape to moray eels and have a long fin which travels along the length of the back, starting just behind the head. Active hunters, they are rarely seen during the day as they hide under the sand, but are easily approachable at night due to their bad eyesight. The most common of the snake eels found in the Virgin Islands is the sharptail eel (*Myrichthys breviceps*), which is quite distinctive, with its pale yellow spots on its head and flanks and two protruding nostrils on either side of the sharp snout. They are not known to be harmful to humans.

The Royal Mail Steam Packet Company was founded in London in July 1839 and received its first mail contract in 1840. Built by Millwall Iron Works and launched on 11 February 1865, the RMS *Rhone* was one of the company's principal ships. Registering 2738 gross tons, 95m long by 12m wide (310 x 40ft) and able to carry 253 first-class, 30 second-class and 30 third-class passengers, she was regarded as one of the finest ships of the time. Her seafaring capabilities were demonstrated when she survived a hurricane in the Caribbean on 11 January 1866 during which her sister ship, the *London*, sank nearby.

For much of the 1860s Tortola was still a sleepy backwater and it was her neighbour, St Thomas, that served as a bustling port. Charlotte Amalie had a huge natural harbour which could accommodate large numbers of ships. As the principal steamship company at that time, the Royal Mail Steam Packet Company used the refuelling depot on St Thomas. Here also larger freight and passenger ships would dock and transfer their passengers and goods onto the smaller schooners which plied the trade routes between Cuba, Puerto Rico, Jamaica, Honduras, and the Leeward and Windward Islands.

However, when yellow fever broke out on St Thomas in 1865, the transatlantic steamers started avoiding Charlotte Amalie. They shifted their operations to Road Harbour in Tortola and Great Harbour in Peter Island.

On the morning of 29 October 1867 the *Rhone* was at anchor outside Great Harbour on Peter Island. Under the command of Captain Robert F. Wooley, she was in the process of taking on stores for her return journey to Southampton, England. Alongside her lay the RMS *Conway*, commanded by Captain Hammock. Little disturbed the blistering heat of the morning, except the fact that the barometer was steadily falling, indicating a reduction in air pressure likely to herald a storm of some magnitude. Neither captain liked the look of the approaching weather, but both felt they were safe as the hurricane season was thought to be over and,

at worst, it would perhaps only amount to a violent squall. Fortunately the majority of the *Rhone*'s passengers had disembarked when the first indications of the approaching storm were known: she had only 18 passengers, plus a crew of 129, aboard. Wooley resolved to cross the Sir Francis Drake Channel to seek shelter in Road Harbour on Tortola.

THE STORM HITS

By 11:00 the barometer reading suddenly fell to 27.95 and the worst hurricane ever to hit the Virgin Islands descended on the ships from the northwest, tearing at their rigging and causing the anchors on both ships to drag. During a lull in the storm around noon, the *Conway* weighed anchor but, as she crossed the channel to Tortola, the storm hit again, removing her funnel and masts and driving the ship onto the shore of Tortola.

Wooley also weighed anchor. Unfortunately the shackle caught in a hause pipe and parted, dropping the 3000 pound anchor and over 90m (300ft) of chain. Wooley ordered 'full speed ahead' and attempted to take the *Rhone* out to sea to ride out the storm. After she had cleared the first rocky obstacles, however, the wind changed direction to the southeast and struck the ship anew. She foundered on Salt Island, the hull broke in two and she sank immediately, taking with her 17 passengers and 108 crew. Wooley was never seen again. Four of the crew, including a fireman, climbed the rigging and held onto the mast as she sank; they clung there for 17 hours before rescue. The one surviving passenger, an Italian, spent six hours in the water and was eventually swept into a small bay. All other surviving members of the crew were picked up the next day, clinging to bits of the ship which had come free when she sank. There is a mass grave on Salt Island.

AFTERMATH OF THE STORM

The hurricane was so severe that on Tortola only 18 houses were left standing. At least 75 ships and over 500 lives were lost during the storm. On 3 November 1867, just five days after the *Rhone* sank, Captain L. Vasey on HMS *Darwin* was despatched to Tortola with provisions for the starving islanders. The following is part of the report he sent to the Secretary of the Admiralty in Whitehall, London:

'I passed the wreck of the RMS Packet *Rhone*. Her poop rail was close to a large boulder on the W. point, but the hull was standing under water – the foremast was standing, but the vessel herself was broken in two and her head slewed round to the North – 50 yards either way would have put her into a sandy bay. In Tortola Roads I observed the RM Steamer *Conway* dismasted and funnel gone.'

The wreck of the *Rhone* was first dived in 1870 by a team of salvors, the Murphy brothers, who travelled up from St Thomas. The Murphys were renowned for their diving and were engaged in the salvage of many ships sunk on that fateful day.

DIVING THE WRECK OF THE RHONE

In May 1870, the *Port of Spain Gazette* reported the following:

'We paid a visit to the Murphys about two weeks ago, they are at Salt Island diving various things out of the wreck of the Steamer Rhone. I have never seen a diving dress, it was a novelty to all of us; the children were delighted to see Murphy, he certainly cut an awful figure, but when he went overboard and we saw him sinking, sinking until we lost sight of him, it was something horrible – the water is 17 fathoms and you can't see the bottom – he was gone for hours, he sent up 12 bales of Cotton and various other things; amongst other matters, a fine large skull, which must have belonged to a very large man – the Cotton is as good as the day it went down; he also saved the anchor and chains and lots of copper. While he was down he sent a message up to invite the ladies down into the saloon of this Rhone ...

'When dinner was nearly ready, Murphy came up, rested for a few minutes and said

Schools of snapper and grunt congregate around the wreckage of the Rhone.

"Now ladies, as I have nothing to offer you, I will look into the other half of the ship (she is broke in two pieces) and see what can be got." They begged him not to go but off he went and in half an hour we had as much champagne, Beer, Soda Water, Lemonade, Seltzer Water and Brandy as we knew what to do with ...

'The Murphys (three brothers of them) came to St Thomas soon after the Hurricane of 1867 and have been there ever since. When the Rhone was wrecked they saved the species and bullion out of her, and they got a large sum of money from Mr Cameron, some $62,000 for their part; the Steamer had on board some £60,000 in specie and bullion.'

16 BLONDE ROCK
★★★★

Location: Between Dead Chest and Salt Island, within the RMS *Rhone* National Park boundary.
Access: By boat only.
Conditions: Can be some surge and current.
Average depth: 9m (30ft)
Maximum depth: 18m (60ft)
Average visibility: 18m (60ft)

Blonde Rock is actually a set of two pinnacles which rise to within 4m (15ft) of the surface. The name comes from the top covering of pale yellow fire coral (*Millepora alcicornis*) which can easily be seen from the surface. Below this level is a large area of sea fans and plumes, where slender filefish (*Monacanthus tuckeri*) can be found hiding among the waving fronds. On one side of the rock is a vertical wall covered in golden cup corals, tube worms and colourful encrusting sponges. Largely undercut, this wall is a delight to divers who can look upwards through the sponges to small schools of snapper and grunt.

Juvenile spotted drums (Equetus punctatus) are easily recognized by their distinctive gyrations.

17 RMS RHONE
★★★★★★★★★★★

Location: Off Lee Bay, northwest point of Salt Island.
Access: By boat only.
Conditions: Quite strong current to be expected on the deeper portion and some surge in the shallows.
Average depth: Deep Section 20m (66ft); Shallow Section 6m (20ft)
Maximum depth: Deep Section 27m (90ft); Shallow Section 18m (60ft)
Average visibility: 18m (60ft)

The *Rhone* is one of the most famous divable shipwrecks in the world, being open to both experienced and novice divers. The marine life is so profuse and her history so tragic that the area surrounding and including the wreck was declared a Marine National Park in 1980, the first of its kind in the Virgin Islands. Anyone found illegally tampering with the wreck will be deported.

The Royal Mail Steamer *Rhone* was swept to destruction on 29 October 1867 in a sudden hurricane which also destroyed other ships all over the eastern Caribbean. Her captain had attempted to take her to sea to ride out the storm, but her anchor snagged and she was unable to leave for safety fast enough.

Christmas tree worms (Spirobranchus giganteus) often cover large areas of coral heads.

Foundering off the northwestern end of Salt Island, her hull broke in two with the loss of almost everyone on board. Lying in two distinct parts from 6 to 27m (20 to 90ft), the wreck is always done as a twin-tank dive, the first dive on the deeper part and the second on the stern and propeller. Incredibly photogenic, the wreck is festooned in marine life, and large schools of snapper and grunt can be found all over.

The deeper part of the wreck, in 27m (90ft), has the most intact section of the hull, lying on her starboard side with the sharply pointed bowsprit clear of the seabed and her masts stretching up the sloping sand plain to the hard rocky seabed. On your first dive to the ship it is important to be accompanied by a dive guide as the current can be quite severe. This allows you a proper orientation of the ship in case you get split up from your group – which it is easy to do due to the numbers of other divers in the water. The guides all follow a particular route over the hull, down through the square open hatch in her side (now the top) and through her innards to the ripped-apart mid-section where the ship broke her back.

The shaded areas of the ship's hull are completely covered in orange cup corals and small colourful hydroids.

Encrusting corals, small sea fans and plumes adorn the upturned port side of the hull. You can swim under the bowsprit and enter it from the inside. All the wooden decking has now rotted away, allowing easy access throughout the ship. The foremast and crow's-nest are still fairly intact, lying partly on the seabed. The hatchway just to the front of the mast was the one used as the setting for the film *The Deep* (1977). Aft of this fore-section of the wreck can be found the boiler and part of the mid-section.

The second boiler is located midway between the two sections of the wreck. When diving this area

---

DEEP DIVING

The only deep diving that usually takes place in the Virgin Islands is around the islands' main wrecks and on the northern wall off St Croix. All divers should be aware of the increased risks when undertaking deep diving, particularly the effects of nitrogen narcosis and the time-at-depth limitations. Divers should treat each dive as a no-stop dive – one that does not require decompression stops. Even following this practice, most dive leaders will request that a safety stop is done at 3m (10ft) for three minutes at the end of each dive.

- Increase depth slowly
- Dive only with experienced deep divers
- Do not put yourself or others at risk
- Be safe
- Plan your dive and dive your plan

The giant anemone (Condylactis gigantea) is quite rare in some locations.

(generally on your second dive), care must be taken with time and depth – particularly if you go on to the water pump, which is at 20m (65ft). The stern of the ship, with her four-bladed bronze propeller embedded in the reef, is now completely opened up and you can swim the entire length of the propeller shaft to the gear box, which is home to squirrelfish, snapper, banded coral shrimps and various encrusting and brightly coloured corals. Under the stern, next to the rudder, there are generally small schools of snapper. Grouper are dotted around all over the area and white-spotted filefish are common. Two large sections of rib stand upright, making an interesting backdrop for photographs. Again, it is best to be accompanied by a dive guide on your first dive – in this case to be shown the silver spoon embedded in the coral, the rack of huge spanners which were used in the engine room, the cracked porthole and numerous shards of pottery and glass. This shallow section of the *Rhone* is also favoured as a night dive.

All the diving operators in both the US and British Virgin Islands visit the *Rhone* every week and sometimes more often. The wreck is also visited by private charter boats, some of which choose to dive the area before the day boats come and take over.

The wreck of the *Rhone* is without doubt one of the best dives in the Caribbean and, despite being so heavily dived, still has an amazing amount of marine life on and around it. The addition of mooring buoys has removed the threat of anchor damage and ensured that the remains are protected.

18 DRY ROCKS WEST (VANISHING ROCKS)
★★★

Location: Between Salt Island and Cooper Island.
Access: By boat only.
Conditions: Current to be expected.
Average depth: 6m (20ft)
Maximum depth: 15m (50ft)
Average visibility: 15m (50ft)
Swept by the current which passes between Salt Island and Cooper Island, this cluster of boulders is covered in a dense mat of coral growth, mainly sea fans and plumes. Around the bottom of the boulders and coral

ridges there are large numbers of corkscrew anemones (*Bartholomea annulata*). Within their tentacles can be found cleaner shrimps (*Periclimenes pedersoni*) and red snapping shrimp (*Alpheus armatus*), which vigorously defend their territory. It is possible to cover the whole site on a single dive, but care must be taken with the current as it often renders the site undivable.

 MANCHIONEEL ROCK (CISTERN POINT; CISTERN ROCK)
★★★ ☆ ☆ ☆

Location: The southern tip of Manchioneel Bay along northwest Cooper Island.
Access: Can be dived from the shore, but most divers come by boat.
Conditions: Can be some surge and should be dived with the current running from the south.
Average depth: 5m (17ft)
Maximum depth: 12m (40ft)
Average visibility: 15m (50ft)
This is a shallow dive at the southern end of a gorgeous bay. Large schools of snapper, grunt, chromis,

damselfish and wrasse are always found amid the jumble of boulders here. The site is popular with yachtsmen who come by dinghy, but few dive boats visit the area, since there are better sites just a short ride away, such as Thumb Rock (Site 22) and the wrecks in Haulover Bay (sites 20–21).

20 INGANESS BAY WRECK
★★★★

Location: In the middle of the channel near Haulover Bay, western Cooper Island.
Access: By boat only.
Conditions: Strong current to be expected. Divers have to travel down either of the two mooring buoys on the wreck.
Average depth: 21m (70ft)
Maximum depth: 27m (90ft)
Average visibility: 18m (60ft)
The coastal freighter *Inganess Bay* sank off Tortola. It was then cleaned up and re-sunk as an artificial reef on this sand plain, which is home to thousands of garden eels. The wreck is completely accessible and, after only a

The wreck of the Inganess Bay (Site 20) is relatively new, but already being colonised in marine growths.

short time underwater, already has a good covering of algae and small corals. It lies in a north–south direction. The current sweeps upwards past the stern of the ship, and the more sheltered eastern part of the bow now has some large gorgonian sea fans. Fish life is profuse: the wreck has become a natural focus for marine life.

21 THE MARIE L, BARGE & GRILL AND PAT WRECKS (BLUE CHROMIS REEF)
★★

Location: South of Cistern Point on the western side of Cooper Island.
Access: By boat only.
Conditions: Fairly sheltered from current, but some surge to be expected during the spring.
Average depth: 18m (60ft)
Maximum depth: 26m (84ft)
Average visibility: 18m (60ft)
The *Marie L* was a cargo boat sunk in the early 1990s as an artificial reef to create a diving attraction on this otherwise fairly featureless sandy plain. The boat is 23m (75ft) long and has been joined by two other small wrecks, the *Barge & Grill* and the *Pat*, a 21m (70ft) tugboat. The *Barge & Grill* is located to the north of the other two and is rarely visited. The *Marie L* and the *Pat* lie next to each other, bow to stern, and are reasonably photogenic, though not the most interesting of wrecks. Of more interest is the large colony of garden eels (*Heteroconger halis*) which can be found in the surrounding area.

22 THUMB ROCK
★★★

Location: Along the western side of South Bay on southern Cooper Island.
Access: By boat only.
Conditions: Surge to be expected and surface chop as the wind whips around this end of the island.
Average depth: 9m (30ft)
Maximum depth: 18m (60ft)
Average visibility: 18m (60ft)
Thumb Rock sticks out of the water off the southwestern tip of Cooper Island – known as Red Bluff due to the coloration of the rock cliffs. There are hundreds of fissures and cracks around the rock and the boulders which connect it to the shore underwater. There are also lots of gorgonian sea fans on the sides of the rock and shade-loving fish such as French grunt (*Haemulon flavolineatum*) can be found in fairly large numbers, as well as porkfish (*Anisotremus virginicus*), which usually travel in small groups of four or five.

23 MARKOE POINT
★★★

Location: The southeastern tip of Cooper Island.
Access: By boat only.
Conditions: Current to be expected, sweeping north towards Black Bluff; some surge to be expected during the spring.
Average depth: 9m (30ft)
Maximum depth: 18m (60ft)
Average visibility: 18m (60ft)
Often blown out due to oceanic swell which pounds into the point, this site is rarely dived. There is a canyon which sweeps into the point from the mooring buoy, with a nice vertical cliff on one side and undercut ledges on the other. Not known for its fish life, it has nonetheless plenty of lobster in the recesses and shade-loving squirrelfish and snapper are nearly always around.

24 DRY ROCKS EAST
★★★

Location: A barely covered spur of rock which extends east from Dustry Point, near the eastern tip of Cooper Island.
Access: By boat only.
Conditions: Current to be expected and some surge.
Average depth: 12m (40ft)
Maximum depth: 25m (80ft)
Average visibility: 25m (80ft)
This offshore rocky ridge appears to be a natural focus for many species of fish, particularly some of the larger jacks such as horse-eye jacks (*Caranx latus*) and black jacks (*Caranx lugubris*). Large schools of schoolmaster (*Lutjanus apodus*) mix with dog snapper (*Lutjanus jocu*), which have a distinctive 'tear' marking under their eyes. Most of the action is at the eastern tip of the boulders, but there is plenty to see in the many crevices and underhangs to be found at this site.

TURTLES

The most commonly seen turtles in the Virgin Islands are the green turtle (*Chelonia mydas*) and the hawksbill turtle (*Eretmochelys imbricata*). Although fairly similar in shape, there are notable differences between them. The green turtle only has one pair of prefrontal scales (between the eyes), has a round face and no overlapping shell scutes and grows to 1.25m (50in). The hawksbill turtle has two pairs of prefrontal scales, a pointed face and overlapping shell scutes, growing to only 95cm (38in). It is only the male of each of the species which has the long tail.

Above: *Foureye butterflyfish (Chaetodon capistratus) are usually found in their life-long mating pairs.*
Below: *Grey angelfish (Pomacanthus arcuatus) are the largest of the angelfish to be found in this area.*

25 CARVAL ROCK (CARVAL)
★★★★

Location: Between Black Bluff on Cooper Island and Wedgeo Bluff on Ginger Island.
Access: By boat only.
Conditions: Surge and current always to be expected.
Average depth: 15m (50ft)
Maximum depth: 27m (90ft)
Average visibility: 25m (80ft)
This solitary rock has a jumble of boulders on its shallower northern side, which is where most divers tend to head due to the large number of colourful sponges and schools of snapper and grunt which are found. Incredibly colourful, the whole area is swept by quite strong currents and the larger part of Carval's walls is covered in gorgonian sea fans. Fire coral predominates in the shallows, but the site is host also to Christmas tree worms (*Spirobranchus giganteus*), various anemones and secretary blennies (*Acanthemblemaria maria*), which live in discarded worm tubes. Oceanic fish such as durgon, surgeonfish and barracuda are common.

26 ALICE IN WONDERLAND
★★★

Location: Along the western side of South Bay on southern Ginger Island.
Access: By boat only.
Conditions: Can be exposed, but sheltered from all northerly swells.
Average depth: 7m (24ft)
Maximum depth: 25m (80ft)
Average visibility: 15m (50ft)

Leafy roll-blade algae (Padina boergesenii) can commonly be found at the base of sea fans.

The entire western section of this reef is a fairly open spur-and-groove formation, with sandy gullies separating long fingers of mushroom-shaped coral heads. These little coral islands have thousands of nooks and crannies and banded coral shrimps (*Stenopus hispidus*) are very common. Flounders, gurnards, tilefish, parrotfish and snapper are common, as are large numbers of grouper. In the shallow area of the bay to the east there are scattered coral heads on sand, which make for a superb night dive – here squid and octopus are common. On the sea fans, huge basketstars (*Astrophyton muricatum*) extend their thin, branched arms to collect passing plankton.

27 ALICE'S BACK DOOR
★★★★★

Location: Off the northern shore of Ginger Island.
Access: By boat only.
Conditions: Subject to northerly swells.
Average depth: 9m (30ft)
Maximum depth: 18m (60ft)
Average visibility: 18m (60ft)
The northern shore of Ginger Island has a coral field made up of pillar corals, brain corals and star corals, the major reef builders. This forms a gently sloping wall of hundreds of small coral heads, looking slightly untidy with algae growing everywhere, attended by beaugregory (*Stegastes leucostictus*) and yellow damselfish (*Microspathodon chrysurus*). Small grouper, hamlets and sea bass are common and this rarely dived site is profuse in sea fans. The reef eventually opens up to a structure similar to classic spur-and-groove until it reaches the sand plain.

How to Get There

Visitors to these islands arrive only by boat, whether it be a small yacht charter, resort ferry or dive boat. The trip from Tortola to the islands takes about 35–45 minutes. Cooper Island's supply boat leaves Tortola on Mondays at 2.30, and Wednesdays and Fridays at 11am.

Getting Around

There are no rental vehicles, petrol stations – or roads, for that matter. Resorts are isolated and have their own jetties. Most visitors never actually reach land, but stay on board their charter yacht in one of the many sheltered bays which can be found around the islands. The only way to get around is by boat.

Where to Stay

Cooper Island Beach Club, Cooper Island, PO Box 859, Road Town, Tortola; US toll free tel (800) 542 4624; tel (284) 494 3721; http://www.cooper-island.com
12 beachfront rooms located on Manchioneel Bay. Great bar and restaurant. Very exclusive.

Peter Island Resort, Peter Island, PO Box 211, Road Town, Tortola; US toll free tel (800) 346 4451; tel (284) 495 2000; fax (284) 495 2500; website: www.peterisland.com
50 rooms with splendid ocean-front views through palm trees – a superb setting. Popular with yachts. Lively bar and restaurant.

Where to Eat

The two centres of activity are at the resorts on Cooper Island and Peter Island, both of which offer excellent international cuisine (quite often buffet-style). There is nowhere else to go.

Dive Operators

Dive BVI Ltd., Peter Island Hotel, Peter Island; US toll free tel (800) 848 7078; tel 495 5513; fax (284) 495 5347; email: info@divebvi.com; website: www.divebvi.com; also at Leverick Bay, Virgin Gorda and Marina Cay.
Very professional operation with experience around all the islands.

Cooper Island Beach Club, Sail Caribbean Divers, Hodges Creek Marina, Tortola, BVI; tel (284) 495 1675; email: info@sailcaribbeandivers.com; website: www.sailcaribbeandivers.com
Small shop and very knowledgeable staff.

Emergency Services

Virgin Islands Search and Rescue, VHF Channel 16; tel (284) 494 4357, dialling 999 or 911
Peebles Hospital, Road Town, Tortola; tel (284) 494 3497
B&F Medical Pharmacie, Mill Mall Bldg., Wickhams Cay; tel (284) 494 2196
Recompression Chamber, St Thomas; tel (340) 776 8311
Divers Alert Network, tel (919) 684 8111

Local Attractions

Between dives on the *Rhone*, visit the caretaker of Salt Island and buy a bag of locally produced salt. Also worth visiting on Salt Island are the graves of those lost at sea in the sinking of the *Rhone*.

Bluebell tunicates (Clavelina puertosecensis) are difficult to find.

VIRGIN GORDA AND ANEGADA

Approximately half the size of Tortola, Virgin Gorda is situated to its east and can be reached by small aeroplane or by a regular ferry service which takes thirty minutes. The main settlement is Spanish Town, otherwise known as The Valley, located in the south of the island. While the northern part is hilly, the southern half is fairly flat and strewn with unusual granite boulders. At a site known as The Baths, these boulders have come to form intriguing passages and hidden caves. On the east coast, the remnants of an ancient tin mine can be found above a rocky headland. First excavated by the Spanish, the mine was reconstructed between 1838 and 1867 by British miners. Although the mine itself is now considered too dangerous for safe exploration, the old chimney and pumphouse are interesting.

Various rocky islands surround Virgin Gorda, including Fallen Jerusalem, The Dogs, Mosquito Island, Prickly Pear Island, Eustatia and Necker Island. These islands, and particularly the area around the North Sound, are popular with yachting enthusiasts due to the large number of sheltered inlets they offer. The small offshore islands are also home to a myriad of marine life, with regular sightings of humpback whales during the spring.

Approximately 19km (12 miles) to the northeast of Virgin Gorda is Anegada, the second biggest island in the British Virgin Islands group and featuring the largest unbroken barrier reef in the eastern Caribbean. Covering roughly 25km^2 (15 square miles), the island is 16km (10 miles) long by 4km (2 miles) wide. Throughout it is very low-lying, rising only 8m (28ft) above sea level, with two massive salt ponds to the west and numerous other marshes and ponds along the south coast. The island's sunken look was what inspired Christopher Columbus to name it Anegada ('Sunken Island'), though curiously it has freshwater springs, indicating that this ancient sandstone and limestone coral reef was once subjected to a massive upheaval as the result of volcanic activity.

Opposite: *Beautiful Savannah Bay on Virgin Gorda is protected by a barrier reef.*
Above: *The indigo hamlet (Hypoplectrus indigo) has brilliant blue vertical bands over its body.*

VIRGIN GORDA

The feeling, pace of life and overall ambience on Virgin Gorda are slower than on Tortola. The main attraction are The Baths near the southern tip of the island, where huge boulders have created grottos, caves and pools. In addition there are twenty beaches on Virgin Gorda, all accessible to the public. The unhurried way of life is complemented by some of the best diving to be found in the eastern Caribbean. Among the top diving locations is The Invisibles (Site 6), near Necker Island (owned by Virgin tycoon Richard Branson). Coming close to the surface, these offshore granite rocks offer superb diving, although they are dived only in the best of conditions.

Many of the shallower reefs are topped with fire coral (Millepora alcicornis).

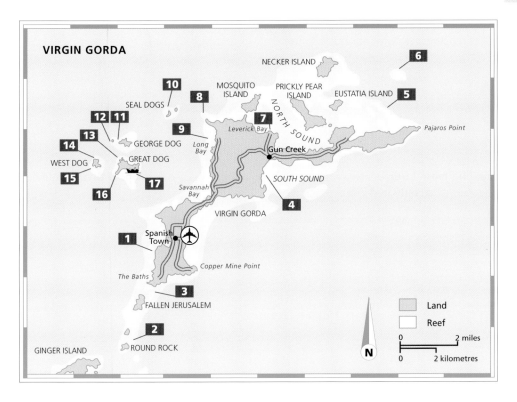

1 THE AQUARIUM
★★★☆☆☆

Location: Between Spanish Town and The Baths in the southeast of Virgin Gorda.
Access: By boat only.
Conditions: Can be choppy in winter, and always a lot of boat traffic; divers and snorkellers should be vigilant when on the surface, or swimming to the surface.
Average depth: 6m (20ft)
Maximum depth: 9m (30ft)
Average visibility: 12m (40ft)

UPSIDE-DOWN JELLYFISH

Two species of upside-down jellyfish are found in the Virgin Islands, the most common being *Cassiopea frondosa*, which can be found amid shallow eel-grass and turtle-grass beds in sheltered bays. They 'pulse' their surrounding skirt against the sea floor, disturbing small creatures and planktonic detritus on which they feed. Mostly resting on the bottom, their arms are aligned vertically to speed the growth of symbiotic single-celled algae called zooxanthellae which grow in their tissues. Upside-down jellyfish receive additional nourishment from these algae. If you look closely at the jellyfish, you may spot a symbiotic shrimp which lives among the fronds for protection.

This is a large jumble of boulders and stones with a light coral covering of small knobby corals, some sea fans and small plumes. Pillar corals (*Dendrogyra cylindrus*) can be found in deeper water and the area has lots of sergeant majors (*Abudefduf saxatilis*) which are fed by snorkellers. Also in the deeper water are small schools of snapper and grunt, and moray eels are common, although they are rather timid.

2 ROUND ROCK
★★★☆☆

Location: Small island at the end of the reef between Fallen Jerusalem and Ginger Island.
Access: By boat only.
Conditions: Can be surge; best snorkelled when it is completely calm.
Average depth: 7m (24ft)
Maximum depth: 18m (60ft)
Average visibility: 18m (60ft)

Just north of Round Rock is a series of boulders lying on top of ancient bedrock, where numerous ledges and underhangs can be found at about 7m (24ft). The current generally flows in a southeasterly direction, making for an enjoyable drift dive. The boulder platform continues all the way to Broken Jerusalem, and the exposed reef there has lots of fire coral (*Millepora alcocornis*). In the passes between the boulders you are likely to find southern stingrays (*Dasyatis americana*), large tarpon (*Megalops atlanticus*) and schools of southern sennet (*Sphyraena picudilla*).

3 THE BLINDERS
★★★☆☆☆

Location: Between the southwestern point of Virgin Gorda and Fallen Jerusalem.
Access: By boat only.
Conditions: Can be current and some surge.
Average depth: 7m (24ft)
Maximum depth: 12m (40ft)
Average visibility: 18m (60ft)
The Blinders is a series of large boulders just off the southern tip of Virgin Gorda. One of the largest boulders breaks the surface, but the others are all underwater, making a blind reef for any unwary boats intending to pass through this narrow channel. The seabed is about 3m (10ft) at its shallowest, and when conditions are right The Blinders makes an excellent site for watching fish and snorkelling.

4 SOUTH SIDE REEF
★★☆☆☆☆

Location: Off South Sound, south of the village of Gun Creek.
Access: By boat, or from the shore by following the road down to the water's edge and snorkelling out from there.
Conditions: Generally sheltered as there is an offshore barrier reef which offers protection to the more fragile inner reef.
Average depth: 3m (10ft)
Maximum depth: 7m (24ft)
Average visibility: 12m (40ft)
This largely protected bay features some excellent corals including staghorn coral (*Acropora cervicornis*), boulder star coral (*Montastrea annularis*) and star coral (*Madracis pharensis*), which is a much more low and encrusting species. The general surrounding area is fished relatively heavily, but there are parrotfish, wrasse, small grouper and many juveniles which gradually move out to repopulate the reefs in the near vicinity.

5 OIL NUT BAY (PAJAROS POINT)
★★★☆☆☆

Location: The reef which stretches across the eastern approaches to Eustatia Sound, between Biras Hill and Pajaros Point.
Access: By boat, but can be reached by swimming from the shore.
Conditions: Often choppy with some surge from the northeast.
Average depth: 5m (17ft)
Maximum depth: 12m (40ft)
Average visibility: 18m (60ft)
Oil Nut Bay is one of the few shallow sites where you always find eagle rays and stingrays as well as large spiny lobsters (*Panulirus argus*) wandering around in the open. Also a popular night-dive site, this shallow coral barrier reef protects the north shore of Virgin Gorda from the might of the Atlantic swell and is difficult to negotiate by boat due to the very shallow coral heads. There are huge stands of elkhorn coral (*Acropora palmata*), enormous sea fans and huge sea plumes (*Pseudopterogorgia* spp.). Finger coral (*Porites porites*) and pillar coral (*Dendrogyra cylindrus*) make up much of the reef and all of these hard corals are home to literally thousands of Christmas tree worms (*Spirobranchus giganteus*). The coral growths are in excellent condition and there is a mass of fish everywhere.

6 THE INVISIBLES
★★★★★

Location: East from Necker Island, towards Pajaros Point at the east end of Virgin Gorda.
Access: By boat only.
Conditions: Only dived when conditions are perfect as the oceanic surge renders this site too dangerous otherwise.
Average depth: 12m (40ft)
Maximum depth: 25m (80ft)
Average visibility: 30m (100ft)
The Invisibles is an offshore group of massive coral-encrusted granite boulders, each one the size of a house, with two individual pinnacles coming very close to the surface. Due to their position, the top 3m (10ft) of the granite blocks are totally overgrown with fire coral (*Millepora alcicornis*) and blade fire coral (*Millepora complanata*), which grows in sheets rather than finger-like projections. On the western side of the boulders, huge curiously shaped protrusions have been carved from this incredibly hard rock and the

undersides of all the boulders are covered in golden cup corals (*Tubastrea coccinea*). Hiding under these natural arches and swim-throughs are large schools of French grunt (*Haemulon flavolineatum*), their vivid electric blue stripes contrasting with the yellow fish and the dark orange and red colours of the rocks. To the north of the boulders, you always encounter a large school of Atlantic spadefish (*Chaetodipterus faber*), black durgon (*Melichthys niger*) and oceanic triggerfish (*Canthidermis sufflamen*). This is an exceptional dive.

7 LEVERICK BAY MOORINGS
★★★

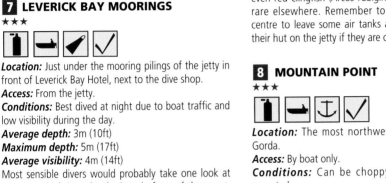

Location: Just under the mooring pilings of the jetty in front of Leverick Bay Hotel, next to the dive shop.
Access: From the jetty.
Conditions: Best dived at night due to boat traffic and low visibility during the day.
Average depth: 3m (10ft)
Maximum depth: 5m (17ft)
Average visibility: 4m (14ft)
Most sensible divers would probably take one look at this site, which is under the jetty in front of the resort, and decide it totally unsuitable for night diving, so, if you choose to try it, you'll get a few curious looks as you enter the water laden with equipment and lights. In fact, this is excellent for a shallow night dive and, as at

Frederiksted Pier (St Croix, Site 3), you can spend ages discovering things which during the day would be overlooked. The pilings supporting the jetty are home to an amazing array of invertebrates, including octopus, banded coral shrimps (*Stenopus hispidus*), arrow crabs (*Stenorhynchus seticornis*), cryptic teardrop crabs (*Pelia mutica*) no bigger than a little fingernail, white-speckled nudibranchs (*Phyllodemium spp*) and numerous juvenile fish which like to hide amid the pilings and rubble under the jetty for protection at night. Also found here are sharp-nosed pufferfish (*Canthigaster rostrata*) and even red clingfish (*Arcos rubiginosus*) – which are very rare elsewhere. Remember to arrange for the dive centre to leave some air tanks and equipment behind their hut on the jetty if they are closing early.

8 MOUNTAIN POINT
★★★

Location: The most northwesterly point of Virgin Gorda.
Access: By boat only.
Conditions: Can be choppy and current to be expected.
Average depth: 9m (30ft)
Maximum depth: 21m (70ft)
Average visibility: 15m (50ft)
Mountain Point is similar to Bronco Billy's (Site 11) in that

Christmas tree worms (Spirobranchus giganteus) are delicate creatures sensitive to pressure and light.

there is a series of wide gullies which split the headland, except that then, as you travel through these and out beyond the coral gardens, there is a steeply sloping wall down to 21m (70ft). Stingrays (*Dasyatis americana*) are always found along this sandy area as well as large numbers of conch shell (*Strombus costatus*). The wall has excellent coral growths and, although there are few fish, those that are present are bright and colourful, with parrotfish, wrasse, butterflyfish and angelfish being the most common species. Closer towards shore there are a couple of long indentations: the first one has a cave at its end, while in the second you pass through a small natural arch into a circular chamber referred to rather unkindly as the Toilet Bowl.

9 LONG BAY REEF
★★★

Location: South of Mountain Point to the reef offshore from northern Long Bay.
Access: By boat only.
Conditions: Can be some surge from the west, but generally quite calm.
Average depth: 7m (24ft)
Maximum depth: 13m (45ft)
Average visibility: 15m (50ft)
This fairly shallow site is found by following a series of three rocks which break the surface near the shore. A wide and gently sloping sand plain rises into the beach and the coral-encrusted boulders are found on either side of the channel, amid large numbers of small coral heads topped with sea fans and plumes. Peacock flounders (*Bothus lunatus*) are common on the sand and around virtually every coral head or piece of coral rubble are countless bridled gobies (*Coryphopterus glaucofraenum*). Parrotfish and wrasse are common in the shallows, as are damselfish, snapper and various species of grunt.

10 SEAL DOG ROCKS
★★★★

Location: To the north of the Seal Dog Rocks, west of Mountain Point.
Access: By boat only.
Conditions: Surge to be expected on this exposed site.
Average depth: 12m (40ft)
Maximum depth: 18m (60ft)
Average visibility: 25m (80ft)
These two lonely rocks (West Seal Dog and East Seal Dog) are visited only when the weather is perfect, due to the exposed nature of the site. The west side of West Seal Dog is the best area for diving, as it offers some shelter. The 'Dog' of the name refers to the barking sounds made

by the Caribbean fur seals (now extinct) which once lived here. This western shore of the rock comprises a series of huge granite boulders and sculpted gullies which cut into the headland. Inside there are glassy sweepers (*Pempheris schomburgki*) and silverside minnows in the summer months. Jacks and large snapper are always cruising along this wall and, although the site is not known for its fish population – or even for good corals – the underwater terrain is dramatic and well worth the dive.

11 BRONCO BILLY'S
★★★★★★

Location: In between Cockroach Island and the western tip of George Dog.
Access: By boat only.
Conditions: Often strong surge makes snorkelling or diving impossible.
Average depth: 7m (24ft)
Maximum depth: 12m (40ft)
Average visibility: 15m (50ft)
This dive is down through a series of underwater channels, caves and archways. The outcrops are volcanic in origin and the sides of the canyons are stripped bare of corals due to the exposed nature of the site, yet the physical grandeur of the site more than makes up for this and once you are out of these gullies there is a beautiful coral garden absolutely teeming with life. Though lacking in coral growth, the sides of the gullies are a mass of differently coloured encrusting sponges, bryozoans and tunicates. Brilliantly coloured queen angelfish (*Holacanthus ciliaris*) are common here. At one part of the dive, the grotto is actually a cul-de-sac where you can come to the surface surrounded by rock, have a chat, and then drop back down and out through a winding passageway.

12 THE VISIBLES
★★★★

Location: Southwest corner of Cockroach Island, west of George Dog.
Access: By boat only.
Conditions: Surge and current to be expected; dived only in perfect conditions.
Average depth: 6m (20ft)
Maximum depth: 25m (80ft)
Average visibility: 21m (70ft)
A mooring buoy has been placed on a submarine pinnacle to the southwest of Cockroach Island, from

The Invisibles (Site 6) is a cluster of huge granite boulders forming caves and caverns.

where this dive usually begins (although live-aboard boats like the *Cuan Law* may drop you off on the northwestern corner and allow the southerly current to take you around to the mooring). There is a whole series of ledges, caves, shallow tunnels and huge overhangs which have large groups of grunt, snapper and squirrelfish in hiding. Barracuda are common, and on the deeper rocky slopes large deep-water gorgonian sea fans (*Iciligorgia schrammi*) and devil's sea whips (*Ellisella barbadensis*) stretch out into the almost permanent current. In the shallows near the shore of Cockroach Island there are literally hundreds of tunnels and fissures that cut into the headland, all covered in brilliantly coloured encrusting sponges and bryozoans.

13 THE CHIMNEY

★★★★☆☆☆

Location: In the bay off the western corner of Great Dog Island.
Access: By boat only.
Conditions: Can be surge.
Average depth: 6m (20ft)
Maximum depth: 13m (44ft)
Average visibility: 15m (50ft)
When the sea is flat, this site rivals any other reef dive in the British Virgin Islands. A rocky headland continues

---

The nurse shark (Ginglymostoma cirratum) is the most common shark around the islands.

down underwater, creating a huge cleft to the north, a small rounded rock and then a shaft or slice, entirely underwater, through the headland. The Chimney is entered over a small cleft in the rocky headland and opens into a vertical shaft with a giant natural archway midway along. Sea fans ring the top of the shaft, while the sides and top of the archway are covered in brilliant sponges and golden cup corals. Round towards the north and in to the island the canyons have sculpted, smooth vertical sides which are very dramatic and great for wide-angle photography. The bottom of the shaft is littered with rounded stones and coral rubble where small gobies and blennies have taken up residence. On the south side and also in towards the island, there is a series of long blind alleys which are wide enough for several divers to pass – again the sides are rather devoid of life, but the tops are all covered in healthy corals.

14 FLINTSTONES

★★★

Location: Off the northwest corner of West Dog Island.
Access: By boat only.
Conditions: Subject to surge and swell; only to be dived when there is no northerly swell.
Average depth: 12m (40ft)
Maximum depth: 21m (70ft)
Average visibility: 18m (60ft)

The name Flintstones comes from the huge mound of rounded boulders and rocks, some of them the size of a house, that characterize this site. There is little good coral growth due to the exposed nature of the site and the sedentary marine life attached to the rocks is all rather stunted, low and encrusting. The rocks give a first impression of being almost devoid of life but, once you switch your diving lights on and peer into the shadows, the true nature of the habitat reveals itself. There are colonial white speck tunicates (*Didemnum conchyliatum*), strawberry tunicates (*Eudistoma* spp.), red sieve sponges (*Phorbas amaranthus*), yellow boring sponges (*Siphonodictyon coralliphagum*) and spiny ball sponges (*Leucetta barbata*). There are also mat zoanthids (*Zoanthus pulchellus*) and shade-loving fish everywhere.

15 WALL TO WALL
★★★

Location: Off the southwest corner of West Dog Island.
Access: By boat only.
Conditions: Affected by surge and swell, generally dived only from April/May to August.
Average depth: 6m (20ft)
Maximum depth: 20m (66ft)
Average visibility: 21m (70ft)
This exposed site gets its name because of the often large concentrations of snapper and grunt: they can be so thick in the water that they appear to be 'wall to wall'. These shoals are located further down the slope of the rocky wall, where a jumble of big boulders has created numerous gullies, canyons and swim-throughs, ideal for fish to move about away from danger from larger predators. The underhanging ledges will always have glasseye snapper (*Priancanthus cruenatus*) lying with their mouths open, inviting the attention of cleaner shrimps. Juvenile Spanish hogfish (*Bodianus pulchellus*) also act as cleaners and there are large numbers of these – their vivid coloration is similar to that of fairy basslets (*Gramma loreto*).

16 JOE'S CAVE
★★★

Location: Southwest corner of Great Dog Island.
Access: By boat only.
Conditions: Surge, oceanic swell and some current to be expected on the surface; little or no surge in the cave.
Average depth: 12m (40ft)
Maximum depth: 22m (75ft)
Average visibility: 21m (70ft)

HERMIT CRABS

The most common of the small crustaceans to be found around the Virgin Islands are hermit crabs. They are similar in some respects to other decapods, but are only armoured on the outer half of the body, with the inner half of the abdomen being long, soft and twisted to follow the coils of its host – usually an empty mollusc shell. The hermit crab's abdomen also has a large constricting muscle, which it uses to retract its upper body parts into the discarded mollusc shell which it uses as a mobile home.

Hermit crabs are opportunistic feeders, performing a vital link in the marine food chain by scavenging on any detritus or decaying matter on the seabed. They can be seen foraging amid turtle-grass beds and over all corals, but are particularly active at night, when they can scavenge in more safety, constantly battling each other over the occupation of shells.

This is a cavern through the bedrock off the headland which can be entered at 6m (20ft) and exited at 22m (75ft). Shafts of light cut into the gloom and, as you turn around to come back up the wall, the view is great, with small schools of blue chromis (*Chromis cyanea*) and creole wrasse (*Clepticus parrai*) swimming above you. The cave's walls are covered in small sponges, tunicates and hydroids, while a large school of glassy sweepers (*Pempheris schomburgki*) can be found.

17 CORAL GARDENS (SOUTH BAY)
★★★★☆☆

Location: On the sheltered southeast corner of Great Dog.
Access: By boat only.
Conditions: Fairly sheltered from the worst of the weather, but silty.
Average depth: 6m (20ft)
Maximum depth: 15m (50ft)
Average visibility: 12m (40ft)
The greater part of this dive is in only 6m (20ft) (where over 80% of all coral species represented in the British Virgin Islands are found). Nearby at 17m (55ft) are the remains of an aeroplane fuselage, which was once used as a prop in a disaster movie. Now home to schools of fish, it makes an excellent, safe dive with little current and a good chance to see barracuda and turtles. The fuselage is open to divers and you can swim through the open doors; there are always fish inside. The seabed is home to hundreds of orange-spotted gobies (*Nes longus*) which live in burrows alongside a commensal snapping shrimp. Garden eels (*Heterconger halis*) are also common and the coral shelf, although silty, is home to an amazing variety of corals.

How to Get There

Daily charter flights fly between Virgin Gorda and San Juan, St Thomas, Fajardo and Culebra; Caribbean Wings also have a regular service from St Maarten and San Juan to Virgin Gorda; tel (284) 495- 309.

Most visitors arrive by the North Sound Express Ferry Service from Beef Island, Tortola. The trip to Spanish Town, Leverick Bay and the Bitter End Yacht Club only takes about 30 minutes. If the ferry is full, overweight bags may be charged for; tel (284) 495 2138, Speedy's sail from Road Town to Spanish Town; tel (284) 495 5240.

Otherwise, visitors generally arrive by private yacht or charter yacht service, mooring at one of the several picturesque bays or booking into a marina.

Getting Around

There are jeeps for hire, but it's unlikely you will want to spend much time exploring the island. A taxi or water taxi arranged by the hotel will take you wherever you need at little expense.

L&S Garage, Taxi and Car Rental, PO Box 1073, The Valley; tel (284) 495 5297
Mahogany Rentals and Taxi Service, Princess Quarters, The Valley; tel (284) 495 5469
Speedy's Car Rentals, PO Box 35, The Valley and Leverick Bay; tel (284) 495 5240; email: speedysbvi@surfbvi.com; website: www.speedysbvi.com

Where to Stay

Most accommodation on Virgin Gorda is aimed at the upper end of the market. Bookings for the high season (Christmas to Easter) should be made well in advance. Facilities cover a wide range, and all resorts include watersports packages plus sailing moorings and facilities. For a full list of accommodation pick up the free Welcome brochure or contact **British Virgin Islands Tourist Board**, Virgin Gorda Yacht Harbour, Spanish Town; tel (284) 495 5181; fax (284) 494 6517; email: info@bvitourism.com; website: www.bvitourism.com

Expensive
Leverick Bay Hotel and Marina, Leverick Bay, PO Box 63, The Valley, Virgin Gorda; US toll free tel (800) 848 7081; tel: (284) 495 7421; fax (284) 495 5518; email: info@leverickbay.com; website: www.leverickbay.com
Built on the hillside, with excellent views over the harbour and jetty. Accommodation ranging from hotel rooms to villas and two-bedroom condominiums. Swimming pool, tennis, watersports. Dive BVI is on the premises. The complex includes a branch of

the well known restaurant Pusser's.
Bitter End Yacht Club, PO Box 46, The Valley, Virgin Gorda; US toll free tel (800) 872 2392; tel (284) 494 2745/6; fax (284) 494 4756; email: binfo@beyc.com; website: www.beyc.com
Busy resort popular with the yachting fraternity. Features a wide range of water-oriented facilities – sailing school, windsurfing, yacht charters and on-site Kilbride's Sunchaser Scuba Ltd. Accommodation ranging from rooms to luxuriously outfitted villas with sea views. Spread out over a wide area, with three restaurants.

Biras Creek Estate, PO Box 54, North Sound, Virgin Gorda; tel (284) 494 3555; fax (284) 494 3557; email: biras@caribsurf.com; website: www.biras.com
60ha (150 acre) resort reached only by boat, and possibly the most exclusive on the island. Beautifully decorated guest cottages and suites, with wonderful views over the North Sound and Berchers Bay, especially from the split-level bar and restaurant. Small pool on the edge of the ocean and a sheltered beach. Tennis, watersports, sailing.

Rosewood Little Dix Bay Hotel, Little Dix Bay, PO Box 70, Virgin Gorda; US toll free tel (800) 928 3000 tel (284) 495 5555; fax (284) 495 5661; email: littledixbay@rosewoodhotels.com; website: www.littledixbay.com
Luxurious resort built by Laurence Rockefeller, with comfortable rooms and amenities set in extensive and well manicured grounds. Good beach with watersports facilities. No dive shop, but nearby operators will pick up clients from the dock. Also features chic shops and the enormous Pavilion restaurant.

Nearby Exclusive Island Resorts
Necker Island, northwest of Virgin Gorda; US toll free tel (800) 557 4255; tel (284) 494 2757; fax (284) 494 4396; UK tel (+44) (0) (171) 727 8000; website: www.neckerisland.com
Owned by Virgin magnate Richard Branson. Guests fly into Virgin Gorda from St Thomas, then by private ferry pick-up to the ultra-private 30ha (74 acre) island. If you want to stay here, bring another 23 guests with you! You can only book the resort as a whole.

Mid-range
Bayview Vacation Apartments, PO Box 1018, The Valley, Virgin Gorda; tel (284) 495 5329; email: Nora@BayViewbvi.com; website: www.bayviewbvi.com
Two-bedroom efficiency apartments,

perfectly located for exploring the southern end of the island.

Guavaberry Spring Bay Villas, PO Box 20, The Valley, Virgin Gorda; tel (284) 495 5227; fax (284) 495 5283; email: gsbhomes@surfbvi.com
21 wooden, self-catering cottages perched on stilts on the hillside, not far from The Baths.

Mango Bay Resort, PO Box 1062, Mango Bay, Virgin Gorda; tel (284) 495 5672; fax (284) 495 5674; email: mangobay@surfbvi.com; website: www.mangobayresort.com
Small resort with just eight villas, decorated in a light, contemporary style. Overlooks a thin, sandy beach and has great sea views.

Olde Yard Inn, PO Box 26, The Valley, Virgin Gorda; tel (284) 495 5544; fax (284) 495 5986; email: oldeyard@surfbvi.com; website: www.oldeyardinn.com
14 rooms beside a nice pool and a lunchtime-only restaurant. Out-of-the-way resort, with horseback riding – and a good library.

Where to Eat

Visitors staying here rarely venture out of their resorts due to the high standards maintained within them: Biras Creek, Little Dix Bay and the Bitter End Yacht Club in particular are renowned for their gourmet cuisine. Those who do want a change will find there are a few small restaurants in The Valley, and of course on Saba Rock. A large number of restaurants can be reached only by private yacht charter. A free BVI restaurant guide is available at most bookstores or tourist points.

Giorgio's Table, Mahoe Bay, Virgin Gorda; tel (284) 495 5684; email: georgiostable@surfbvi.com
Excellent Sicilian-style pastas, salads and desserts, served with the best Italian wines.

The Rock Café, The Valley, Virgin Gorda, British Virgin Islands; tel (284) 495 5482; website: www.mangobayresort.com/rockcafe
Situated among the rocks between the Baths and Spanish Town, The Rock Café provides this popular BVI tourist destination with fine Italian cuisine and Caribbean dishes served in an open-air setting.

Top of the Baths, P.O.Box 1133, The Valley, Virgin Gorda, BVI; tel (284) 495 5497; fax (284) 495 5411; email: thebaths@thebathsbvi.com; website: www.topofthebaths.com
The Top of the Baths is on a hill overlooking one of the best beaches in the world and

The aeroplane wreck off Great Dog (Site 17) is a popular site for exploration, next to an excellent reef.

includes a restaurant, bar, pool, and collection of shops - all with panoramic views of the British Virgin Islands.

Dive operators

Dive BVI Ltd., PO Box 1040, Leverick Bay, Virgin Gorda; US toll free tel (800) 848 7078; tel 495 5513; fax (284) 495 5347; email: info@divebvi.com; website: www.divebvi.com; also at Peter Island Hotel and Marina Cay. Very professional operation with huge experience around all the islands.

Kilbride's Sunchaser Scuba Ltd, PO Box 46, Bitter End Yacht Club, Virgin Gorda; US toll free tel (800) 932 4286; tel (284) 495 9638; fax (284) 495 9369; email: sunchaser@surfbvi.com; website: www.sunchaserscuba.com
Great location for northeastern reefs and rocks, video editing suite on site, good shop, well trained staff. PADI courses.

Kilbride's Sunchaser Scuba Ltd, PO Box 40, Bitter End Yacht Club, Virgin Gorda; US toll free tel (800) 932 4286; tel (284) 495 9638; fax (284) 495 9369; email: sunscuba@caribsurf.com

Emergency Services

Virgin Islands Search and Rescue, VHF Channel 16; tel (284) 494 4357, dialling 999 or 911
Peebles Hospital, Road Town, Tortola; tel (284) 494 3497
Medicure Pharmacy and Health Centre, The Valley, Virgin Gorda; tel (284) 495 5479
Island Drug Centre, The Valley, Virgin Gorda; tel (284) 495 5449
Recompression Chamber, St Thomas; tel (340) 776 8311
Divers Alert Network, tel (919) 684 8111

Local Highlights

Little Fort National Park can be found at the south of the island and was formerly the site of a Spanish Fort; some of the old walls still remain inside this 14ha (36-acre) wildlife sanctuary. Over on the southwest tip can be found the remains of an **old copper mine**. Founded originally by the Spanish, it was rebuilt by Cornish miners between 1838 and 1867 and the remains of the chimney, boiler house, cistern and mine shafts can still be seen on this exposed headland.
The **Gorda Peak National Park**

contains a wide variety of indigenous plants and, although it was deforested at one time, has now been replanted with mahogany and many exotic species. South of the widely spread-out original settlement of Spanish Town, now known as The Valley, can be found **The Baths**, a series of gigantic granite boulders. There are a few trails in, around and under the boulders at The Baths and many can be reached only by swimming. This small beach is popular with tourists and is always busy.

When staying at the Bitter End Yacht Club, you can hire a small skiff to putter out to **Saba Rock**, once the home of the legendary wreck and treasure hunter Bert Kilbride (see page 147). There is a small bar and fun restaurant, only accessible by boat. The rock is mid-channel between the Bitter End Yacht Club and Prickly Pear Island. You can do this trip on the way back from a day at deserted **Deep Bay**, where mangroves hug the waterside and a stretch of golden beach extends east to Oil Nut Bay.

The early years of conquest and colonization in the Caribbean brought ships from all over coastal Europe, and particularly Spain. The Spanish proceeded to capture and enslave many of the indigenous natives of the eastern Caribbean to work in the gold mines of Santo Domingo. As their influence spread, the Spanish moved their base ports from these islands down to Venezuela and Colombia where fresh water, produce and good wood for ships' repairs was more readily available. Nevertheless, the trade route back across the Atlantic still required them to travel up through the eastern Caribbean and north towards Bermuda, before turning to starboard with the trade winds to assist them on their journey home. This route brought many of their ships through the Virgin Islands, up through the Turks and Caicos and onwards through the eastern Bahamas and past the Florida Straits.

Bert Kilbride (right) has charted over 150 wrecks around Anegada.

SHIPS LOST

For every 'legitimate' ship travelling this route to Europe – often with a hold laden with spices, hardwoods, gold, silver and precious jewels – there would be at least another five privateers or filibusters engaged in active harassment and pursuit, either for their own gain or to benefit the coffers of a rival sovereign. Many galleons escaped the privateers only to perish on treacherous reefs. The submerged barrier reefs which stretch for many kilometres east of Anegada in the British Virgin Islands laid claim to the highest proportion of all.

One early report in Spanish archives from about 1705 told of a Spanish Galleon laden with treasure and wrecked accidentally off Anegada. The crew buried the treasure nearby, where it remained, according to legend. Another note, written in 1775 on a chart of the Virgin Islands and found inside a merchant's book, added: 'On Anegada is Ye Treasure Point, so called by ye freebooters from the gold and silver supposed to have been buried there abouts after the wreck of a Spanish Galleon.'

However, many of the ships lost off the reefs of Anegada were laden not with jewels but with slaves. Ships came from Africa packed with men, women and children who – if they survived (they were so tightly packed aboard that the death-toll was appallingly high) – were destined to work on the newly formed sugar plantations of the surrounding islands. Tragically, numerous Africans died in this way on Anegada's reefs.

WRECK SURVEYING

There are reported to be over 300 wrecks around Anegada's Horseshoe Reef area alone. This massive barrier has laid claim to ships over the centuries. The remains of the wooden hulls have long since rotted away, but piles of ballast can still be found. All the wrecks are now protected, though in the past they have yielded fascinating artefacts – gold doubloons and the like – to wreck hunters.

Anegada's formidable Horseshoe Reef has taken a heavy toll on shipping in the past.

One such wreck enthusiast was Herbert 'Bert' Kilbride (March 8, 1914–January 8, 2008), the self-proclaimed 'Last Pirate of the Caribbean'. He was a larger-than-life character who wore a bandana and a gold cutlass earring and resembled the archetypal buccaneer. Originally a spear-fisherman like many of his contemporaries, he gave that up for active conservation work and the dream of finding treasure while diving around the British Virgin Islands. Of the 250 wrecks around Anegada listed by Lloyds of London, Kilbride located over 150, many of which are stacked like a deck of cards on top of each other, having sunk in exactly the same position centuries apart.

It took Kilbride five years to locate the majority of the wrecks. One area of Horseshoe Reef which is littered with cannon particularly drew his attention. In 1960 he went to the Spanish National Archives in Seville to research the area, and found the manifests of 32 Spanish ships, all lost at the same time as the famous shipwrecks discovered by Mel Fisher off Florida – which revealed the greatest treasure horde yet to be found underwater. The possibility of a connection between the two has tantalized Kilbride, and many like him, for years.

Kilbride was appointed Receiver of Wrecks by the Queen in 1967. He had moved to St Croix, USVI, in 1956 and to the British Virgin Islands in 1964 where he lived until 2005. He was a diver for almost a century, a treasure seeker for over 50 years and owned a SCUBA diving tour business for 30 years. In the 1960s, he created the 'Resort Course' for beginners interested in SCUBA diving that is now taught worldwide under the name 'Introductory SCUBA Course'.

In the 1990s, the governor of the British Virgin Islands called Kilbride a 'living legend' and in 2004, at 90, the Guinness Book of World Records proclaimed him the oldest scuba diver in the world. He died in Etna, California, at the age of 93.

ANEGADA

Located 19km (12 miles) north of Virgin Gorda, Anegada is one of the largest coral islands in the eastern Caribbean and rises only 8.5m (28ft) above sea level. The island has just 160 inhabitants, most of whom are clustered around The Settlement. Anegada's one hotel lies further west, towards Setting Point; nearby is an extensive salt pond where flamingoes can be seen.

Anegada is famous for the huge number of ships that have foundered around its shores. Horseshoe Reef (Site 2), to the southeast of the island, is the main resting place for many of these wrecks – some 250 are recorded by Lloyds of London as having sunk here. Some of them lie stacked one on top of the other, having sunk in exactly the same position centuries apart. Unfortunately, until recently this massive reef system was off-limits to divers due to a ban imposed as a result of pressure by local fishermen, who had convinced the government that the divers were chasing away the fish and reducing their catches. However, it has become apparent that the reverse is the case, overfishing being the main culprit, and some dive sites have now been opened up again.

Spotted moray eels (Gymnothorax moringa) may be found on most reefs and are unafraid of divers.

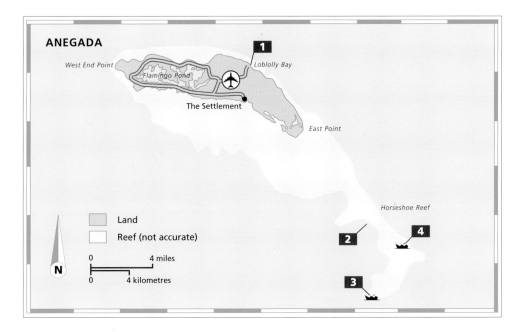

ANEGADA

West End Point
Flamingo Pond
The Settlement
Loblolly Bay
East Point
Horseshoe Reef

Land
Reef (not accurate)

0   4 miles
0   4 kilometres
N

1 LOBLOLLY BAY

★★★☆☆☆☆☆☆

Location: On the northern shore of Anegada.
Access: From the beach.
Conditions: Sheltered from surge due to offshore barrier reef, but still exposed in the winter months.
Average depth: 1m (3ft)
Maximum depth: 6m (20ft)
Average visibility: 15m (50ft)
This sheltered bay is protected from oceanic surge and swell by the offshore barrier reef, creating an aquarium-like lagoon which is home to a myriad of juvenile fish. Sadly much of the outer reef has been overfished, but the area is still a delight. Damselfish and small angelfish and butterflyfish are common, as are bottom algae feeders such as wrasse, and even stingrays can be found in the shallows hunting small molluscs and crustaceans.

2 HORSESHOE REEF

★★★☆☆☆

Location: Huge shallow reef southeast of Anegada.
Access: By boat only.
Conditions: Exposed to Atlantic swell and surge.
Average depth: 9m (30ft)
Maximum depth: 25m (80ft)
Average visibility: 25m (80ft)

At present few dive boats venture out to Horseshoe Reef – the exceptions being infrequent visits by the *Cuan Law* and passing yachts – but it is hoped that the moratorium on diving will soon be lifted altogether and the National Parks Trust and BVI Diving Operators' Association will then be able to install mooring buoys to protect the reef from potential anchor damage. Although fairly extensive, the reef is not as pristine as one would expect, since it is constantly battered by storms; nevertheless, it does boast some huge stands of elkhorn and pillar corals.

3 ROCUS (GRAVEYARD WRECK; BONE WRECK)

★★★★☆

Location: Southern corner of Horseshoe Reef.
Access: By boat only.
Conditions: Can be strong surge; snorkellers are advised to be doubly cautious due to the large and jagged stands of elkhorn coral in the shallows.
Average depth: 9m (30ft)
Maximum depth: 12m (40ft)
Average visibility: 18m (60ft)
The *Rocus* was a Greek cargo vessel carrying a cargo of animal bones from Trinidad to a fertilizer factory in Baltimore when she ran aground and sank in 1929 on the southern corner of Horseshoe Reef. This steel ship, now lying on her starboard side, was originally 116m (380ft) long, but sadly the impact of some severe hurricanes over the last few years has completely

Peppermint gobies (Coryphopterus lipernes) are often perched on coral heads.

destroyed the ship, spreading her remains and animal bones all over the seabed. The bow is now below the surface and the stern is in 11m (36ft), the propeller having been removed in the 1970s. There are some large sea fans on the wreck and short stubby hard corals. Her winches and boilers are still recognizable. Various species of jacks and oceanic triggerfish (*Canthidermis sufflamen*) are common, as are barracuda, preying on lots of small damselfish and sergeant majors (*Abudefduf saxatilis*). The wreck is very difficult to find without specific knowledge.

CUTS AND ABRASIONS

Care should always be taken underwater to avoid blundering into coral accidentally, not only because of the damage you may cause the coral. Cuts or abrasions from old pieces of wreckage can be particularly nasty, especially if you are stung by fire coral at the same time. Wounds should be treated and sterilized immediately on exiting the water. In some instances a visit to the local hospital may be required due to the high amounts of planktonic bacteria to be found in warmer waters.

4 PARAMATTA

★★★☆☆

Location: North of the southern corner of Horseshoe Reef.
Access: By boat only.
Conditions: Can be strong surge and current to be expected.
Average depth: 6m (20ft)
Maximum depth: 12m (40ft)
Average visibility: 18m (60ft)

The *Paramatta* was a former Royal Mail Steam Packet Company ship which foundered on Horseshoe Reef in 1859. At 100m (330ft) long, she was an impressive steel-hulled ship with two massive paddle wheels. She was left high and dry for over a month of failed salvage attempts, and her crew eventually had to abandon her to her fate. Picked clean by the locals, the ship was eventually pounded flat and her stern is now in 12m (40ft). Her unique square portholes are lovely to see. Huge sea fans and boulder corals are all over the wreckage and the surrounding reef, with various small schools of wrasse and parrotfish. Rarely dived, it is only in the best of conditions that divers can visit this exposed section of the reef in safety.

HOW TO GET THERE

There is a small airstrip on Anegada northwest of the Settlement (reached via the Ruffin Point Road) with a regular daily service from Beef Island Airport on Tortola with Fly BVI Ltd.; tel (284) 495 1747. Gorda Aero also have a regular daily service to the island; tel (284) 495 3371 Most other visitors arrive by private or charter yacht.

GETTING AROUND

There are no paved roads on the island. A dirt track runs all the way around the island, and traverses it at the Jack Bay Road, just north of the airport. Bicycles are available at the Anegada Reef Hotel.

WHERE TO STAY

Anegada is a great place to come for those who really want to get away
from it all and listen to the tall tales of the visiting yachties who collect around the bars in the evening.

Anegada Reef Hotel, Ruffin Point Rd, West End, Anegada; tel (284) 495 8002; fax (284) 495 9362; email: info@anegadareef.com; website: www.anegadareef.com
16-room hotel, with its own anchorage. Lively bar and a good restaurant, where candle-lit dinners (reservations required) feature specialities such as locally caught lobster.

Mac's Place Camping, The Settlement, Anegada; tel (284) 495 8020
Tents and cleared pitches available.

Showers, toilets and dining area.

Neptune's Campground, The Settlement, Anegada; tel (284) 495 9439
Prepared pitches with linen and mattresses. Restaurant, showers and toilets.

WHERE TO EAT

There are very few restaurants open at any one time, so it is hard to compile any list of recommendations: those described here are typical, and may be open during your visit. Always call ahead to avoid disappointment.

Pamato Point Restaurant, Pamato Point, Anegada; tel (284) 495 8038
Relaxed, friendly restaurant and bar on the beach near the Anegada Reef Hotel, towards Pamato Point.

The Big Bamboo, Loblolly Bay, Northside, Anegada; tel (284) 495 2019
Very popular beach bar in a pleasant setting, offering conch, lobster, shrimp, steaks and chicken. Great atmosphere and very friendly.

DIVE OPERATORS

Anegada Reef Hotel offers dive packages in conjunction with We Be Divin'. Anegada, given its name 'sunken island' by Christopher Columbus, is the BVI's only completely coral island and We Be Divin' has been granted exclusive rights to dive the Horseshoe Reef for the first time in over 15 years.

EMERGENCY SERVICES

Virgin Islands Search & Rescue, VHF Channel 16; tel (284) 494 4357, dialling 999 or 911
Peebles Hospital, Road Town, Tortola; tel (284) 494 3497
Medicure Pharmacy & Health Centre, The Valley, Virgin Gorda; tel (284) 495 5479
Recompression Chamber, St Thomas; tel (340) 776 8311
Divers Alert Network, tel (919) 684 8111

LOCAL HIGHLIGHTS

There's not a lot to do on Anegada other than **snorkelling** along the barrier reef's sheltered north shore. The beach here is also excellent for beachcombing. In 1992 a group of **Caribbean flamingoes** was re-introduced to Anegada from Bermuda. (They had previously been wiped out from Anegada.) These are best seen from Flamingo Pond along the West End Road.

Yellow lobed tube sponges (Pseudoceratina crassa) can be found.

The Marine Environment

As with all eastern Caribbean reefs, the sublittoral regions of the Virgin Islands can be divided into a number of different areas or habitats. The majority of the underlying reefs in the Virgin Islands are made of hard bedrock and huge boulders sculpted by time. True coral reefs are found only in more sheltered areas between the smaller islands north of St Thomas and St John, as well as around Anegada and St Croix. The other localities have a light encrusting growth of corals and sponges.

TYPES OF REEF

Directly out from the shore you will encounter a **fringing reef**. In the Virgin Islands this slopes steeply away from the rocky shore down to about 12m (40ft), where it meets the sand plain. This reef is made of hard corals topped by sea fans. It is one of the most prolific areas for fish and invertebrates.

The main island archipelago is quite shallow, with an average depth of only 18m (60ft), and comprises a flat sand plain covered in a meadow of eel grass and dotted by boulders and true corals. The boulder ridges are known as 'breakers' and many have names synonymous with their hidden dangers, such as The Invisibles (Virgin Gorda, Site 6). The coral blocks in these areas are known as **patch reefs** and this is generally where you will find the highest proportion of marine life during your diving. Any night diving you do will probably be in this environment. The various ships sunk deliberately as artificial reefs are always located on the sand plain, though near to good reefs to encourage the growth of corals.

On northern Anegada and St Croix there are classic Caribbean reef structures known as **spur-and-groove reefs**. Always running perpendicular to the shore, the spur is a ridge of hard coral growth usually topped by sea fans, with its often vertical sides covered in sponges. The groove is a coral rubble and sand channel that has been sculpted out of the reef by the constant surge of the waves. Both spurs and grooves generally lead over the edge of the wall or drop off and are regarded as among the best attractions for visiting divers who can often only experience deep diving in these locations in the Virgin Islands. Because spur-and-groove reefs always run perpendicular to the shore, if you get disoriented on a dive you should be able to find your way into shallow water.

These types of coral growths may eventually form a much larger **barrier reef**, comprising elkhorn, boulder, star, brain and staghorn corals. Examples of barrier reefs are the one found off northeastern Virgin Gorda and the massive Horseshoe Reef (Anegada, Site 2), which stretches southeast from Anegada. The latter is reputed to be one of the longest unbroken reefs in the Caribbean. These barrier reef systems in fairly shallow water present a hazard to navigation, as many parts of the reefs come close to the surface and are difficult to see in low light. Barrier reefs tend to grow parallel to the coastline.

The only island with a true **reef wall** or **drop-off** is St Croix, where the coral lip located at the northern edge of the island is part of the continental shelf and drops many hundreds of metres, making for some spectacular diving, quite different from the rest of the Virgin Islands. Walls and drop-offs are not on the diving list of any of the northern resorts.

CORALS

The Virgin Islands are home to some superb true coral reefs, such as Horseshoe Reef, the entire north-shore deep wall off St Croix and amid the northern islands. Wherever there is a lee shore and tidal conditions are optimum for regeneration, corals survive and healthy reefs are able to propagate. However, with the greater part of the Virgin Islands being in fact rock-based, it is more common to find underwater boulders colonized by corals and sponges suited to this substrate and similar to the species which first attach onto wrecks. The corals are mainly small encrusting species; sea fans are also common, requiring only a small base, yet able to extend into the current to filter-feed plankton.

With the exception of the offshore islands of St Croix and Anegada, the waters around the Virgin Islands are not as clear as in other areas of the Caribbean, due to the fact that much of the shelf on which the rocky islands sit is very shallow, resulting in greater turbidity. Although there are no major rivers, the very nature of the islands creates quite heavy rainfall during hurricane season and the rainwater run-off from the steep-sided mountains can have an effect on the quality of the corals. The corals predominating on the rocky boulders are generally low and encrusting and very sturdy as sea conditions can get rough seasonally.

Fed by the Gulf Stream, there are over 120 species of coral, including luxuriant growths of sea fans and plumes. Remember that these are incredibly delicate organisms which can be damaged or killed by a misplaced hand, fin or camera attachment. The major proportion of the reef is actually a crust of living organisms building over the ancient skeletons of their ancestors, changing in shape and structure as the environment changes around it.

In shallow waters and forming barrier reefs, the largest of the branching corals is the elkhorn coral (*Acropora palmata*). Each individual colony can grow

---

Opposite: *This typical Virgin islands reef scene includes sea whips, sponges and corals.*

up to 3m (10ft) and they frequently have small schools of snapper and grunt sheltering under their extended branches. Branching finger coral (*Porites porites*) is common, although it forms much smaller clumps; it is often associated with yellow pencil coral (*Madracis mirabilis*).

On boulder outcrops, small ten-rayed star corals (*Madracis decactis*) form large encrusting sheets. Rose corals such as *Manicina areolata* form small clumps and closely resemble brain corals, although the latter are generally much more spherical in shape. The species whose form most resembles the convolutions of the human brain is *Diploria labyrinthiformis*. The most common coral in these areas (and perhaps one of the most untidy) is the corky sea finger (*Briareum asbestinum*), which, with the polyps extended, looks totally different from the stubby yellowish tips that you see amid dense growths of algae on the reef tops.

On the deeper walls off northern St Croix, large overhanging sheet corals such as *Agaricia lamarki* and scroll coral (*Agaricia undata*) can be found on the outer edges of the wall, tumbling into the depths. Interspersed along walls are long, thin sea whips, often referred to as wire coral (*Cirrhipathes leutkeni*). Spiralling up from the depths, these corals are closely related to the true black corals which grow in large bushes in areas of fast-moving water.

What many divers remember most about the Virgin Islands are the sheer walls of colour found on the undersides of boulders, in shaded areas of the reef and on the various wrecks. This colour comes from golden cup coral (*Tubastrea coccinea*), which has long golden polyps that extend during twilight hours to sift the plankton. Gorgonian sea fans can be found on the tops of all the reefs and boulders on the lower slopes, on the sides of wrecks and wherever there is strong current. Although not a true coral, fire coral (*Millepora alcicornis*) also dominates many of the offshore rocks such as The Invisibles, Blonde Rock (Little Sisters, Site 16) and Carrot Shoal (Little Sisters, Site 9). Always be careful when approaching these corals as they can cause painful burns if you bump into them when there is a strong underwater surge.

A FRAGILE ECOSYSTEM

Reefs are living communities made up of many thousands of species and tens of thousands of individuals, and the reefs around the Virgin Islands are no exception. To damage one part damages the whole ecosystem. Over 1000 species of animals and plants may be found in the near-shore waters and many of the animals are interdependent.

The major inhabitants are the corals and algae. Algae grow much faster than coral (in fact, one of the fastest growing living things is a marine alga). If a coral is accidentally damaged, algae take a very fast grip on the damaged area and can soon smother and

kill the coral. These two groups are in constant competition with each other.

Certain varieties of coral such as staghorn and elkhorn coral are more regularly encountered by divers and snorkellers and are thus particularly vulnerable. The living tissue found in corals is on and just below the surface and if this is damaged the entire coral may die. It is imperative that divers maintain full control over their buoyancy, as a misplaced fin or equipment console can seriously wound or kill the coral. Even placing your hand on the coral can remove the protective mucus and expose the coral to stress and damage. The average yearly growth of coral is incredibly small –brain coral grows about 1cm (⅓in) each year. Elkhorn can grow up to 10cm (4in) each year, and staghorn slightly faster, but not enough to compensate for damage caused by careless actions.

PROTECTING OTHER MARINE LIFE

The geographical position of the Virgin Islands, bordering both the Caribbean and the western Atlantic and fed by the nutrient-rich waters of the Gulf Stream, has resulted in a very high diversity of marine species. So much so, in fact, that several universities and marine biological groups are studying the marine flora and fauna to be found here. Project REEF uses amateur divers, well tutored in fish identification, to take observations on every dive throughout the year, recording seasonal anomalies, species distribution and sudden changes in density of underwater populations (which may indicate an approaching hurricane or breeding aggregations).

When approaching marine life you must do so sensitively and with empathy. Try and understand that what you are looking at is just one small link in one of the most complex ecosystems on earth. Divers MUST master the art of self control and buoyancy technique to keep well clear of the reef and its inhabitants.

Turtles, for example, are fascinating and graceful creatures, but do not try to hold onto them. If you find one sleeping at night, stay well clear because to grab hold of it could give the creature such a shock that it might blunder into a cave and be drowned, or seriously damage itself and the corals around it.

Pufferfish should also be left untouched. They have a natural defence mechanism of sucking in water very rapidly until they are balloon-sized with any defensive spines jutting out. They may look comical when inflated and cannot swim properly, but continual handling of these fish will remove the protective mucous membrane from their skin, and let infection set in that can kill the fish.

Long-spined black sea urchins must be treated with caution. Apart from the very obvious danger of getting spines embedded in soft parts of your flesh due to lack of diver control, it is also illegal to cut up these creatures to feed other animals on the reef. The urchins play an important part in controlling algae and are only just beginning to recover after being almost completely wiped out in the Caribbean due to disease in 1983.

Barrel sponges should be treated with respect. Some of the larger species can grow to over 2m (7ft), but to climb inside one can kill it.

Generally, most fish are slow in their growth patterns and, if the marine habitat of a particular fish or invertebrate, such as coral, is damaged, the spin-off on the rest of the reef's population can be catastrophic. A small reduction in the coral community can not only make the reef look less inviting or pretty to a visiting diver, but may also drastically reduce fish stocks and populations of other creatures such as shrimp, lobster and octopus.

COMMON INVERTEBRATES OF THE VIRGIN ISLANDS

Anemones (phylum Cnidaria, class Anthozoa, order Actinaria)

The most common species of anemone found around the islands is the corkscrew anemone (*Bartholomea annulata*). It is often home to snapping shrimps and cleaning shrimps which live with immunity among the stinging tentacles. The largest is the giant anemone (*Condylactis gigantea*) which has long, thick tentacles tipped with a purple or green knob. The branching anemone (*Lebruna danae*) is common around Painted Walls off Dead Chest Island (Little Sisters, Site 14), while amid the grass beds there are tiny turtle-grass anemones (*Viatrix globulifera*).

Crabs (phylum Crustacea, section Anomura, Brachyura)

The largest of the crustaceans is the channel clinging crab (*Mithrax spinosissimus*), which only comes out onto the reef top at night. Nimble spray crabs, sometimes referred to as sally lightfoots (*Percnon gibbesi*), are found in association with long-spined sea urchins in shallower water. The comical-looking arrow crab (*Stenorhynchus seticornis*) is the crab most associated with the Caribbean.

Lobsters (phylum Crustacea, suborder Panilura)

Spanish lobsters (*Scyllarides aequinoctialis*) and spotted spiny lobsters (*Panulirus guttatus*) inhabit the reef ledges. Always hiding from direct sunlight, they actively forage at night. They can retreat rapidly by fast movements of their tail, propelling them backwards.

Shrimps (phylum Crustacea, order Decapoda)

Under the protective tentacles of corkscrew anemones, snapping shrimp (*Alpheus armatus*) can be found in many locations. The spotted cleaner shrimp (*Periclimenes yucatanicus*) is more associated with the giant anemone, while one of the species associated with cleaning fish of parasites is the cleaning shrimp (*Pereclimenes pedersoni*). At night, the red night shrimp (*Rhynchocinetes rigens*) may be spotted by its green reflective eyes.

Snails (phylum Mollusca, class Gastropoda, subclass Prosobranchia)

Quite rare in other areas of the Caribbean, the fingerprint cyphoma (*Cyphoma signatum*) can be found off Cane Bay (St Croix, Site 15) and in many locations in the British Virgin Islands. Netted olive shells (*Oliva reticularis*) can be found amid the turtle grass and conch, of course, are common sand plain inhabitants.

Sponges (phylum Porifera)

The branching tube sponge (*Pseudoceratina crassa*) and the azure vase sponge (*Callyspongia plicifera*) are commonly found on the reefs. Under the offshore boulders and in shaded caverns, the walls of the rocks are covered in red encrusting sponges (*Diplastrella megastellata*) and spiny ball sponges (*Leucetta barbata*).

Starfish and brittlestars (phylum Echinodermata, class Crinoidea, Asteroidea, Ophiuroidea)

Starfish are uncommon in the Caribbean, preferring to come out and feed only at night. An exception is the cushion sea star (*Oreaster reticulatus*), which is associated with eel-grass beds. The largest of the brittlestars is the basketstar (*Astrophyton muricatum*), while a common species is the sponge brittlestar (*Ophiothrix suensonii*) which tends to inhabit sea plumes and sponges.

Tunicates (phylum Chordata, class Ascidiacea)

Tunicates or sea squirts are largely overlooked and are quite common, particularly in areas of fast-moving water, where you will find the lightbulb tunicate (*Clavelina picta*), which is often a deep purple in colour.

REEF ENVIRONMENTAL EDUCATION FOUNDATION (PROJECT REEF)

The Reef Environmental Education Foundation, now recognized by PADI International, is a far-reaching scheme to maintain people's interest in diving activity, travel and environmental awareness, while at the same time contributing to scientific knowledge about marine life. At its heart is a scheme to encourage divers to monitor the state of the reef – by completing survey sheets recording marine life in the area they have just dived. There are varying degrees of involvement and you can become a member free just by filling out an application form and completing one REEF Fish Survey per year. It costs $30 to become a Contributing Member; to become a Survey Volunteer you need to complete a Reef Fish Identification Course and fill in at least six Fish Survey forms annually. To become a Survey Specialist you must participate in a five-day REEF Field Survey and complete at least twelve Fish Survey forms during a year. There are regular Field Surveys throughout the Caribbean. These, plus a quarterly newsletter and further information on REEF, can be obtained from: The REEF Environmental Education Foundation, PO Box 246, Key Largo, Florida 33037; tel (305) 451 0312; email: reefhq@reef.org; website: www.reef.org

Foureye butterflyfish (*Chaetodon capistratus*)

Threespot damselfish (*Stegastes variabilis*)

Spotted drum (*Equetus punctatus*)

Whitespot filefish (*Cantherhines macrocerus*)

Peacock flounder (*Bothus lunatus*)

COMMON FISH OF THE VIRGIN ISLANDS

Butterflyfish (family Chaetodontidae)
All the butterflyfish species are recorded in the Virgin Islands. Two of the prettiest are the reef butterflyfish (*Chaetodon sedentarius*) and the foureye butterflyfish (*Chaetodon capistratus*). The foureye butterflyfish has a distinctive large eye marking near the tail and is marked with numerous dark thin lines and a darker bar through the eye. The longsnout butterflyfish (*Chaetodon aculeatus*) is one of the smallest species.

Chromis/Damselfish (family Pomacentridae)
Common all around the Caribbean, chromis and damselfish are generally small and oval in shape, cultivating a 'garden' of algae among the coral which they defend with a passion. On the reef top, yellowtail damselfish (*Microspathodon chrysurus*) are very common, as are threespot damselfish (*Stegastes planifrons*), whose juveniles are brilliant yellow with a black splodge under the mid-dorsal fin.

Drum (family Sciaenidae)
Spotted drums (*Equetus punctatus*) are timid fish living under coral overhangs and in shaded areas. The juveniles are the ones that will attract most of your attention, due to their active gyrations and beautiful long 'striped' dorsal fins. A similar species is the highhat (*Equetus acuminatus*), which is almost identical at the juvenile stage, though later develops many more stripes than the drum.

Filefish/Triggerfish (families Balistidae, Monacanthidae)
The commonest of the filefish found amid the swaying sea fans is the slender filefish (*Monacanthus tuckeri*). Black durgon (*Melichthys niger*) are common on the outer reefs, often in quite large numbers. The largest of the filefish is the white-spotted filefish (*Cantherhines macrocerus*), which always travels with its lifelong mate. Oceanic triggerfish (*Canthidermis sufflamen*) are commonly seen in more exposed locations.

Flounders (family Bothidae)
Fairly rare on the sand flats are peacock flounders (*Bothus lunatus*) and eyed flounders (*Bothus ocellatus*), which are quite skittish when approached and take off over the sand plains at great speed. Peacock flounders have one long pectoral fin which has come to serve as a 'dorsal fin', being raised during flight. Both species are known to be preyed on by dolphins.

Gobies (family Gobiidae)

The cleaning goby (*Gobiosoma genie*) typifies the cleaning stations found all over the reef. Often occurring in quite large numbers in some of the larger sponges and coral heads, they wait in groups for fish requiring their services. One of the prettiest of the small gobies is the orange-sided goby (*Gobiosoma dilepsis*) – not to be confused with the orange-spotted goby (*Nes Longus*), which lives in burrows in the sand with its symbiotic partner the snapping shrimp.

Peppermint goby (*Coryphopterus lipernes*)

Hamlets (family Serranidae)

Hamlets are a member of the sea bass family and there are several striking representatives in the Virgin Islands. The most common is the barred hamlet (*Hypoplectrus puella*). The golden hamlet (*Hypoplectrus gummingatta*) is perhaps the brightest of all, with its golden body and curious blue and black markings around its mouth. The blue hamlet (*Hypoplectrus gemma*) is another rare yet beautiful example.

Barred hamlet (*Hypoplectrus puella*)

Jawfish (family Opistognathidae)

Related to blennies and gobies, these bottom dwellers live in burrows amid coral rubble which they pull around the entrance to their lair for added protection. However, they are more commonly observed hovering in mid-water with their tails pointing towards their burrow. They retreat rapidly when approached. Jawfish are one of those curious species that incubate their eggs in their mouths.

Yellowhead jawfish (*Opistognathus aurifrons*)

Lizardfish (family Synodontidae)

Named after their lizard-like heads, lizardfish or sand divers (*Synodus* spp.) are bottom dwellers, often partially submerged in sand as they sit and wait for their prey to swim by and be gulped down. They will not move unless you come too close to them. Found all over the Caribbean and western Atlantic, they are often seen near schools of silversides.

Lizardfish (*Synodus intermedius*)

Moray Eels (family Muraenidae)

Moray eels are common around all of the reefs, with the green moray (*Gymnothorax funebris*) the largest of the eels to be found in the eastern Caribbean. Several large species are well known in St Croix, where regular fish-feeding takes place. The viper moray (*Enchelycore nigricans*) looks particularly fearsome, the up-turned side of its mouth exposing its teeth. The colourful chain moray (*Echidna catenata*) has a large dark-brown-to-black body with irregular yellow bars and yellow eyes.

Goldentail moray (*Gymnothorax miliaris*)

OTHER COMMON FISH OF THE VIRGIN ISLANDS

Angelfish (family Pomacanthidae)
There are four species of angelfish in the Virgin Islands, including the rock beauty (*Holacanthus tricolor*) with its yellow face and tail and wide black body. Growing up to 30cm (12in), it is perhaps the most difficult to photograph. The most colourful of all is the queen angelfish (*Holacanthus ciliaris*) which can grow up to 45cm (18in) and is identifiable by a very distinctive 'crown' on the forehead. Perhaps the rarest species encountered is the grey angelfish (*Pomacanthus arcuatus*); of a similar size is the French angelfish (*Pomacanthus paru*), which is dark blue-grey-black with yellow rims on the scales and a bright yellow ring around the eye.

Barracuda (family Sphyraenidae)
The largest of the silvery predators on the reef is the great barracuda (*Sphyraena barracuda*), which usually leads a solitary existence. A smaller relative, the southern sennet (*Sphyraena picudilla*) is seen in large numbers amid the shallower reefs.

Basslets (family Grammidae)
The fairy basslet (*Gramma loreto*) is one of the most strikingly colourful fish to be found on any reef, with its golden-headed front and violet rear. It is usually found in recesses and under shaded areas of the reef.

Blennies (families Clinidae, Blennidae, Tripterygiidae)
Blennies are similar to gobies, in that few have swim bladders and they tend to perch on coral heads and rubble. Most live in cracks or in holes vacated by another marine organism, which they defend vigorously. One of the commonest species in the Virgin Islands is the roughhead blenny (*Acanthemblemaria aspera*). A similar species is the secretary blenny (*Acanthemblemaria maria*) which prefers to live in brain corals.

Garden Eel (family Congridae)
The garden eel (*Heteroconger halis*) lives in large social congregations in flat sand plains and can be seen on most dives wherever there is moving water to bring the planktonic tidbits on which they feed. Very common all over the Virgin Islands, they are extremely shy and withdraw into their burrows long before you reach them for a closer look.

Goatfish (family Mullidae)
Spotted goatfish (*Pseudupeneus maculatus*) can be found in small groups, often resting at night under overhanging coral heads. They excavate in soft sand with incredibly sensitive whisker-like barbels, searching for small crustaceans and worms. Although normally skittish, they can be approached more easily at night.

Grouper/Sea bass (family Serranidae)
Grouper, sea bass and soapfish form a very large family. The commonest is the coney (*Cephalopholis fulvus*), which comes in various colour forms, all of them striking. The largest of the groupers to be encountered is the jewfish (*Epinephelus itajara*), which is often found hiding under wrecks.

Grunt/Margate (family Haemulidae)
Found in large shoals under boulder overhangs and elkhorn coral, French grunt (*Haemulon flavolineatum*) and white margate (*Haemulon album*) can be seen swimming in close proximity with mutton snapper. Grunt are named after the grunting noise they make underwater.

Gurnards (family Dactylopteridae)
Flying gurnards (*Dactylopterus volitans*) are uncommon reef dwellers, often found in fairly shallow water of under 10m (33ft). They tend to be in their lifelong mating pairs and are seen skimming over the surface of the sandy sea bed with large extended pectoral fins, or 'walking' over the seabed with the modified spines from their ventral fins.

Hogfish/Razorfish (family Labridae)
Very closely related to wrasse and parrotfish, the common hogfish (*Lachnolaimus maximus*) and the Spanish hogfish (*Bodianus rufus*) are both represented in this area of the Caribbean. Juveniles of the Spanish hogfish act as cleaners to many reef species, often swimming out into open water to service passing jacks which posture by 'standing' on their tail and opening their mouths. The juveniles resemble fairy basslets with a purple head leading to a yellow-gold belly and tail.

Jacks (family Carangidae)
Black jacks (*Caranx lugubris*) are commonly found swimming along the edge of the drop-off, often in hunting packs of only three or four individuals. Horse-eye jacks (*Caranx latus*) form much larger groups and will congregate in open water wherever there is a divergence of current, bringing many other fish species into the same area. Blue runners (*Caranx crysos*) are particularly common amid the shallow reefs, often near large schools of silversides.

Parrotfish (family Scaridae)
All parrotfish begin life as females and grow through various colour changes, until some eventually attain a supermale size. Bucktooth parrotfish (*Sparisoma radians*) are quite small, living among the eel grass and well camouflaged by their mottled green coloration. A

common parrotfish all over the reefs is the queen parrotfish (*Scarus vetula*). All parrotfish have several colour phases before they reach the supermale size. The largest of all is the rainbow parrotfish (*Scarus guacamaia*) which can grow to over 1m (3ft).

Pufferfish/Boxfish (families Tetraodontidae, Diodontidae, Ostraciidae)
Pufferfish and boxfish are very common all over the Virgin Islands and should never be handled, since this removes the protective mucus on the skin and can lead to disease. The bridled burrfish (*Chilomycterus antennatus*) is rather timid, hiding under boulders during daylight hours, while the sharp-nosed pufferfish (*Canthigaster rostrata*) can always be found during night dives resting in sponges or on sea fans.

Rays (order Rajiformes)
The spotted eagle ray (*Aetobatus narinari*) is often seen cruising along the northern wall of St Croix and through the various passages between the northern islands, particularly when there is any current. This large ray has a spotted back and a snout somewhat like a pig's. It uses the snout to dig and forage beneath the sand for crustaceans and molluscs. Golden stingrays (*Urolophus jamaicensis*) are the most common of the rays found in the Virgin Islands and can be seen in shallow water all round the coastline, growing to a maximum of only 50cm (15in). The ray most commonly associated with the eastern Caribbean is the southern stingray (*Dasyatis americana*).

Sand Tilefish (family Malacanthidae)
Sand tilefish (*Malacanthus plumieri*) live on the sand plain amid coral rubble and are easily spotted as they hover over their large coral rubble nests, darting into their nests whenever divers approach too close. They are long and white with a pale yellow, crescent-shaped tail.

Scorpionfish (family Scorpaenidae)
Scorpionfish generally inhabit shallower waters under piers and jetties or amid algae-covered stones where their near-perfect camouflage renders them virtually invisible. These sedentary fish have venomous spines along their dorsal fins and, although stings from them are not lethal, they offer a good enough reason to control your buoyancy and keep well clear of the reef at all times. One of the more common small species is the plumed scorpionfish (*Scorpaena grandicornis*).

Sharks (families Rhincodontidae, Sphyrnidae)
As in most other areas of the Caribbean, sharks are rarely seen except on some of the more isolated sea mounts. However, tiger sharks (*Galeocerdo cuvier*) are not uncommon around St Croix. The most frequently sighted is the nurse shark (*Ginglymostoma cirratum*) which is an active feeder at night.

Silversides (families Atherinidae, Clueidae, Engraulididae)
The smallest of the silvery fish most likely to attract your attention are silversides. These fish grow to only about 8cm (3in). During their juvenile stage they are at their most vulnerable. Among the gullies and caves of the patch reef you will find them grouping together in huge shoals in a mixture of species, including anchovies, herring and scad.

Snapper (family Lutjanidae)
Always swimming in mixed shoals with grunt, mutton snapper (*Lutjanus analis*) are often seen congregating in large numbers in early May during the breeding season. Grey snapper (*Lutjanus griseus*) are usually seen under the branches of elkhorn coral in shallower waters. Perhaps the most common of all is the yellowtail snapper (*Ocyurus chrysurus*), which will greet divers on most dives and is always around when fish-feeding takes place.

Squirrelfish/Soldierfish (family Holocentridae)
Squirrelfish and soldierfish are active hunters at night and are found on the reefs during the day under overhangs and in crevices, usually in small congregations. The longspine squirrelfish (*Holocentrus rufus*) has white triangular markings on the tips of its dorsal spines and is a metallic silver and red in colour. The blackbar soldierfish (*Myripristis jacobus*) is a close relative and is usually a uniform dark red in colour, with a dark vertical band across the gill coverings. It often congregates in large numbers and enjoys the protection offered by wrecks.

Trumpetfish (family Aulostomidae)
Trumpetfish (*Aulostomus maculatus*) are very common all over the Virgin Islands and can grow up to 1m (3ft). This is another of the many fish species that are able to alter their coloration to suit their environment or even that of other fish species within their vicinity. The trumpetfish is distinguished by its trumpet-shaped mouth.

Wrasse (family Labridae)
Most wrasse feed on small invertebrates. Bluehead wrasse (*Thalassoma bifasciatum*) are very commonly found foraging on the reefs, constantly moving in small groups; the females are bright yellow with a black spot on the front of the dorsal fin. The supermale of the species is blue (in fact, three different shades of blue separated by dark vertical bands). When diving on the deeper wall, the wrasse you will most commonly see in open water is the creole wrasse (*Clepticus parrai*), which forms large, constantly moving schools travelling along the reef crest.

Underwater Still Photography

Underwater photography requires thinking about before entering the water. You cannot change films, memory cards or prime lenses in this environment, so if you have a clear idea of what you wish to photograph before you take the plunge, you are likely to get better results.

PHOTOGRAPHIC EQUIPMENT
Film Cameras
If the water is calm you can carry two camera outfits, one for wide-angle and another for close-up or macro. Look for non-reflex waterproof cameras with Through-The-Lens (TTL) automatic exposure systems and dedicated flash guns.

Housings
Land cameras of various types can be used underwater in specialist metal or plexiglas housings. Metal housings are strong, reliable, work well at depth and will last a long time if properly maintained. They are heavy to carry, especially when travelling by air, but have buoyancy in water. Their higher cost is justified if you're using an expensive camera that deserves the extra protection.

Plexiglas housings are cheaper but more fragile and require careful handling, both above and below the water. Some models compress at depth, making the control rods miss the camera controls. As most underwater photographs are taken near to the surface, however, this drawback is not too serious. These housings are lightweight to carry on land, but often too buoyant in the water and you may have to attach extra weights to them.

The specially designed Nikonos lenses give sharper results underwater than any housed lenses, but the lack of reflex focusing makes it difficult to compose pictures, and it is easy to cut off part of a subject. Remember that the focusing scale on the 35mm and 80mm is inscribed in 'in-air' distances, while that on the 15mm, 20mm and 28mm underwater lenses are inscribed in underwater distances.

Housings without controls, which are designed for auto-everything cameras, require fast ISO speeds to obtain reasonable shutter speeds and lens apertures in the low ambient light. Autofocus systems that work on contrast (not infrared) work underwater, but only on high contrast subjects and not on those that have large areas of one colour.

Nikonos Lenses
Nikonos lenses range from 15mm to 80mm in focal length, but these must be changed on land. The 35mm and 80mm are really only useful underwater when fitted to extension tubes or close-up outfits. You should consider the 28mm as the standard lens

for underwater photography. Independent companies supply lenses, lens converters, extension tubes and housing for fish-eye and superwide land camera lenses that fit the Nikonos. Lens converters are convenient as they can be changed underwater, as can the Nikonos close-up kit.

Seals
Underwater cameras, housings, flash guns and cables have 'O' ring seals. These and their mating surfaces or grooves must be kept scrupulously clean. 'O' rings should be lightly covered with special grease to prevent flooding. Be aware that too much grease will attract grit and hairs, and do not use silicone spray. When not in use it is best to store any removable 'O' rings off the unit to avoid them becoming flattened. The unit itself should then be sealed in a plastic bag to keep out moisture. User removable 'O' rings are best replaced every 12 months, while non-user removable 'O' rings should be serviced every 12–18 months. 'O' rings on housings usually last the life of the housing.

Batteries
Some digital cameras can consume their battery power very quickly. There are two types of camera: those that accept standard AA batteries and those that use a rechargeable proprietary battery of a different shape. AA-compatible cameras can work with disposable alkaline batteries. These are acceptable emergency backups but you will get a better performance and longer life out of rechargeable nickel metal hydride (NiMH) batteries.

A major problem for travelling photographers and videographers is keeping up with battery charging. If your equipment can use AA or D cell batteries, these will be available at most mainland towns – but be warned that they may be old or stored in poor conditions. If you can carry the weight it is best to take a fresh supply with you.

Despite their memory problems, rechargeable nickel cadmium batteries have advantages in cold weather, can recharge flash guns much more quickly and can usually be used again if flooded. NiMH batteries do not have memory problems. Make sure that you carry spares and have chargers of the correct voltage and Hertz for your destination. Quick chargers are useful as long as the electric current available is strong enough. Most video cameras and many flash guns have dedicated battery packs, so carry at least one spare and keep it charged.

Film
For black and white photography, fast 400 ISO film is the first choice. For a beginner wishing to use

colour, negative print film is best as it has plenty of exposure latitude. Reversal film is preferred for reproduction, but requires very accurate exposure. Kodachrome films are ideal for close work but with mid-water shots they produce a blue/green water background; although this is accurate, people are conditioned to a 'blue' sea. Ektachrome and Fujichrome produce blue water backgrounds, and 50–100 ISO films are the best compromise between exposures and grain. Pale yellow filters will cut down the blue.

UNDERWATER PHOTOGRAPHY
What you photograph depends on your personal interests. Macro photography with extension tubes and fixed framers is easiest to get right as the lens-to-subject and flash-to-subject distances are fixed and the water sediment is minimized. If using film, expose a test film at a variety of exposures with a fixed set-up; the best result will give you the exposure to use for all future pictures for this setting.

Light and Filters
When the sun is at a low angle, or in choppy seas, much of the light fails to enter the water. To take advantage of the maximum light available it is best to photograph two hours either side of the sun's highest point. Sunlight can give spectacular effects underwater, especially in silhouette shots, but generally you should keep the sun behind you and on your subject.

When balancing flash with daylight, cameras with faster flash synchronization speeds (1/125 or 1/250 of a second) give sharper results by avoiding the double images associated with fast moving fish.

Water acts as a cyan (blue/green) filter, cutting back red, so colour film will have a blue/green cast. For available light photography in either cold or tropical waters, different filters are sold to correct this, but they reduce the already limited amount of light available. Flash will put back the colour and increase apparent sharpness.

Flash guns used on or near to the camera will light up suspended matter in the water like white stars in a black sky (back scatter). The closer these particles are to the camera, the larger they will appear. The solution is to keep the flash as far as possible above and to one side of the camera. Two narrow angle flash guns, one on each side of the camera, often produce a better result than a single wide-angle flash gun, but the resulting picture may appear flat.

Although objects appear closer to both your eye and the camera lens under water, the flash must strike the subject directly to illuminate it. Narrow angle flash guns must therefore be aimed behind the apparent subject, to hit the real subject. Built-in aiming/focusing lights, or a torch strapped to the flash, will help with both this problem and with focusing during night photography. Built-in aiming/focusing lights are best powered by a separate battery, or the system will not last for a complete dive.

Fish scales reflect light in different ways that vary with the angle of the fish to the camera. Silver fish reflect more light than coloured fish and black fish almost none at all; therefore, you should bracket exposures. With automatic flash guns you can do this by altering the film speed setting.

UNDERWATER SUBJECTS
Some fish are strongly territorial. Surgeonfish, triggerfish and sharks will make mock attacks on a perceived invader and these situations can make strong pictures if you are brave enough to hold your ground. Manta rays are curious and will keep coming back if you react quietly and do not chase after them. Remember that if an eye is in the picture it must be lit and sharp; it is acceptable for the rest of the animal to be slightly blurred. Angelfish and butterflyfish will swim off when you first enter their territory, but if you remain quietly in the same place they will usually return and allow you to photograph them.

Divers and wrecks are the most difficult to photograph. Even with apparently clear water and wide-angle lenses there will be back scatter, and flash is essential to light a diver's mask. Flash guns with a colour temperature of 4500 Kelvin will give more accurate skin tones and colour.

Night photography underwater is another world. Focusing quickly in dim light is difficult and many subjects will disappear when lit up, so pre-set your controls. Many creatures only appear at night and some fish are half asleep, making them more approachable.

Remember not to touch coral and do not wear fins over sandy bottoms as they will stir sand up. Photographers do not swim around much, so wear a wetsuit for warmth.

If underwater photography sounds too difficult, try video. Macro subjects require extra lighting but other shots can be taken with available light and improved afterwards if necessary. Back scatter is much less of a problem and the results can be played back on site and shot again if necessary.

DIGITAL CAMERAS UNDERWATER
Digital cameras are gradually taking over from film cameras because without the cost of film they appear to work out cheaper. They particularly appeal to underwater photographers because they can get a lot more shots onto a memory card than they could on a film. They can discard any failures and can keep on photographing a subject, so long as it doesn't move. Digital images can also be adjusted and corrected later by computer.

However, electronics carry more problems in a saltwater environment. You'll have to carry a portable computer or several memory cards to download the images, and if used professionally (ie heavily), the camera's service life is only about three years, so the saving in film costs is soon negated.

Digital cameras often produce images that lack the punch, contrast or sparkle that a film-based model delivers. The results can be wishy-washy and lack detail in the highlights, and so you may have to 'up' the colour depth and contrast with image manipulation software.

Files of the images are stored in a variety of file formats, eg uncompressed as TIFFs (Tagged Image File Format) or compressed as JPEGs (Joint Photographic Experts Group), which can reduce the file size if required. Most modern cameras allow storage as RAW – the raw data as it comes directly off the sensor. There is no standard for this; it uses the proprietary software of the camera manufacturer. RAW images have the best quality, as no adjustments have yet been made to the image. It is worth saving the images in RAW format so that any future software enhancements can be applied to the original image later. However, RAW files do take up more room on memory cards.

Most digital cameras have much smaller image sensors than 35mm cameras, so lenses appear to have a longer focal length. Canon and Kodak have brought out true full-frame sensors that cover the same area as 35mm film, but there are still problems with these and wide-angle lenses because of the angle at which the light from the outer edge of the lens strikes the sensor. Unless corrected, this leads to reduced sharpness at the edges of the picture. For this and other reasons, Nikon and other manufacturers have so far preferred to stick with the smaller sensors and manufacture special lenses for them. However, critics will also point out that because these lenses cover a smaller area than 35mm film, they are cheaper to produce.

Digital and Optical Zoom

Digital zoom is electronic enlargement of the image coupled with cropping to emulate 'zooming in' closer with the lens, whereas in reality all that is being done is enlargement of the pixels. An optical zoom 'brings the subject closer' optically before recording the image on the sensor – thus giving better resolution and a higher quality result.

Image-capture, Noise, Temperature, ISO Speeds and White Balance

Noise is the visible effect of electronic interference; it often appears similar to the grain in fast film. Two of the major causes are temperature, where high equals worse and low equals better, and ISO (International Standards Organization) sensitivity

where again, high equals worse and low equals better. The latest high-end digital cameras act better than film at high ISO settings.

All digital cameras, including video cameras, have an automatic white balance setting that enables the camera to calculate the correct colour balance for the image. Some have pre-set values for different types of lighting, either by colour temperature on professional models or such settings as sunny, cloudy or fluorescent lighting on amateur models. For underwater use some divers use the 'cloudy' setting, or you may have to experiment with 'manual' using a white plastic card as the subject. Some divers use the RAW image format for the freedom of adjusting the white balance setting after the dive.

Flash with Digital Cameras

Most, but not all, digital cameras are incompatible with normal TTL flash guns as they cannot read the flash reflected off film. This is addressed with either a light sensor on the camera body to judge proper exposure or with special flash guns for different digital cameras, many of which send out several pre-flashes and read their intensity when they are reflected back from the subject (DTTL). You can still use manual flash, shoot the picture, review it, make the necessary adjustments and shoot the picture again, but this takes time and the subject may have moved. There are answers to TTL flash problems for underwater photography. One is to house a land flash gun that is dedicated to your digital camera; the problem with this is they will not cover the field of view of very wide-angle lenses, though they are fine for close shots. A second solution is that independent manufacturers of wide-angle underwater flash guns now have models featuring special electronic circuitry for use with the newest digital cameras. They are still compatible with the popular film cameras used underwater, including the Nikonos.

Shutter Lag

Most cheaper digital cameras suffer from 'shutter lag'. There is a time lag between pressing the shutter release and the shutter actually firing, as the camera has to change mode and write to memory or the storage media. This means that if you are aiming for an expression on a face or a moving fish, these can be lost by the time the shutter fires, making action photography difficult. More expensive cameras speed things up by saving to a buffer (extra memory).

Dust on Sensors

Where digital cameras have interchangeable or zoom lenses, tiny bits of dust and lint are attracted to the sensor due to its static. Some cameras have a vibrating cleaning system but all require the sensor to be cleaned occasionally.

Health and Safety for Divers

The information on first aid and safety in this part of the book is intended as a guide only. It is based on currently accepted health and safety guidelines, but it is merely a summary and is no substitute for a comprehensive manual on the subject – or, even better, for first aid training. We strongly advise you to buy a recognized manual on diving safety and medicine before setting off on a diving trip, to read it through during the journey, and to carry it with you to refer to during the trip. It would also be sensible to take a short course in first aid.

We urge anyone in need of advice on emergency treatment to see a doctor as soon as possible.

WHAT TO DO IN AN EMERGENCY

- Divers who have suffered any injury or symptom of an injury, no matter how minor, related to diving, should consult a doctor, preferably a specialist in diving medicine, as soon as possible after the symptom or injury occurs.
- No matter how confident you are in making a diagnosis, remember that you are an amateur diver and an unqualified medical practitioner.
- If you are the victim of a diving injury do not let fear of ridicule prevent you from revealing your symptoms. Apparently minor symptoms can mask or even develop into a life-threatening illness. It is better to be honest with yourself and live to dive another day.
- Always err on the conservative side when treating an illness or an injury. If you find that the condition is only minor you – and the doctor – will both be relieved.

FIRST AID
The basic principles of first aid are to:
- do no harm
- sustain life
- prevent deterioration
- promote recovery.

If you have to treat an ill or injured person:
- First try to secure the safety of yourself and the ill or injured person by getting the two of you out of the threatening environment: the water.
- Think before you act: do not do anything that will further endanger either of you.
- Then follow a simple sequence of patient assessment and management:
  1 Assess whether you are dealing with a life-threatening condition.
  2 If so, try to define which one.
  3 Then try to manage the condition.

Assessing the ABCs:
Learn the basic checks – the ABCs:
A: for AIRWAY (with care of the neck)
B : for BREATHING
C: for CIRCULATION
D: for DECREASED level of consciousness
E: for EXPOSURE (a patient must be exposed enough for a proper examination to be made).

- **Airway (with attention to the neck):** check whether the patient has a neck injury. Are the mouth and nose free from obstruction? Noisy breathing is a sign of airway obstruction.

- **Breathing:** look at the chest to see if it is rising and falling. Listen for air movement at the nose and mouth. Feel for the movement of air against your cheek.

- **Circulation:** feel for a pulse (the carotid artery) next to the windpipe.

- **Decreased level of consciousness:** does the patient respond in any of the following ways?
  A - Awake, aware, spontaneous speech.
  V - Verbal stimuli: does he or she answer to 'Wake up'?
  P - Painful stimuli: does he or she respond to a pinch?
  U - Unresponsive.

- **Exposure:** preserve the dignity of the patient as much as you can, but remove clothes as necessary to carry out your treatment.

Now, send for help
If, after your assessment, you think the condition of the patient is serious, you must send or call for help from the nearest emergency services (ambulance, paramedics). Tell whoever you send for help to come back and let you know whether help is on the way.

Recovery position
If the patient is unconscious but breathing normally there is a risk that he or she may vomit and choke on the vomit. It is therefore critical that the patient be turned on one side with arms outstretched in front of the body. This is called the recovery position and is illustrated in all first aid manuals.

If you suspect injury to the spine or neck, immobilize the patient in a straight line before you turn him or her on one side.

If the patient is unconscious, does not seem to be breathing, and you cannot feel a pulse, do not try to turn him or her into the recovery position.

Do **NOT** give fluids to unconscious or semi-conscious divers.

If you cannot feel a pulse

If your patient has no pulse you will have to carry out CPR (cardiopulmonary resuscitation). This consists of techniques to:

- ventilate the patient's lungs (expired air resuscitation)
- pump the patient's heart (external cardiac compression).

CPR (cardiopulmonary resuscitation)
Airway

Open the patient's airway by gently extending the head (head tilt) and lifting the chin with two fingers (chin lift). This lifts the patient's tongue away from the back of the throat and opens the airway. If the patient is unconscious and you think something may be blocking the airway, sweep your finger across the back of the tongue from one side to the other. If you find anything, remove it. Do not try this if the patient is conscious or semi-conscious because he or she may bite your finger or vomit.

Breathing: EAR (expired air resuscitation)

If the patient is not breathing you need to give the 'kiss of life', or expired air resuscitation (EAR) – you breathe into his or her lungs. The 16 per cent of oxygen in the air you expire is enough to keep your patient alive.

1 Pinch the patient's nose to close the nostrils.
2 Place your open mouth fully over the patient's mouth, making as good a seal as possible.
3 Exhale into the patient's mouth hard enough to make the chest rise and fall. Give two breaths, each given over one second.
4 If the patient's chest fails to rise, try adjusting the position of the airway.
5 Check the patient's pulse. If you cannot feel one, follow the instructions under 'Circulation' below. If you can, continue breathing for the patient once every five seconds, checking the pulse after every ten breaths.
- If the patient begins breathing, turn him or her into the recovery position (see page 163).

Circulation

If, after giving expired air resuscitation, you cannot feel a pulse, you should try external cardiac compression:

1 Kneel next to the patient's chest.
2 Rescuers should place their hands in the centre of the chest, rather than spend more time positioning their hands using other methods.
3 Place the heel of your right hand on your left hand.
4 Straighten your elbows.
5 Place your shoulders perpendicularly above the patient's breast bone.
6 Compress the breast bone 4–5cm (1½–2in) to a rhythm of 'one, two, three . . .'
7 Carry out 30 compressions.

Carry on using a ratio of compressions to rescue breaths of 30:2 for all casualties. The aim of CPR is to keep the patient alive until paramedics or a doctor arrive with the necessary equipment.

Check before you dive that you and your buddy are both trained in CPR. If not, get some training – it could mean the difference between life and death for either of you or for someone else.

DIVING DISEASES AND ILLNESSES
Acute decompression illness

Acute decompression illness is any illness arising from the decompression of a diver – in other words, by the diver moving from an area of high ambient pressure to an area of low pressure. There are two types of acute decompression illness:

- decompression sickness (the bends)
- barotrauma with arterial gas embolism.

It is not important for the diver or first aider to be able to differentiate between the two conditions because both are serious, life-threatening illnesses, and both require the same emergency treatment. The important thing is to be able to recognize acute decompression illness and to initiate emergency treatment. The box on page 165 outlines the signs and symptoms to look out for.

The bends (decompression sickness)

Decompression sickness or the bends occurs when a diver has not been adequately decompressed. Exposure to higher ambient pressure underwater causes nitrogen to dissolve in increasing amounts in the body tissues. If this pressure is released gradually during correct and adequate decompression procedures, the nitrogen escapes naturally into the blood and is exhaled through the lungs. If the release of pressure is too rapid, the nitrogen cannot escape quickly enough and bubbles of nitrogen gas form in the tissues. The symptoms and signs of the disease are related to the tissues in which the bubbles form and it is described by the tissues affected – joint bend, for example.

Symptoms and signs include:
- nausea and vomiting
- dizziness
- malaise
- weakness
- pains in the joints
- paralysis
- numbness
- itching of skin
- incontinence.

Barotrauma with arterial gas embolism

Barotrauma is the damage that occurs when the tissue surrounding a gaseous space is injured following a change in the volume of air in that space. An arterial gas embolism is a gas bubble that moves in a blood vessel; this usually leads to the obstruction of that blood vessel or a vessel further downstream.

Barotrauma can occur in any tissue surrounding a gas-filled space. Common sites and types of barotrauma are:

- ears (middle ear squeeze) → burst ear drum
- sinuses (sinus squeeze) → sinus pain/nose bleeds
- lungs (lung squeeze) → burst lung
- face (mask squeeze) → swollen, bloodshot eyes
- teeth (tooth squeeze) → toothache.

Burst lung is the most serious of these since it can result in arterial gas embolism. It occurs following a rapid ascent during which the diver does not exhale adequately. The rising pressure of expanding air in the lungs bursts the delicate alveoli – air sacs in the lungs – and forces air into the blood vessels that carry blood back to the heart and, ultimately, the brain. In the brain these air bubbles block blood vessels and obstruct the supply of blood and oxygen to the brain. This causes brain damage.

ROUGH AND READY NONSPECIALIST TESTS FOR THE BENDS

If you suspect a diver may be suffering from the bends, carry out these tests. If the results of your checks do not seem normal, the diver may be suffering from the bends and you must take emergency action. Take the appropriate action outlined on page 164 even if you are not sure of your assessment – the bends is a life-threatening illness.

1 Does the diver know:
   who he/she is?
   where he/she is?
   what the time is?
2 Can the diver see and count the number of fingers you hold up? Hold your hand 50cm (20in) in front of the diver's face and ask him/her to follow your hand with his/her eyes as you move it from side to side and up and down. Be sure that both eyes follow in each direction, and look out for any rapid oscillation or jerky movements of the eyeballs.
3 Ask the diver to smile, and check that both sides of the face have the same expression. Run the back of a finger across each side of the diver's forehead, cheeks and chin, and ask whether he/she can feel it.
4 Check that the diver can hear you whisper when his/her eyes are closed.
5 Ask the diver to shrug his/her shoulders. Both should move equally.
6 Ask the diver to swallow. Check that the adam's apple moves up and down.
7 Ask the diver to stick out his/her tongue at the centre of the mouth – deviation to either side indicates a problem.
8 Check the diver has equal muscle strength on both sides of the body. You do this by pulling/pushing each of the diver's arms and legs away from and back toward the body, asking him/her to resist you.
9 Run your finger lightly across the diver's shoulders, down the back, across the chest and abdomen, and along the arms and legs, feeling upper and underside surfaces. Check that the diver can feel your finger moving along each surface.
10 On firm ground (not on a boat) check that the diver can walk in a straight line and, with eyes closed, stand upright with feet together and arms outstretched.

The symptoms and signs of lung barotrauma and arterial gas embolism include:

- shortness of breath
- chest pain
- unconsciousness.

Treatment of acute decompression Illness:

- ABCs and CPR (see pages 163-4) as necessary
- position the patient in the recovery position (see page 163) with no tilt or raising of the legs
- give 100 per cent oxygen by mask or demand valve
- keep the patient warm
- remove to the nearest hospital as soon as possible – the hospital or emergency services will arrange for recompression treatment.

Carbon dioxide and carbon monoxide poisoning

Carbon dioxide poisoning can occur as a result of skip breathing (diver holds breath on SCUBA), heavy exercise on SCUBA or malfunctioning rebreather systems. Carbon monoxide poisoning occurs as a result of: exhaust gases being pumped into cylinders; hookah systems; air intake too close to exhaust fumes.

Symptoms and signs of carbon monoxide poisoning include:

- blue colour of the skin
- shortness of breath
- loss of consciousness.

Treatment of carbon monoxide poisoning:

- get the patient to a safe environment
- ABCs and CPR (see pages 163-4) as necessary
- 100 per cent oxygen through a mask or demand valve
- get the patient to hospital.

Head injury

Any head injury should be treated as serious.

Treatment of a head injury:

- the diver must surface and do no more diving until a doctor has been consulted
- disinfect the wound
- if the diver is unconscious, contact the emergency services
- if breathing and/or pulse have stopped, administer CPR (see page 164)
- if the diver is breathing and has a pulse, check for bleeding and other injuries, and treat for shock (see page 167)
- if the wounds permit, put the injured person into the recovery position and, if possible, give 100 per cent oxygen
- keep the patient warm and comfortable and monitor pulse and respiration constantly.

Hyperthermia (raised body temperature)

A rise in body temperature results from a combination of overheating, normally due to exercise, and inadequate fluid intake. A person with hyperthermia will progress through heat exhaustion to heat stroke, with eventual collapse. Heat stroke is an emergency: if the diver is not cooled and rehydrated he or she will die.

Treatment of hyperthermia:
- move the diver as quickly as possible into a cooler place and remove all clothes
- call the emergency services
- sponge the diver's body with a damp cloth and fan him or her manually or with an electric fan
- if the patient is unconscious, put him or her into the recovery position (see page 163) and monitor the ABCs as necessary
- if the patient is conscious you can give him or her a cold drink.

Hypothermia (low body temperature)

Normal internal body temperature is just under 37°C (98.4°F). If for any reason it falls much below this – usually, in diving, because of inadequate protective clothing – progressively more serious symptoms may follow, and the person will eventually die if the condition is not treated rapidly. A drop of 1C° (2F°) causes shivering and discomfort. A 2C° (3F°) drop induces the body's self-heating mechanisms to react: blood flow to the hands and feet is reduced and shivering becomes extreme. A 3C° (5F°) drop results in memory loss, confusion, disorientation, irregular heartbeat and breathing and eventually death.

Treatment of hypothermia:
- move the diver as quickly as possible into a sheltered and warm place; *or:*
- prevent further heat loss: use an exposure bag; surround the diver with buddies' bodies; cover his or her head and neck with a woolly hat, warm towels or anything else suitable
- if you have managed to get the diver into sheltered warmth, remove wet clothing, dress your patient in warm, dry clothing and wrap him or her in an exposure bag or heat blanket; however, if you are still in the open, the diver is best left in existing garments
- if the diver is conscious and coherent administer a warm shower or bath and a warm, sweet drink
- if the diver is unconscious, check the ABCs (see page 163), call the emergency services, make the patient as warm as possible, and treat for shock (see page 167).

Near-drowning

Near-drowning is a medical condition in which a diver has inhaled some water – water in the lungs interferes with the normal transport of oxygen from the lungs into the bloodstream. A person in a near-drowning condition may be conscious or unconscious.

Near-drowning victims sometimes develop secondary drowning, a condition in which fluid oozing into the lungs causes the diver to drown in internal secretions, so all near-drowning patients must be monitored in a hospital.

Treatment of near-drowning:
- get the diver out of the water and check the ABCs (see page 163); depending on your findings, begin EAR or CPR (see page 164) as appropriate
- if possible, administer oxygen by mask or demand valve
- call the emergency services and get the diver to a hospital for observation, even if he/she appears to have recovered from the experience.

Nitrogen narcosis

Air contains about 80 per cent nitrogen. Breathing the standard diving mixture under compression can lead to symptoms very much like those of drunkenness (nitrogen narcosis is popularly known as 'rapture of the deep'). Some divers experience nitrogen narcosis at depths of 30–40m (100–130ft). Down to a depth of about 60m (200ft) – which is beyond the legal maximum depth for sport-diving in the UK and the USA – the symptoms are not always serious; but below about 80m (260ft) a diver is likely to lose consciousness. Symptoms can occur very suddenly. Nitrogen narcosis is not a serious condition, but a diver suffering from it may do something dangerous.

Treatment of nitrogen narcosis: the only treatment for this condition is to get the diver to ascend immediately to shallower waters.

TRAVELLING MEDICINE

Many doctors decline to issue drugs, particularly antibiotics, to people who want them 'just in case'; but a diving holiday can be ruined by an ear or sinus infection, especially in a remote area or on a live-aboard boat, where the nearest doctor or pharmacy is a long and difficult journey away.

Many travelling divers therefore carry with them medical kits that could lead the uninitiated to think they were hypochondriacs. Nasal sprays, ear drops, antihistamine creams, anti-diarrhoea medicines, antibiotics, sea-sickness remedies . . . Forearmed, such divers can take immediate action as soon as they realize something is wrong. At the very least, this may minimize their loss of diving time.

Always bear in mind that most decongestants and remedies for sea-sickness can make you drowsy and therefore should never be taken before diving.

Shock

Shock is a medical condition and not just the emotional trauma of a frightening experience. Medical shock results from poor blood and oxygen delivery to the tissues. As a result of oxygen and blood deprivation the tissues cannot carry out their functions. There are many causes; the most common is loss of blood.

Treatment for medical shock:
This is directed at restoring blood and oxygen delivery to the tissues:
- check the ABCs (see page 163)
- give 100 per cent oxygen
- control any external bleeding by pressing hard on the wound and/or pressure points (the location of the pressure points is illustrated in first-aid manuals); raise the injured limb or other part of the body
- use a tourniquet only as a last resort and only on the arms and legs
- if the diver is conscious, lay him/her on the back with the legs raised and the head to one side; if unconscious, turn him or her on the left side in the recovery position (see page 163).

MARINE-RELATED AILMENTS

Sunburn, coral cuts, fire-coral stings, swimmers' ear, sea-sickness and bites from various insects are perhaps the most common divers' complaints – but there are more serious marine-related illnesses you should know about.

Cuts and abrasions

Divers should wear appropriate abrasive protection for the undersea environment. Hands, knees, elbows and feet are the areas most commonly affected. The danger with abrasions is that they become infected, so all wounds must be thoroughly washed and rinsed with water and an antiseptic as soon as possible after the injury. Infection may progress to a stage where antibiotics are necessary. If the site of an apparently minor injury becomes inflamed, and the inflammation spreads, consult a doctor immediately – you may need antibiotics to prevent the infection spreading to the bloodstream.

Swimmers' ear

Swimmers' ear is an infection of the external ear canal caused by constantly wet ears. The condition is often a combined fungal and bacterial infection. To prevent it, always dry your ears thoroughly after diving. If you know you are susceptible to the condition, insert alcohol drops after diving. If an infection occurs, the best treatment is to stop diving or swimming for a few days and apply ear drops such as:
- 5 per cent acetic acid in isopropyl alcohol; *or*
- aluminium acetate/acetic acid solution.

FIRST-AID KIT

Your first-aid kit should be waterproof, compartmentalized and sealable, and, as a minimum, should contain the following items:
- a full first-aid manual – the information in this appendix is for general guidance only
- contact numbers for the emergency services
- coins for telephone
- pencil and notebook
- tweezers
- scissors
- 6 large standard sterile dressings
- 1 large Elastoplast/Band-Aid fabric dressing strip
- 2 triangular bandages
- 3 medium-size safety pins
- 1 pack sterile cotton wool
- 2 50mm (2in) crepe bandages
- eyedrops
- antiseptic fluid/cream
- bottle of vinegar
- sachets of rehydration salts
- sea-sickness tablets
- decongestants
- painkillers
- anti-AIDS pack (syringes/needles/drip needle)

Sea or motion sickness

Motion sickness can be an annoying complication on a diving holiday involving boat dives. If you suffer from motion sickness, discuss the problem with a doctor before your holiday – or at least before boarding the boat. But bear in mind that many medicines formulated to prevent travel sickness contain antihistamines, which make you drowsy and will impair your ability to think quickly while you are diving.

Biting insects

Some regions are notorious for biting insects. Take a good insect repellent and some antihistamine cream to relieve the effects.

Sunburn

Be sure to take plenty of precautions against sunburn, which can cause skin cancer. Many people get sunburned on the first day of a holiday and spend a very uncomfortable time afterwards recovering. Pay particular attention to the head, the nose and the backs of the legs. Always use high-protection factor creams, and wear clothes that keep off the sun.

Tropical diseases

Visit the doctor before your trip and make sure you have the appropriate vaccinations for the regions you intend to visit on your trip.

Fish that bite

- **Barracuda** These very rarely bite divers, although they have been known to bite in turbid or murky, shallow water, where sunlight flashing on a knife blade, a camera lens or jewellery has confused the fish into thinking they are attacking their normal prey.

  Treatment: clean the wounds thoroughly and use antiseptic or antibiotic cream. Bad bites will also need antibiotic and anti-tetanus treatment.

- **Moray eels** Probably more divers are bitten by morays than by all other sea creatures added together – usually through putting their hands into holes to collect shells or lobsters, remove anchors, or hide baitfish. Once it bites, a moray often refuses to let go, so you may have to persuade it to by gripping it behind the head and exerting pressure with your finger and thumb until it opens its jaw. You can make the wound worse by tearing your flesh if you pull the fish off.

  Treatment: thorough cleaning and usually stitching. The bites always go septic, so have antibiotics and anti-tetanus available.

- **Sharks** Sharks rarely attack divers, but should always be treated with great respect. Their attacks are usually connected with speared or hooked fish, fish or meat set up as bait, lobsters rattling when picked up, or certain types of vibration, such as that produced by helicopters. The decomposition products of dead fish (even several days old) seem much more attractive to most sharks than fresh blood. Grey reef sharks can be territorial. They often warn of an attack by arching their backs and pointing their pectoral fins downward. Other sharks often give warning by bumping into you first. If you are frightened, a shark will detect this from the vibrations given off by your body. Calmly back up to the reef or boat and get out of the water.

  Treatment: a person who has been bitten by a shark usually has severe injuries and is suffering from shock (see page 167). If possible, stop any bleeding by applying pressure. The patient will need to be stabilized with blood or plasma transfusions, so get the diver to hospital. Even minor wounds are likely to become infected, so the diver will need antibiotic and anti-tetanus treatment.

- **Triggerfish** Large triggerfish – usually males guarding eggs in 'nests' – are particularly aggressive and will attack divers who get too close. Their teeth are very strong, and can go through rubber fins and draw blood through a 4mm (⅙in) wet suit.

  Treatment: clean the wound and treat it with antiseptic cream.

Venomous sea creatures

Many venomous sea creatures are bottom dwellers – they hide among coral or rest on or burrow into sand. If you need to move along the sea bottom, shuffle along, so that you push such creatures out of the way and minimize the risk of stepping directly onto sharp venomous spines, many of which can pierce rubber fins. Antivenins require specialist medical supervision, do not work for all species, and need refrigerated storage, so they are rarely available when they are needed. Most of the venoms are proteins of high molecular weight that break down under heat.

General treatment: tie a broad bandage at a point between the limb and the body and tighten it. Remember to release it every 15 minutes. Immerse the limb in hot water (perhaps the cooling water from an outboard motor if no other supply is available) at 50°C (120°F) for two hours, until the pain stops. Several injections around the wound of local anaesthetic (such as procaine hydrochloride), if available, will ease the pain. Young or weak people may need CPR (see page 164). Remember that venoms may still be active in fish that have been dead for 48 hours.

- **Cone shells** Live cone shells should never be handled without gloves: the animal has a mobile, tubelike organ that shoots a poison dart. This causes numbness at first, followed by local muscular paralysis, which may extend to respiratory paralysis and heart failure.

  Treatment: tie a bandage between the wound and the body, tighten it, and release it every 15 minutes. CPR (see page 164) may be necessary.

- **Fire coral** Corals of the genus *Millepora* are not true corals but members of the class Hydrozoa – i.e., they are more closely related to the stinging hydroids. Many people react violently from the slightest brush with them – producing blisters sometimes as large as 15cm (6in) across, which can last for as long as several weeks.

  Treatment: bathe the affected part in methylated spirit or vinegar (acetic acid). Local anaesthetic may be required to ease the pain, though antihistamine cream is usually enough.

- **Fireworms** These worms with white hairs along their sides display bristles when touched. These easily break off in the skin, causing a burning feeling and intense irritation.

  Treatment: bathe the affected part in methylated spirit, vinegar (acetic acid) or hot water.

- **Jellyfish** Most jellyfish sting, but few are dangerous. When seasonal changes are favourable you can encounter the Portuguese man-of-war (*Physalia physalis*). These creatures are highly toxic and continued exposure to the stinging cells may require hospital treatment. Sea wasps (*Carybdea alata*) can be found in shallow warm water at night and are attracted to light. These creatures often swarm and stings can be severe, causing muscle cramps, nausea and breathing difficulties. Whenever the conditions are favourable for thimble jellyfish (*Linuche unguiculata*), there is always the chance of much smaller and almost invisible micro-organisms in the water column. Wear protection such as a wet suit or the new style of Lycra skin suit.

Treatment: in the event of a sting, the recommended treatment is to pour acetic acid (vinegar) over both animal and wounds and then to remove the animal with forceps or gloves. CPR (see page 164) may be required.

- **Scorpionfish** These are not considered dangerous in Caribbean waters, but care should always be taken of the spines on top of their dorsal fin.

Treatment: inadvertent stinging can be treated by bathing the affected part of the body in very hot water.

- **Sea urchins** The spines of some sea urchins are poisonous and all sea urchin spines can puncture the skin, even through gloves, and break off, leaving painful wounds that often go septic.

Treatment: for bad cases bathe the affected part of the body in very hot water. This softens the spines, making it easier for the body to reject them. Soothing creams or a magnesium sulphate compress will help reduce the pain, as will the application of the flesh of papaya fruit. Septic wounds need to be treated with antibiotics.

- **Stinging hydroids** Stinging hydroids often go unnoticed on wrecks, old anchor ropes and chains until you put your hand on them, when their nematocysts are fired into your skin. The wounds are not serious but they are very painful, and large blisters can be raised on sensitive skin, which can last for some time.

Treatment: bathe the affected part in methylated spirit or vinegar (acetic acid). Local anaesthetic may be required to ease the pain, though antihistamine cream is usually enough.

- **Stinging plankton** You cannot see stinging plankton, and so cannot take evasive measures. If there are reports of any in the area, keep as much of your body covered as you can.

Treatment: bathe the affected part in methylated spirit or vinegar (acetic acid). Local anaesthetic may be required to ease the pain, though antihistamine cream is usually enough.

- **Stingrays** Stingrays vary considerably in size from a few centimetres to several metres across. The sting consists of one or more spines on top of the tail; although these point backward they can sting in any direction. The rays thrash out and sting when they are trodden on or caught. The wounds may be large and severely lacerated.

Treatment: clean the wound and remove any spines. Bathe or immerse in very hot water and apply a local anaesthetic if one is available; follow up with antibiotics and anti-tetanus.

- **Other stinging creatures**
Venoms can also occur in soft corals, the anemones associated with clownfish and the nudibranchs that feed on stinging hydroids. If you have sensitive skin, do not touch any of them.

Cuts

Underwater cuts and scrapes, especially those caused by coral, barnacles and sharp metal, will usually, if they are not cleaned out and treated quickly, go septic; absorption of the resulting poisons into the body can cause more serious medical conditions.

After every dive, clean and disinfect any wounds, no matter how small. Larger wounds will often refuse to heal unless you stay out of seawater for a couple of days. Surgeonfish have sharp fins on each side of the caudal peduncle; they use these when lashing out at other fish with a sweep of the tail, and they occasionally use them to defend their territory against a trespassing diver. Their 'scalpels' may be covered in toxic mucus, so wounds must be cleaned and treated with antibiotic cream.

As a preventive measure against cuts in general, the golden rule on the reef is: do not touch. Be sure to learn good buoyancy control so that you can avoid touching anything unnecessarily – never forget for an instant that every area of the coral you touch will inevitably be killed.

Bibliography

Arneborg, Carol *A Guide to The BVI National Parks* (1996) Island Publishing Ltd., Tortola

Berg, Daniel and Berg, Denise *Tropical Shipwrecks* (1989) Aqua Explorers Inc., New York

Bushell, T. *'Royal Mail' 1839–1939* Trade and Travel Publications Ltd.

Colin, Dr Patrick I. *Caribbean Reef Invertebrates and Plants* (1978) T. F. H. Publications Ltd

Cummings, Suzanne and Stuart *Diving and Snorkelling Guide to the United States Virgin Islands* (1992) Gulf Publishing Co., Texas

Helleberg Fields, Meredith (editor) *Yachtsman's Guide to the Virgin Islands* (1996) Tropic Isle Publishers, New Jersey

Humann, Paul *Reef Coral Identification* (1993) New World Publications, Florida.

Humann, Paul *Reef Creature Identification* (1993) New World Publications, Florida.

Humann, Paul *Reef Fish Identification* (1993) New World Publications, Florida

Lewisohn, Florence *The Romantic History of St Croix* (1964) St Croix Landmark Society

Littler, Littler, Bucher and Norris *Marine Plants of the Caribbean* (1984) Smithsonian Institution Press

Marler, George and Luana *The Royal Mail Steamer* Rhone (1978) Marler Publications Ltd, Tortola

Marx, Robert F. *Shipwrecks of the Western Hemisphere 1492–1825* (1971), World Publishing Company, New York

Megnin, Judy (publisher) *'Meet the Virgins' – The Settler's Handbook* 11th edition (1995) Megnin Publications Inc., St Croix

Obradovich, John and Betty (publishers) *Bahamas and Caribbean Pilot's Guide* (1997) Pilot Publishing, Glendale, California

Sefton, Nancy and Webster, Steven K. *Caribbean Reef Invertebrates* (1986) Sea Challengers, California

Seyfarth, Fritz *Pirates of the Virgin Islands* (1986) Spanish Main Press, St Thomas

Sorensen, Linda *Diving and Snorkelling Guide to the British Virgin Islands* (1991) Gulf Publishing Co., Texas

Varlack, Pearl and Harrigan, Norwell *American Paradise* (1992) Research and Consultancy Services, St Thomas

Verbruggen, Jan (Editor) *The World Dive Guide* (1998) Compuprint Publishing, Belgium

Vine, Peter *Caribbean Divers' Guide* (1991) Immel Publishing, London

Williams, Jeff *The Guide to Diving and Snorkelling in the British Virgin Islands* (1991) DIVEntures Publishing, Hopkinton, MA

Wood, Lawson *Top Dive Sites of the Caribbean* (1998) New Holland Publishers (UK) Ltd, London

Index